POWER, IMPARTIALITY AND JUSTICE

Power, Impartiality and Justice

PETER G. WOOLCOCK
University of South Australia

Ashgate

Aldershot • Brookfield USA • Singapore • Sydney

Published by
Ashgate Publishing Ltd
Gower House
Croft Road
Aldershot
Hants GU11 3HR
England

Ashgate Publishing Company
Old Post Road
Brookfield
Vermont 05036
USA

British Library Cataloguing in Publication Data
Woolcock, Peter G.
    Power, impartiality and justice. - (Avebury series in
    philosophy)
    1. Ethics
    I. Title
    170

Library of Congress Catalog Card Number: 98-71966

ISBN 1 84014 506 6

Printed in Great Britain by The Ipswich Book Company, Suffolk

Contents

v

Acknowledgements

I would like to express my thanks to those people whose help has contributed to the gestation of this book - to my mother for introducing me early to the idea of a better world; to my father for the possibilities he kept open; to Julius Kovesi for sparking my interest in philosophy as a vocation; to my brother-in-law Winston Nesbitt for making philosophy a matter of pleasure as well as of passionate seriousness; to John Chandler and Harry Beran for their knowledgeable comments on the doctoral thesis which eventually mutated into this book; to Alan Smithson for his enthusiastic interest and insight; to George Couvalis for many hours of intense and productive discussion; to my colleagues at Flinders and Adelaide Universities for their feedback at research seminars on the various papers I have given over the years; to my colleagues in Philosophy and History of Education at the University of South Australia for providing a stimulating working environment; to Linda Blackstone for her patience, good will and professional skill in word-processing matters - she has probably learnt more from my errors than she ever wished to know; to the University of South Australia for allowing me to benefit from its excellent 'adjunct scholar' programme; to my children Dylan and Buffy for the escape their rich musical and artistic lives provided from my musings; to Jarrah for his unerring eye for the 'silly'; and most of all, to my wife Iris who has tolerated my obsessions with good humour, love and wry wit.

The passage on p.122 from *Moral Thinking* (pp.128-129) by R.M. Hare (1981) is quoted by permission of Oxford University Press.

Preface

Unlike thinkers in the Christian and Jewish traditions and their secular descendants such as Hegel, Marx, and Toynbee, I do not believe that history has a grand plan, any unfolding design. Nonetheless, there are trends and tendencies. One of these, it seems to me, is a gradual improvement in our moral understanding. The evidence for this is the gradual elimination of a whole range of attitudes from the realm of defensible value positions, beginning with the repudiation of religious discrimination that arose from the clash between Catholicism and Protestantism in Reformation Europe, extending to the right of the common people to select their own government in post-revolutionary America, the denial of hereditary privilege in the French Revolution, the abolition of slavery in the 19th Century, and a gamut of innovations in the twentieth century such as universal suffrage, rejection of discrimination on the basis of race, sex, sexual proclivity or political affiliation, the development of international agreements to limit the kinds of behaviour permissible in war, recognition of the right of working people to withdraw their labour, and the extension of moral concern to those unable to advocate their own rights such as children, the handicapped and animals. These, together with the development of institutions, such as parliamentary democracy and the United Nations, which function to make these improvements politically secure, indicate that there has been moral progress - an insecure progress, to be sure, with many a backward step along the way, but progress nonetheless.

   In calling it 'progress', of course, I am expressing my own approval of it. The main purpose of this book is to justify such approval. It is to show that innovations like the ones listed above are derivable from the best account of how we ought to act and why. In essence, my theory is that our actions in the real world should, as far as possible, match those that would be agreed to by people in a hypothetical position of equal power. I will not spell out here all the ins and outs of such a theory as that would be to steal my own thunder. However, I am probably not giving too much away when I say that such a theory helps to explain the kind of moral progress I have just outlined. As power in any particular domain has equalised between the contending parties, so they have been forced to recognise each other's rights, at least in the sense that they had to show a public commitment to such rights, even if some of them in their hearts of hearts have resented doing so and have plotted to return themselves to the kind of situation of superior power where their own real preferences could triumph. Most, however, I think, have not done this but have come to accept these new values as the proper standards by which to conduct our relationships with each other. The theory fits well the case of religious persecution, where no particular sect had sufficient of a monopoly of power to feel safe in practising its faith, but also applies to those situations where the power of different social classes starts to balance out as a result of improved education, greater access to the media or greater purchasing power. It also applies in the cases where nations find themselves unable to indulge without penalty in gunboat diplomacy, either because the force of international opinion has become more effective or because their own citizens have become less jingoistic and less inclined to die for causes they themselves have not democratically endorsed.

My theory, then, is not merely a theory about how we ought to act, although that is its main purpose. It is primarily a normative theory, a theory that helps us judge, of the world as it is, whether or not it should stay that way or be changed. It aims to help us decide, when we are faced with a number of courses of action, which are the ones we should choose. However, even though it is first and foremost an action-guiding theory, it also has explanatory consequences in that, as people find themselves in positions that approximate closer to equal power in the real world, so their public judgements about what is right and wrong should parallel the judgements that would be reached in the hypothetical position of equal power. In addition to being a theory of metaethics, it may even provide the basis for a theory of sociology. In this book, however, I confine myself to its metaethical dimension.

The book begins with an overview of the theory, spelling out the conditions that make an agreement an unforced one, including the features of the contracting position itself and the qualities needed by the people occupying it if agreement is to be possible. In the course of the first chapter we are introduced to a number of characters who play an important role in the remainder of the book such as the egoist, the sectarian, the noncoercionist, the monist, and the impartialist. Reasons are given as to why the issues the theory deals with are moral ones and the question 'Why should we be moral?' is given what I believe to be its only plausible answer. It is then argued that agreement on the adoption of utilitarian principles to resolve conflicts of desires would be a forced agreement, something that people would not accept in a position of equal power.

The concern with utilitarianism is taken up in Chapter 2, where it is argued that the notion of freedom as the capacity to further one's interests, a notion that would seem to fit well with utilitarianism, is incompatible with impartialism because of the implications it has for the status of slaves. This chapter, in a sense, 'motivates' the book. It aims to demonstrate the importance of the issues involved.

In the third chapter, the theory spelt out in Chapter 1 is applied to a contemporary case of a conflict of desires, namely, the conflict between those who want to build a bridge at Hindmarsh Island in South Australia and those who want to ban such an enterprise on the grounds that it infringes the rights of the indigenous people there. Impartialism is applied to the reasons offered for banning the bridge to see whether or not the principles involved would be agreed to by the parties in a position of equal power.

Chapter 4 examines the scope of impartialist theory - does it apply only to conditions of moderate scarcity or is it supposed to tell us how people should act in extreme circumstances such as those where they can only survive by cannibalism? Does it apply only to people in social groupings or does it deal with how the isolated individual such as Robinson Crusoe should act? Can it answer such questions from within its own resources or must it appeal to additional principles that are independent of its basic assumptions but that are neutral between theories that make these assumptions and theories that do not? This chapter, as is the case with many of the following chapters, unfolds its topic by comparing the impartialist position with that adopted by John Rawls, especially in his book *A Theory of Justice*.

The fifth and sixth chapters begin the task of spelling out what moral or political conclusions follow from impartialism. They focus on what freedoms would be treated as basic by the parties in the position of equal power and what institutions they would see as fundamental to a polity.

Chapter 7 deals with questions related to the distribution of opportunities. For example, when, if ever, would the parties in a position of equal power be prepared to sacrifice a freedom for a gain in wealth or status? Under what conditions, if any, would they allow some people to have greater wealth than others?

Chapter 8 examines the stance that the parties in a position of equal power would take on religious freedom, both in the circumstance when they all believed one particular religion to be the true one and in the circumstance when the truth of any particular religion was a matter of dispute among them. This discussion raises some epistemological issues which lead on to Chapter 9 where impartialist theory is applied to whether or not education should be compulsory and, if it is, what its content and manner should be.

Chapter 10 considers what impartialism has to say about international law, contrasting the recommendations of the parties in the position of equal power with those made by Rawls in his article 'The Laws of Peoples'.

Chapters 11 and 12 look at what impartialism has to say about the rights of beings that are not themselves able to participate in the discussion in a position of equal power, such as foetuses, the mentally impaired, and animals. These issues are also used to investigate whether or not impartialism rests on any contentious metaphysical assumptions, as Vinit Haksar suggests is the case with Rawls.

Chapter 13 continues the scrutiny of metaphysical assumptions, arguing that impartialism is not committed to denying Derek Parfit's theory of personal identity. The account of ethics I offer contends that people such as egoists may well be immoral but that, in itself, does not make them irrational. Chapter 14 criticises a minbar of arguments meant to demonstrate the irrationality of egoism. Chapter 15 looks at two accounts of how ethical theories are to be justified, namely the account offered by John Rawls and the one offered by R.M. Hare and rejects both in favour of the procedure sketched earlier for impartialism. The final chapter proposes that there is a distinction between what can be rationally justified *simpliciter* and what it is rational to try to justify publicly, and that this distinction has an important role to play in explaining why the demands of morality seem to be categorical rather than hypothetical. In the process I criticise arguments offered by R.S. Peters and Michael Smith. It concludes with a brief discussion of the extent to which nature or nurture determines whether or not we are moral.

1 The Equal Power Perspective

1.1 Introduction

This book is primarily about those situations in which there is a conflict of desires between two or more people or groups of people. These conflicts are ones where one party wants to perform some particular action and the other party opposes this, especially by trying to make such an action illegal and ensuring that any attempts to perform it are effectively punished. My concern will be with how we are to decide who of the two is to have its way. Who, if either, is morally in the right? What is the just and fair resolution of the conflict?

My aim is to propose a theory that answers these questions, not only for our society and our time but across all cultures and all eras. It is a theory intended to give us answers that are as objective as possible, ones that are not merely matters of personal opinion, grounded in subjective preferences, but that hold for all sane rational adult human agents. While our principal focus will be on when it is justifiable to ban a type of act, we will also look at cases of when an act is to be morally condemned even though it is inappropriate to involve the legal process. The theory, then, is meant to be a comprehensive moral theory with a theory of justice as its dominant component.

To get the exposition of the theory under way, consider the case of dispute between a woman, Ann, who wants the law to allow abortions and a man, Ben, who wants the law to ban them. We have here what I will call an 'external' conflict of desires, that is, a disagreement between two parties over what should happen in a particular circumstance. Such 'external' conflicts of desire are to be distinguished from 'internal' ones, that is, ones where there is a clash of desires within the one person, for example, when Ben's desire to go to a party on the night before his exams clashes with his desire to pass the exam.

1

In looking at how to resolve such external conflicts of desires we will not want to deal a-new with each case. Rather, we will be interested in the reasons that the parties offer for their position in the conflict in order to be able to generalise across cases. We do not just want to know that Ann favours legalising abortion whereas Ben wants it criminalised. We also want to know the justifications they have for their stands. What is the principle on which Ann bases her support for legal abortion? What is the principle underlying Ben's opposition? Under what conditions might it be possible for Ben, say, to get Ann to change her mind and agree with his principle?

At first sight, there appear to be two different ways in which he might do so. Firstly, he could try to show her that there is something she values even more highly than the legalisation of abortion such that it will only be able to be achieved if abortion is against the law, that is, he could try to give her a reason from her own perspective to persuade her to voluntarily and sincerely change her mind. Secondly, he could try to force her to agree with him or, at least, force her to act as if she agrees with him in that her behaviour conforms with his position on the matter, even if she does not sincerely endorse it.

The most obvious way in which he could force her to appear to agree with him is through the use of intimidatory force. He could, for example, threaten to torture her. In these circumstances Ann has a choice of a kind. Given that she believes he can put his threat into effect, then she can choose either to disagree with him and risk being tortured or she can make sure she isn't tortured by saying that she agrees with him. If she chooses the latter option, then, in a sense, Ben has got her to agree with him, but her agreement here is a 'forced' and insincere agreement. It may be that what Ben has got her to do is what she should have done anyway but he has done nothing to convince her that his position on what the law should be was the right one. Nonetheless, forced agreement is one way to arbitrate such a dispute.

Another option is unforced agreement, one in which the agreement between the parties is a genuine consensus, accepted sincerely, a manifestation of consent, not of intimidation and threat. Intimidatory force, however, is not the only kind of force that Ben could have used. Suppose he had secretly drugged the water supply with a chemical that made everyone agree with him no matter what he proposed. Ann, then, would regard herself as voluntarily accepting his point of view, seeing herself as a rational agent who has exercised her free will in changing her mind. She would not regard herself as a victim of coercion, but surely she would be mistaken about this. The issue, then, of what makes an agreement forced or unforced may turn out to be more vexed than we, at first, suspect.

However, if we put tricky cases like the one above to one side for the moment, the obvious way for Ann and Ben to resolve their conflict by a means other than force is to resolve it by argument, by offering each other reasons to behave in one way rather than another. Of course, when Ben threatened to torture Ann if she didn't agree with him, he offered her a kind of argument, namely, the argument 'If you don't agree with me, then I will torture you, which is something that you will dislike even more than you dislike agreeing with me.' He gave her a reason to act as he preferred.

As is probably clear by now, what I am after in this theory is an account of when an agreement between people counts as a noncoercive one, one that does not amount to a substitute for straightforward physical compulsion. On my account, it is the fact that people would reach noncoercive agreement on the desirability of certain laws that makes those laws the morally justifiable ones, although I will leave until later an explanation of why exactly this is the relevant feature for their moral justification.

There are a number of requirements that an argument needs to meet to count as a noncoercive one, avoiding the kinds of problems sketched above. I will call the first of these requirements 'the neutrality requirement'. Why it is required will be explained in the next section.

1.2   The Neutrality Requirement

If Ann and Ben conduct their argument in the real world, it may well be the case that the outcome of the argument is determined by whoever has the greater power. In the situation we have described so far, Ben appears to have greater power than Ann because he, presumably, is able to put his threat to torture her into operation whereas there seems to be little she can do to stop him. Although Ben may have the greater power in the real world, it remains the case that he cannot guarantee to win the dispute with Ann. Even someone with relative weak power can find a pistol and ambush a powerful figure, or poison his food, or whatever. The real world can be regarded as a situation of 'uncertain' power.

Even so, as a rule, the person with the greater power will be able to force his or her preferred solution to any disagreement on the other party. In order to overcome this bias in the argument, we will need to consider how the parties would behave if they were no longer located in a situation of unequal power. We need to imagine them removed from the real world of uncertain safety, where force rather than reason can be the determinant of the outcome, into one where the conditions of the discussion are fair to them both, that is, where the context of the argument is neutral with respect to each party.

I will now turn to the second requirement that an agreement needs to meet if it is count as an unforced one. For reasons that will become clear in the next section, I will call this requirement 'the comparability requirement'.

1.3   The Comparability Requirement

When Ann and Ben argue as if they are no longer in location in a position of uncertain power, they are to be treated as if they have equal power with each other.[1] Having equal power means that neither of them has an 'advantage' over the other in terms of winning the argument, that is, it is not the case that there is some difference between them such that, when Ann has this property, she wins the argument against Ben but when Ben has it he wins against her yet, when each of them has it to an equal extent, they can only resolve the argument by appeal to logic and the truth of claims.

Greater physical force is a typical advantage, as is greater intelligence, or being a more skilful liar, or being more bloody-minded or having greater patience or charisma, or being party to information denied the other. If Ben is physically stronger than Ann, then he can use this advantage to get her to agree with him in situations where she would not have agreed with him if their physical force had been equal. Having greater physical force enables him to exercise sanctions against her. If she doesn't act as if she agrees with him, even if insincerely, then he is able to do things to her that she doesn't want done whereas she cannot do such things, or even equivalently unpleasant things, to him in return.

All advantages can be translated into physical force terms. If Ben is able to get agreement due to some advantage then, were he and Ann equal with respect to this advantaging characteristic and with respect to all others except physical force, then he would only be able to get the same agreement from her by resorting to the use of, or threatening the use of, sanctions. It may be that other advantages also have this convertibility value, being able to be substituted for force in some or even all circumstances, but it will be convenient to take physical force as the standard as it is the most readily recognised and familiar.

None of the above should be taken to mean that deceiving people, for example, is always as morally bad as threatening them with some violent consequence or physically manhandling them until they do what you want. Most people will desist from their efforts to gain an advantage over others if strategies such as deceit no longer work. They will not resort to the violence that would otherwise be necessary to produce the same result but this in no way mitigates the exploitative nature of their original intent. Nonetheless, it is a salutary reminder to those who engage in practices such as deceit to realise that, if the deceit had failed, just how much violence they would have had to have used on other people to have obtained the same result.

Within our model, then, Ann and Ben would not be able to settle their disagreement by force if neither had any advantages over the other. In such a situation their power is equal. As a consequence, if they are able to settle their disagreement at all, it will have to be by noncoercive argument. Even here, neither of them is to gain an advantage over the other by greater proficiency at argument as such.

Why, then, is there need for argument, given that each party knows whatever the other knows and has the same reasoning capacities? The point of argument is to ensure that there is genuine consent, that those involved willingly accept the principle that will govern their actions. Even though they are to be conceived as being equally intelligent, they may well not configure their knowledge in the same way as each other. They may reach different conclusions because their interests lead them to see the links between what they know in terms of what is important from their perspective rather than from the other person's. The role of the other party is to ensure that his or her perspective is taken into account, that it is not sidelined but is given due attention, that the enterprise is a mutual one, not one in which one party sets up the premises to be considered and does the derivation of conclusions.

In the position of equal power, then, Ann will offer arguments to Ben as to why the law should allow her to have the abortion, say, and Ben will offer arguments why it should not. Usually this will involve her showing him that allowing the abortion falls under some general principle, then arguing that he, as well as her, has good reasons for adopting this general principle. The aim of the discussion is to find a principle that both of them accept.

Should such a principle be found, the understanding is that each of them has contracted to treat as legitimate only those laws in the real world whose legitimacy is agreed to in the position of equal power. The principle, then, becomes the criterion of what makes a particular law on the subject under consideration morally right and wrong in the actual world. In this instance, the principle becomes the criterion of when, if at all, it is morally right or wrong to ban or permit abortions.

One requirement, then, that must apply to the argument between Ann and Ben if any agreement they reach is to be unforced is that the agreement is one they would accept in a position of equal power, that is, when the parties to the debate are conceived of as being comparable in their ability to manipulate the outcome in their own favour.

I will now turn to the third requirement for an agreement to count as unforced, which I will call the 'symmetry' requirement.

1.4   The Symmetry Requirement

In the real world we may propose a principle as a resolution of a conflict of desires because we think that we can trick other people into thinking that the principle is to their benefit when it is not. If we are arguing as if we are in a position of equal power, however, we have to argue as if other people know whatever we know. If we know that this principle is not to their benefit then so do they. Moreover, as knowledge of our own motives gives us an advantage over others, we also have to argue as if our motives are transparent. As a consequence, we cannot propose principles if the only plausible explanation for our doing so is that we are assuming superior power in real life. To do so indicates that our commitment is to the use of force if it is on our side, not to the resolution of the conflict by a means other than force. We must sincerely be prepared to accept the principle even if it applies to us when we have inferior power in the real world.

In order to demonstrate that we have proposed a particular principle in good faith, not merely because we expect it to benefit us in the power conditions in the real world, it has to be the case that we would find the principle acceptable even if the power conditions in the real world were reversed. We must still be prepared to advocate this principle even if it operates when the superior power belonged to the other party. We must be prepared to endorse the principle when it is applied symmetrically to both the situation in which we have the superior power and to the situation when the other party has the superior power. We must prefer what I will call the 'symmetrified' form of this principle to the symmetrified form of any competing principle.

Another aspect of symmetrification is the requirement that we must be prepared to accept that we should be penalised in the real world if we break the agreements reached in the position of equal power. It cannot be the case that we agree to a system of punishment because we assume that we will have superior power in the real world and , therefore, it never will apply to us. Rather, we must argue as if we were sincerely committed to all people who transgress impartialist agreements being apprehended and punished, including ourselves.

1.4.1   The Egoist

To see how this works, it will be useful to look at the kinds of people that the parties in the position of equal power might be. The first kind of person that Ann, say, could be is an egoist. As it happens, she could be one of two kinds of egoists, either a universalist one or a particularist one. If she is a particularist one, then her basic value, the fundamental principle which underlies her actions, is that everyone should do what serves her particular self-interest. If she is a universalist egoist, then her most basic motivation is that each person should do whatever is most in his or her own self-interest, which has, as a corollary that she, Ann, should give Ann's own self-interest priority over everyone else's. (Certain philosophers have argued that either form of egoism is logically incoherent. I reply to these claims in Chapters 14 and 16.)

1.4.2   The Particularist Egoist

I will consider the case of Ann as a particularist egoist first. The principle that drives her actions is that everyone ought to do what serves her personal self-interest. There is, however, no point in Ann offering such a principle to Ben in a position of equal power as the basis for resolving their conflict over abortion (or any other dispute, for that matter). Ben will not have Ann's self-interest as the determining goal of his actions. Whatever his goals are, then, it will entirely fortuitous if the satisfaction of Ann's self-interest turns out to be the means that a rational agent with those goals should choose. As Ann has no capacity in the position of equal power to force Ben to agree to her particularist egoist principle, and as following it may well prevent him achieving what he most values, he will reject it as a way of arbitrating between the proposal that abortion be legalised and the proposal that it not be. It will fail the comparability test.

1.4.3   The Superfan Requirement

It is conceivable, however, that people other than Ann might govern their lives by the principle 'Do whatever best serves Ann's self-interest'. Sadly for Ann, such people are rarely, if ever, found in the real world. Perhaps, if she were a rock star with a following as dedicated as Elvis's, or a religious guru or political messiah or some such, then she may evoke sufficient fervour in some people, whom I will call her 'superfans', to cause them to sacrifice all their own interests in her service. Her superfans, however, are not in dispute with her over questions of fundamental value. They share with her a common principle for guiding their lives, namely, maximising the satisfaction of Ann's self-interest. The only source of disagreement between them, or between them and Ann, will be over the best means for achieving it.

Questions about the best means for achieving an agreed-upon goal, however, are not the questions for which the position of equal power is designed. Instead, it is intended to arbitrate between otherwise irresolvable disagreements. It is to be taken as an assumption of the equal power model that neither party in the position of equal power is the superfan of the other. They are to be regarded as being in genuine conflict over a basic value. Ben, therefore, is not to be conceived of as one of Ann's superfans. He is in conflict with her at more than just the instrumental level of how to achieve some common goal. Their very goals differ.

This point also makes clear that one of the conditions that the parties must meet to be situated in the position of equal power is that they be agents whose goals are, ultimately, independent of each other, that is, each of them is an 'autonomous' agent. The conflicts between them cannot only be technical ones but must ultimately, be ones where each of them is, as a distinct subject, capable of endorsing values incompatible with those of the other. Another requirement, then, that an agreement must meet in order to count as unforced is what I will call the 'superfan' requirement.

1.4.4 The Universalist Egoist

Suppose, however, that Ann was a universalist egoist instead, that is, she sincerely holds the principle that everyone ought to maximise their own personal self-interest. If she puts forward this principle as one that Ben should consider, she is not proposing that he pursue her self-interest in preference to his own, as she was when she put forward the particularist version. The position of equal power by itself doesn't seem to rule out universalist egoism. As a consequence, Ben may well find such a principle attractive.

1.4.5 Symmetrification

However, it cannot be the case that he finds it attractive because he thinks that he will be in a position of superior power in the real world and, thereby, able to get away with benefiting himself at the expense of other people. Were the real world scenario to be the other way round so that Ann, say, was the one with the superior power, then it cannot be the case that he would no longer be interested in agreeing in the position of equal power that universalist egoism be the principle that governed disputes in the real world. In other words, were we to make Ann's position in the real world symmetrical to the one he envisages for himself, then he must be prepared to accept the reverse application of it.

If he is not prepared to accept the symmetrified version of the universalist egoist principle, then he is a pseudo-universalist egoist. He is just a particularist egoist in disguise. In recommending a principle, even if it is a universal one, just because he thinks he will have the advantage in the real world under such a principle, he shows himself to be committed to the resolution of conflicts between people by force and not by reason and argument.

If Ben is a sincere universalist egoist, that is, he not only accepts the application of the principle when he is in a position of superior power but also when superior power is possessed by parties who further their own self-interest at the expense of his, then his universal egoism cannot be excluded from the position of equal power on the grounds of the symmetry test alone. As we shall see, however, there are other reasons why it is not an acceptable part of the position of equal power.

Symmetrification as a procedure works as follows:- Suppose a principle is proposed, say Principle P. Ann, say, is to consider how the adoption of P would impact on her values if she were in a position of inferior power as well as in a position of superior power. However, she must also ask herself, 'Is there some other principle Q which, when the same process is applied to it, will give her a better outcome in the position of inferior power?' If the answer is 'Yes', then Q is to be preferred to P. The same, however, is to be done for Ben, so the final principle that the two of them must adopt is the one that maximises the values of each of them, with respect to the particular item of contention, when each of them looks at the situation in terms of their being the one in the situation of inferior power. If, for example, the item of contention is choice of religion, then the situation where each of them is free to practise their religion with consenting others, and to preach it, but not to engage in forceful conversion, will be the best inferior power option for each of them, provided (as we shall see) that neither of them cares most about converting others. It may be, however, that the conflict is between religionists and atheists. If so, then the principle will not be about religion as such but about what plays the same role as religion in the lives of the two groups.

1.4.6   The Sectarian

The egoist is closely related, as a kind of person, to an individual I will call the 'sectarian'. Exactly why these two are closely related will become clear when I discuss their respective attitudes to the equal worth of people. For the moment, the important thing to note about the sectarian (say, Ben) is that his fundamental value is devotion to a particular cause. The object of a sectarian's devotion can be secular as well as religious. For example, someone whose life is committed to the triumph of a political party or the achievement of artistic perfection is as much a sectarian in this sense as someone who worships a particular religious concept of God. What is important about this cause is that the sectarian is dedicated to pursuing it regardless of whether or not the parties in the position of equal power agree to it.

1.4.7 The Particularist Sectarian

Sectarians, like egoists, can come in either particularist or universalist forms. If Ben is a particularist sectarian, then he will hold the principle that everyone ought to do whatever is necessary to consummate his particular cause. As we have seen, Ann is to be conceptualised in the position of equal power as in dispute with Ben at the level of fundamental values so she will not agree to this principle. She may, for example, be an egoist who wants her own self-interest maximised and it would be entirely fortuitous that this should correspond to consummating Ben's cause. Alternatively, she may be a sectarian whose cause is quite different to Ben's. Again, any correspondence between courses of action conducive to the realisation of both their goals would be entirely coincidental. As Ben has no capacity in the position of equal power to force her to agree to his principle, and as following his principle may well prevent the achievement of what she most values, she will reject it. It will have failed the commensurability test.

1.4.8 The Universalist Sectarian

Ben, however, might modify his sectarian principle so that it is universalist rather than particularist. He might suggest that all people should pursue the triumph of their own cause over that of everyone else's, in the sense that the triumphant cause eliminates the others. It does not coexist peacefully with them but replaces them entirely. As a sincere universalist sectarian, however, he would have to endorse the principle both when his cause has superior power and when it does not. Only if he is prepared to do this will he meet the symmetry requirement. Otherwise, he just shows himself to be committed to resolving conflicts of desire by force and not by reason, as we saw with the pseudo-universalist egoist.

    To illustrate this point, consider a case in which Ben worships the god Zeus, and believes that his religion is the only permissible one. Suppose further that Ann worships the god Osiris. If Ben only recommends the adoption of universal sectarianism because he thinks that the Zeusists in the real world would be able to eradicate all other religions, including Osirisism, then he is really a partialist egoist dressing up his partialism in a pseudo-universalist garb. Were the symmetrical counterpart of the principle to apply, that is, were the Osirisists to have superior power in the real world, he would reject universal sectarianism. This, however, contravenes the symmetrification requirement.

The genuine universalist sectarian seems somewhat similar to the kind of character that R.M. Hare (1963, pp.159-185) calls 'the fanatic' in that both are prepared to accept a principle even when it turns out that they are the losers under the principle rather than the winners, that is, they are prepared to 'universalise' their principle. Hare's example is of a Nazi who advocates the principle that all Jews should be killed and who, when he discovers that he himself is a Jew, offers himself up to the Nazi authorities.

It is now time to turn to the fifth requirement, which I will call the 'nonconcerionist requirement'.

1.5   The Noncoercionist Requirement

1.5.1   The Coercionist

As we have seen, the parties in the position of equal power could be egoists or sectarians. This list, however, does not exhaust the possibilities, another of which is the person whom I will call the 'coercionist'. If Ann, for example, were a coercionist then she would be the kind of person who wanted to coerce other people more than she wanted them not to coerce her. Her desire to control their lives is greater than her desire that they don't control her life. She is willing to accept the risk that people who want to coerce her more than they want her not to coerce them have the same right to do so as she does. She holds the symmetrical principle that everyone be free to try to coerce others to conform to their will. If she turns out to have the superior power, then she will make people do as she wishes but if others have the superior power and compel her in ways injurious to her personal self-interest or to the causes she espouses then she acknowledges that this is consistent with the principle she has endorsed.

If Ann were to propose this principle in the position of equal power, then Ben is to be conceptualised as opposing it. In effect, as he is bound by the symmetry requirement, this means that he is committed to the alternative principle that neither party be free to coerce the other. I will call people like Ben by the name 'noncoercionists.'

In the position of equal power, then, either Ann could seek to convince Ben to become a coercionist or Ben could seek to convince her to become a noncoercionist. Given that the two positions seem incompatible, how is the dispute between them to be resolved? If it is not resolvable, then, on the premises of the theory I am offering, there is no way to show that coercionism is morally wrong. The reason for this is that an act will only be morally wrong on this theory if the parties in the position of equal power agree to reject the principle from which it is derived. But the disagreement between the coercionist and the noncoercionist seems to be so fundamental that there appears to be no way in which they will ever reach agreement to reject one of these principles and support the other.

I said at the beginning of this chapter that our principal focus will be on when it is justifiable to ban acts of certain kinds. The case we have used to illustrate this kind of issue has been the case of legalising or banning abortion. We have been looking at various principles that Ann and Ben might propose in order to resolve the dispute in their respective favours. One principle that either might propose in the position of equal power is that they each be free in the real world to try to impose their preferred outcome on the other, that is, that each be free to try to coerce the other.

It seems unlikely that this principle would pass the symmetry test because we would only expect someone to propose it if they thought they would have superior power in the real world and, therefore, be able to impose their preferred outcome on the other party. However, it would pass the symmetry test if the person who proposed it (say, Ann) was sincerely prepared to accept it even if she were in the position of inferior power in the real world. She accepts that fairness in the form of the comparability and symmetry conditions requires her to take the risk that she will not have the superior force essential to compelling others to conform to her preferences. Such a person may be rare but she does not seem to be logically impossible. In effect, she is an idealist whose ideal is that disputes between persons be decided in favour of whoever has the greater power.

It seems clear enough that Ann, if she is a coercionist, is not the kind of person who can be one of the parties in the position of equal power. The point of the position of equal power is to reach agreement on conflicts of values by means other than force. The sincere coercionst, however, is committed to resolving them by force even when she is the loser in such a scenario. The parties in the position of equal power, then, must be noncoercionists.

1.5.2   Determinate Answers

However, we can see a further reason to exclude the coercionist from the position of equal power if we return to the function such a position is supposed to serve.   Its purpose is to enable us to decide whether a particular action is such that people in the real world should be stopped from performing it.   Consider the case in which Ben wants to murder Ann, say.   Murdering Ann counts as a case of coercion.   It amounts to forcing her to lose her life against her will.   There may be cases where Ben can take her life noncoercively, that is, cases where she willingly allows herself to be killed, but such cases do not usually get called 'murder'.

Now, if the noncoercionist principle were to be adopted by the parties in the position of equal power, then it would produce a determinate answer to the question 'Should Ben's desire to murder Ann take precedence over Ann's desire not to be murdered?' The answer would be 'No.'   By contrast, the coercionist principle is not able to give us a determinate answer to this question.   Whose desire takes precedence will be entirely a matter of the respective natural capacities of Ann and Ben, and luck.   This means that, in most cases, whichever of the two of them happens to have the superior power will be the one whose desire is satisfied, the exception being that sometimes even superior power can be trumped by sheer bad luck.

Our whole enterprise, however, was to find a method other than superior power for deciding whether an act should be performed or stopped.   We, therefore, must reject the coercionist principle.   Moreover, if we discover that the person we are arguing with is a coercionist, the appropriate strategy would appear to be to abandon the argument or, at least, no longer treat it as a genuine argument, and get ourselves the necessary superior power.   As a consequence, coercionists can be regarded as excluded from the position of equal power.   They are not genuine seekers of a resolution of a conflict between people by means other than force.

In order, then, for an agreement to be an unforced one, it must be made between parties who cannot argue as if one or both of them were coercionists.   They have to argue as they were noncoercionists.   If a principle would only be proposed because its advocate wanted to coerce others more than he or she wanted not to be coerced, then that principle is unacceptable in the position of equal power.   The parties must argue as if they were the kinds of people who want not to be coerced by others more than they want to engage in coercing others.

When we left the universalist egoist and sectarian in the previous section, we had seen that neither the comparability requirement nor the symmetry requirement excluded them from the position of equal power, which meant that agreement in that position seemed impossible. Now that we have been introduced to the coercionist and seen that he or she is committed to the resolution of conflicts of desires by force and not by reason, we are in a position to determine the equal power acceptability of characters like the universalist egoist and sectarian. I will begin with the universalist egoist.

The particularist egoist (say, Ann) offered her principle regardless of whether or not she would have superior power in the real world. In effect, then, she is saying that any conflict of egoistic desires between herself and Ben should be resolved in favour of whoever has the superior force in the real world. As such, her position is a coercionist one and is to be rejected in the position of equal power for the same reasons. In like vein, the universalist sectarian Ben is proposing that any conflict between his cause and some incompatible cause be resolved in favour of whichever has the superior power in the real world. He, too, is committed to coercionism and, so, cannot be one of the parties in the position of equal power. I will now look at the sixth and final requirement for an agreement to count as an example of genuine consent, which I will call the 'nonmonist requirement.'

1.6   The Nonmonist Requirement

One particular form that coercionism can take is what I will call 'monism'. The parties in the position of equal power will not be able to reach agreement if one or both of them is so committed to some value that they are prepared to destroy each other, or everyone (themselves included), when their power is equal, rather than settle for less of what they value. It could also be called the 'mutual destruction' condition.

As an example, let us return to the case of Ben who is a Zeusist and Ann who is a Osirisist. Suppose Ben so strongly valued his Zeusist religion that he would rather die than live in a nonZeusist world. Let us assume further that it is part of Zeusism that everyone must become a Zeusist. Now, if Ben was a noncoercionist, that is, he wanted not to be coerced more than he wanted to coerce, then this situation would not arise because he would be prepared to practice those elements of Zeusism that were available to the individual worshipper.

Ben, however, in this example, is a monist, that is, he would rather die than live in a world that does not have his value or values fully instantiated (the 'monist' term here refers to the fact that it is his value or values that must be fully instantiated, that is, the values of only one of the parties to the debate are to be met). Moreover, it matters to him more that he coerce everyone into adherence to these values than that he be left free to practise those of them that can be engaged in by consenting parties.

There is, as a consequence, nothing that the other parties in the position of equal power can argue with him about. They cannot show him that there is some other value he has that is better served by some mutually beneficial principle, or that there is some range of values that is so served. Ben is a monist and what is needed in the position of equal power is a nonmonist or, if people are monists, then they must be noncoercionist monists, that is, they must limit the methods they use in pursuit of their single value to those acceptable to the parties in a position of equal power.

It should be noted, however, that what is at issue here is a monism of values brought into the position of equal power. Once the parties in the position of equal power have determined that some principles or values are the right ones, then it is not a monist issue on this account that a person would rather die than see a world that did not instantiate his or her 'equal power' values, although it would be a matter to be settled in a position of equal power whether this ever justified mutual destruction. It seems highly unlikely that the parties in a position of equal power, given that they must be noncoercionists, would rather see themselves and their opposition killed than allow a world where equal power values had been totally suppressed.

We have, now, spelt out all the requirements for an agreement to count as an unforced one. These can be regarded as the axioms at the basis of the impartialist system. In summary, they are:-

(1) the neutrality requirement;
(2) the superfan requirement;
(3) the comparability requirement;
(4) the symmetry requirement;
(5) the noncoercionist requirement; and
(6) the nonmonist requirement.

There are, however, a few additional features of the theory that need to be developed at this point to make later exposition and analysis more readily comprehensible, for example, it will be helpful to be introduced to the fourth kind of person whom we will find in the position of equal power - a character that I will call the 'impartialist'.

1.7   The Impartialist

The people in the position of equal power can adopt one of two attitudes towards whatever principles they eventually agree on. Either they can be the kind of person who will act in accord with those principles in real life or else they can be the kind of person who will ignore what was agreed to in a position of equal power and, if they have superior power in the real world, will pursue whatever principle they personally preferred. The first kind of person is the impartialist. The second kind of person I will call a 'partialist'.

Agreements reached in the position of equal power as to what principle should be followed in the real world or which of two conflicting desires should be met in the real world are agreements that are impartial between the disputants. They are fair resolutions of the conflict. Anyone who opts for an outcome other than one that would be endorsed in the position of equal power is acting in a biased, prejudiced, unfair and unjust manner. They are being partial to one side of the argument rather than impartial to all participants. As we have seen, egoists, sectarians, coercionists and monists are not being impartial in this sense.

The differences between these four kinds of personalities can be summarised in terms of their attitude to when the use of force is permissible. Impartialists believe that might is right only when it is used to enforce whatever has been agreed without any exercise of might, that is, whatever is agreed to in the position of equal power. The egoist believes that might is right only when he or she has it, or it serves their self-interest. The sectarian believes that might is right only when it is possessed by his or her ideal or cause and its adherents or serves its interests, and the coercionist believes that might is always right, regardless of who has it, even someone other than him or herself.

If impartialism is the method by which we determine the morality of an act, then an act will be morally permissible if the parties in the position of equal power agree that people are allowed to do it in the real world. It will be morally obligatory if they agree that it be required in the relevant circumstances and it will be morally forbidden if they agree to ban it. It will be morally wrong to do any act in the real world that is forbidden by impartialism, or to fail to do any act that is obligatory. It will be morally right to do any act that is obligatory and to either do or not do any act that is permitted.

As I said two paragraphs ago, impartialists believe that might is right only when it is used to enforce whatever has been agreed without any exercise of might, that is, whatever is agreed to in the position of equal power. Impartialists, then, are prepared to accept that it is sometimes necessary to use force. To avoid any misunderstanding on this point, it is worth spelling it out in more detail, as I will do in the next section.

1.8   Impartialist Force in the Real World

Impartialists will condone the use of force in the real world if it is used to ensure compliance with the principles agreed to in the position of equal power. When, and how, force should be used in the real world to ensure obedience to impartialist principles is itself a question to be debated from an equal power perspective. There will different views, different principles proposed on the matter, so the issue needs to be conceptualised as a debate under equal power conditions between those who favour a particular principle and those who oppose it.

However, the equal power conditions are to be understood as ensuring that the protagonists for each side have not closed their minds to the possible merits of the alternative principles. Which principle to adopt is an open question for them in a way that is not true of partialists. Egoists are never sincere in agreeing to any principle that might result in their being forced to act against their own self-interest. If they make such an agreement, then it is a hypocritical one and they will break it as soon as the opportunity presents itself.

This is just as true of universalist egoists as it is of particularist ones. While the universalist egoist (say Ann) accepts that other egoists are right to benefit themselves at her expense when they have superior power, this does not mean that she will honour any agreement they force on her using their superior power. The moment she has the power to get away with breaking this agreement, she will do so. This is quite consistent with her universal egoism.

Likewise for sectarians. Both particularist and universalist sectarians are never sincere in agreeing to any principle that commits them to being forced to sacrifice part or all of their ideal or cause. The universalist sectarian (say, Ben) will sincerely accept the right of other sectarians to force him into agreements, when they have superior power, that benefit their cause at the expense of his, but it will be perfectly consistent with his universalist sectarianism for him to dishonour such an agreement as soon as he has the power to do so. All the varieties of egoists and sectarians are coercionists and, as we have seen, while coercionists sincerely endorse the right of whoever has the greater power to use it, they will pursue power for themselves to force their own preferences on others.

The only kind of person who sincerely says that he or she agrees to be forced to adhere to one principle rather than another because it has been agreed to from an equal power perspective is the impartialist. This doesn't rule out impartialists behaving with weakness of will in the real world and sometimes acting like egoists or sectarians but it does rule out their thinking such behaviour to be acceptable rather than a matter for shame and remorse.

It should be noted that, even though the impartialist (say, Ann) realises that any partialist in the real world (say, Ben) only uses argument as a substitute for force, she is limited in the ways she can respond to this fact by her own impartialism. She will be entitled to use force to ensure he adheres to impartialist principles but the kind and degree of force has to be acceptable to the parties in a position of equal power. Moreover, the parties are likely to insist that she and her fellow impartialists still engage in argument with partialists in order to model the appropriate process for the resolution of conflicts of desires to ensure that he understands the reason for any eventual resort to coercion and to make apparent to themselves that their course of action is a publicly justifiable one that is fully thought through and that has had an opportunity to be contested.

I have treated all conflicts of desires so far as if they were two-party conflicts. However, there can be many positions that people can adopt on a particular dispute. One case we have used frequently is the abortion debate. People can range in their views on this matter from those who want all abortions legalised to those who want none, with positions in between such as those who would allow abortions in the first trimester, or those who would allow it if the woman had been raped, and so on. Nonetheless, I still think that such a range of opinions can be dealt with by the two-party approach and will look at how in the next section.

1.9   Two-Party Conflicts of Desire

I have cast the discussion so far in terms of two parties because all conflicts of desire involving more than two parties can be reduced to conflicts between two parties. Consider the abortion case referred to above. Let us suppose that one of the parties to this dispute is in favour of legalising all abortions. They will be opposed, as we saw, by those who want all abortions banned, as well as those who want all abortions banned except those where the woman was raped, or those who want all abortions banned except where the mother's life is at risk, and so on.

All of these groups, however, can be treated as one group, namely, the group that opposes legalising all abortions. Let us call these two groups Group 1 and Group 2 and let us suppose that, in a position of equal power, the parties agree that Group 1 is wrong. (Again, this is only an example. I am not saying that impartialists would actually agree that it is wrong to legalise all abortions.) The conflict of desires, now, narrows down to a conflict that was previously within Group 2. This conflict can be also be turned into a two-part dispute. We can focus on whichever view within Group 2 interests us and treat the protagonists of that view as Group 3 and all those who oppose that view as Group 4.

Hopefully, when the parties to the dispute consider it as if they were in a position of equal power, they will come to a decision about the correctness or otherwise of Group 3's view. If they reject Group 3's position, then there will be a new conflict of desires to be considered from within the parties that comprised Group 4, and this in its turn can be formulated as a two-party dispute between the Group 5 part of Group 4 and those in Group 4 who oppose the Group 5 position (that is, those who would make up a Group 6) and so on, until there is a group (which may consist of only one person) whose opinion would be accepted by the parties in a position of equal power.

None of this is meant to suggest that the adoption of the impartialist procedure guarantees that we will come to a consensus in real life or that, if we do, the consensus we reached actually is the decision that the parties in the position of equal power would make. Consensus in the real world can be prevented by the resistance of egoists and sectarians, by differences between us in knowledge, reasoning ability, patience, etcetera. Even if we reach consensus, it could be because we all shared a false belief, or did not know all the facts, or were blinded by a common prejudice. In the next section I will look at the implications of our fallibility in more detail.

1.10   Fallible and Infallible Impartialists

Even though we argue with each other as if we were constrained by the requirements of the equal power perspective, we cannot avoid bringing to the argument whatever limitations we possess. The conclusions we will reach, no matter how conscientious we are, may turn out to be quite different to those that noncoercionists without these limitations would reach in a position of equal power. Just because we try to reason as if we were impartialists - in fact, even if we are impartialists - we still retain our own restricted knowledge, our own susceptibilities to logical error, etcetera.

At our best, then, we will still be very fallible rational agents. This fallibility will affect which principles it is that we reach unforced agreement on. What we will get in the real world, then, as a result of people applying the impartialist method, is a set of provisional impartialist principles. They are provisional because they are not necessarily the principles that sincere impartialists would agree upon if they had their facts right, had included all the relevant facts, had made no logical errors, had suffered no delusions about their motives for adopting a principle, and so on.

While these provisional principles are the ones that we will have to work with in any particular place at any particular time, we would prefer to follow the set of unprovisional principles if we could generate them. They are the ideal to which we, as impartialists, aspire but we can never know when we have actually obtained them, just as scientists can never know when they have reached the final truth about the nature of empirical reality. Nonetheless, the more we know about the relevant facts, the more we have scrutinised our logic, the more our motives have been exposed to examination, the more likely it is that our principles correspond to the ideal. It would be most unlikely, for example, that the principle that it is always wrong to torture people for fun should turn out to be mistaken, just as it is highly unlikely that the inverse law for attraction between masses should turn out to be wrong in physics.

In a way, then, when we argue with each other about which act is the right one to do in a particular situation, we are out to demonstrate that this is the act that the parties in a position of equal power would agree should govern this kind of conflict of desires were they infallible and omniscient. If we are sincere impartialists, we will amend our opinions in the direction of whichever principle has the best credentials as the unprovisional impartialist principle. If one of us can show the others that their proposal to resolve a conflict of desires rests on a factual or logical error or oversight, then the rest of us should modify our position.

It is worth noting that, while impartialism is an objectivist theory, that is, it treats some moral claims as true and others as false, it is not an absolutist theory. It does not offer us principles that we are to hold to regardless of our situation, that is, its principles are situation-sensitive, although it may well offer us principles where a situation that would justify a variation to the principle is hard to imagine, such as the principle that it is wrong to torture people for fun. There will, however, be many principles which can be honoured with quite different practices, for example, different cultures may well be expressing the same principle of respect for the dead in practices as different as burying the dead, cremating them, leaving their bodies out to be picked clean by vultures, etcetera. The only principle, then, that impartialism holds absolutely is the impartialist principle itself, that is, the principle that one should act in accord with whatever would be agreed to by the parties in a position of equal power.

Even if all that I have said so far about impartialists and partialists is true, it could still be the case that there is no more justification for being one rather than the other. Why be an impartialist rather than an egoist or a sectarian? This question is part of the metaethics of impartialism, which I will look at in the next three sections.

1.11 Why be an Impartialist?

Metaethical questions about impartialism will be of two kinds. Firstly, questions of how to justify impartialism. Secondly, questions of the meaning of impartialist claims, especially whether they are to be understood as claims that are just expressions of subjective feeling or claims that are either true or false. I will begin with the issue of justification. Can we show that it is rational to be an impartialist and irrational not to be? If we could, then this would be the most powerful kind of justification for it that we could present.

When we try to answer the above questions, we arrive at what I will call the 'partialist' paradox. The partialist has been defined in such a way that a person (say, Ben) will only count as a partialist if he is committed to the resolution of disagreements by force rather than by argument. As a consequence, the question 'Why prefer impartialism to partialism?' amounts to the request to provide an argument why argument should be preferred to force.

Suppose Ben is asking for a logical demonstration of the rational superiority of impartialism. In effect, he is saying that he wants to resolve the disagreement between partialists and impartialists by argument. Whoever sincerely wants to settle this disagreement by argument has already decided that at least one disagreement should be settled by argument rather than by force, that is, has already committed themselves to at least a limited impartialism. It is not possible to seriously entertain this question with an open mind as to what the outcome will be. One either enters this dispute with the view that disagreements should be settled by argument or one doesn't. In so far as disagreements are resolvable by argument they must be disagreements other than ones about whether argument is ever to have binding force as the resolution of disagreement.

In the end, then, we have only two choices - whether we are going to regard ourselves as bound to follow those principles chosen by argument under impartialist conditions even when we have superior power or whether we will abuse a position of superior power to enforce those principles that we held prior to any argument. Which we do will depend on the kind of person we are - on our intuitions, as the current terminology puts it.[2] Nonetheless, if my argument in this book is correct, we are restricted to two grand intuitions, just as Oscar Wilde suggested there were only two kinds of tragedy - either the tragedy of not getting what we want or the tragedy of getting it. In much the same way, we are restricted to either the grand intuition that conflicts of desires are to be resolved by force or to the alternative grand intuition that they are not Any lesser intuitions fall in either one camp or the other and are rejected or accepted on the basis of whether or not they fit the grand intuition.

Once we have identified ourselves with the impartialist camp, for example, then the logic of the impartialist requirements itself acts to narrow down the range of morally acceptable principles available to us. In practice, the problem is unlikely to be serious. Few people will publicly admit to partialism. As a rule they will attempt to dress their egoistic or sectarian interests up in an impartialist disguise because any other approach publicly demonstrates their commitment to having their own way. They will be disinclined to show that they regard those who disagree with them with contempt unless their power is so great they can ignore what others think. This rarely happens. As a matter of practicality, then, there is constant pressure on people to argue in accordance with impartialist standards and push for principles with an impartialist plausibility. Even white supremacists, for example, will not put forward arguments that their protection of white privilege is just self-interested or rank ideology. They appeal to such notions as 'desert' and 'the best interests of the blacks'. This could be called the 'pragmatic' justification of impartialism.

Another way to approach the question of the justification of impartialism is to elaborate the idea that the partialist (Ben, say) is committed to having his own way, that he has no genuine respect for others as equal partners into an endeavour to arrive at a mutually acceptable resolution of a conflict of desires. I will look at this approach to the justification of impartialism in the next section.

1.12   Justification and the Equal Worth of Persons

Consider a case in the real world where Ann and Ben have incompatible desires but Ann has superior power to Ben. Suppose Ann sincerely believes in the principle that abortions ought to be allowed whereas Ben sincerely wants all abortions to be illegal. Suppose, further, that both Ann and Ben know that, in a position of equal power, Ann would not agree to making all abortions illegal and Ben would not agree to allowing any to be legal. Should Ann use her superior power in the real world to get Ben to agree with her, and to publicly say that everyone should agree, that abortions are morally permissible, even if his agreement is insincere? To do this, of course, Ann and her supporters would need to control the government or the military. (It should be noted that this is only an example. I am not saying that the parties in the position of equal power do actually know that agreement on the rights and wrongs of abortion is impossible but, for the purposes of illustration, let us suppose that they do know this.)

If Ann does force Ben to say publicly in the real world that he thinks abortions should be legal, then she does so even though she cannot give Ben any reason that he would find acceptable in a position of equal power, which means that she cannot give any reason that he would find acceptable in a position where both he and Ann are equally capable of determining which principle governing the rights and wrongs of abortion is the better principle. Ann certainly has not convinced Ben that hers is the better principle just because, in the real world, she can intimidate him into public agreement. Ben is as capable as she is, in this scenario, of assessing the merits of the two principles and he is not convinced that hers deserves priority over his.

If Ann, then, having the superior power in the real world, chooses to enforce the principle that abortions be legal, given the story we have told so far, Ben can only interpret this choice as being based on who holds the principle, not on any quality internal to the principle itself. If Ann had sincerely proposed to Ben in a position of equal power that a principle be chosen solely because it was her principle, then Ben would have rejected it.

But in this case, there would be no disagreement between Ann and Ben over ultimate principles As long as there is a disagreement between Ann and Ben over ultimate values, Ben could not, as a rational agent, accept it as a reason for choosing the legalisation of abortion over its criminalisation that it can be derived from the principle that whatever Ann wants to be the law should be the law. This would be for Ben to accept that a principle had priority regardless of its nature merely because of who endorsed it. As a rational agent with desires in conflict with Ann's, Ben could not agree to this.

In forcing Ben to agree to the legalisation of abortion just because she has superior power, even though Ben refused to agree to it in a position of equal power, Ann shows herself to be the kind of person who believes that whatever principles she holds are to have priority over any principles that Ben holds, merely because she is the one who holds them rather than him. If this is so, then what really matters to Ann is not that everyone follow her principle of legalising abortion but that everyone follow whatever principle she happens to endorse. It is really a case of Ann placing herself above any principle.

Whether Ann realises it or not, if this is how she behaves, then she derives her principle from the meta-principle that any principle that she holds is to be preferred to any different principle held by anyone else. She also ranks herself as more important than, or superior to, anyone else when it comes to deciding what actions anyone should do in a particular situation. She is claiming that her views have priority over everyone else's regardless of whether or not other people see that there is good reason why this should be so. She is dismissing the idea that other people be seen as equal, or even significant, contributors to the decision. No wonder, then, that, in a position of equal power, she fails to convince them. She has no genuine arguments.

The equal power perspective, then, is a perspective from which Ann has to treat Ben, and vice versa, as a person worthy of the same respect as herself. She has to give Ben's desires the same consideration as her own. She must treat Ben as an end in himself, not just as a means to her own ends. She cannot ride roughshod over Ben's interests or values in pursuit of her own. When she proposes a principle she must take into account whether it serves Ben's interests as much as her own. She must give Ben's concerns equal weighting with her own if she wants to get Ben's cooperation in a position of equal power, and she needs his cooperation if her own values are to be given any degree of implementation.

If Ann is prepared to make Ben agree in a position of unequal power to what he refused to accept in a position of equal power, then she does not regard Ben as a person whose worth is equal to her own. In fact, she regards his priorities as totally subservient to her own. She may not be vindictive to Ben, that is, she may not frustrate his desires just out of malicious pleasure but, whenever his desires conflict with her own, she has no compunction in sacrificing his highest priorities for her most trivial ones. At least, this is so if Ben is incapable of sanctioning her sufficiently. When it comes to arguing, then, as to whose preferences are to prevail, she has already decided the issue, and her decision is only alterable by sanctions or their equivalent.

A further crucial difference between the impartialist (Ben) and the partialist (Ann) is that he is genuinely open in the position of equal power about which of the principles under discussion he expects everyone to follow in real life. This is true even when he believes himself committed to one of these principles prior to the argument. Should the argument in the position of equal power lead to an agreement that everyone should follow some different principle, then he will change his mind and expect everyone, including himself, to follow this other principle.

The impartialist, then, is not wedded irrevocably to it being the case that everyone follows the principle that he preferred prior to the argument just because it is his principle, just because he is the person preferring it. Even if the impartialist has superior power in the real world, he will enforce the principle agreed to in a position of equal power, regardless of whether or not he held the other principle prior to the equal power agreement.

On the other hand, the partialist is wedded irrevocably in the real world to a principle just because it is her principle. The fact that this principle was rejected in a position of equal power will make no difference to her if she finds herself with sufficient superior power in the real world to enable her to impose her own preferred principle. In effect, then, genuine argument with the partialist is not possible. She has reached her conclusion prior to any argument and no discussion that is conducted in a noncoercive situation could make her change her mind.

The partialist, however, rarely finds herself in a position of superior power in the real world where she can just enforce compliance with her preferred principle by the use of naked aggression. Instead, she will attempt to get agreement by argument but her use of argument is manipulative and insincere. She does not endorse the premises she proposes but offers them solely to lend legitimacy to the conclusions she wishes reached.

Argument with partialists, then, is not genuine argument. There is no guarantee that the arguments offered publicly are ones sincerely held and, therefore, no guarantee that the principles reached as the conclusion of these arguments will be honoured. Whenever the partialist has superior power she will use it to force her own principles on others and the only reason she seems to have as to why this principle should be preferred to any other is that it is her principle, that it is she who holds it.

In effect, the partialist does not respect other people as equal participants in the argument. She does not accord others an equal worth or moral dignity. She is committed to her own superiority, either the superiority of her own personal interests as an egoist solely on the grounds that the interests are hers rather than someone else's or the superiority of her own principle or cause as a sectarian on what appear to be no better grounds than the principle is the one she holds.

Of course, sectarians will deny this, claiming that they hold their principle because it is God's will, or in the true interests of the people or some such, but what makes the principle a sectarian one is that they would have been unable to convince people in a position of equal power to adopt it, that is, they would have failed to convince them that God commanded it or that it is their true interests. As a consequence, if they impose it on other people in the real world, it can only be because, of all the principles that might have been ordained by God or in the true interests of people, this is the one that they, the particular advocates of this principle, have chosen.

1.13   Justification and Ordinary Life

Even though Ann and Ben may be able to resolve conflicts of desire if they are in a position of equal power, of what relevance is this to those of us who are almost never in a position of equal power which is true of most people in ordinary life. Nevertheless, even in ordinary life, Ann and Ben may come to argue over which of two ultimate principles people should follow, as we have seen in the example of the principle that all abortions be legal and the principle that none be. Even in ordinary life they can argue *as if* they are in a position of equal power, that is, *as if* they were bound by the impartialist requirements.

People in ordinary life do not need to reach the same agreement as infallible and omniscient impartialists for any agreement they have reached to count as unforced, but they do have to conduct their argument as the parties in a position of equal power would conduct it. Otherwise, their agreement has only occurred because one or the other of them has consciously or unconsciously manipulated the other into agreement, either by deception or by the direct use of the threat of sanctions or by the improper use of some other advantage. In ordinary life, if Ben has agreed to a principle even though he would have not done so in a position of equal power, then it must be the case that Ann has obtained this agreement by deception or sanctions or some other improper advantage.

When we enter into arguments in ordinary life we do not expect the argument to be vitiated right from the start because someone (Ben, say) insists that he be given priority and therefore the argument be settled in favour of his preference. If he had openly declared this at the beginning we could have abandoned any type of argument except ones that threatened sanctions or which amounted to it.

Instead, we assume, when we enter the argument, that those we are arguing with regard their views as having no automatic priority over ours, that the point of the exercise is to arrive freely and willingly at a joint conclusion, that they will value the outcome because it is reached as a result of the genuine consent of both parties. In other words, we assume that it matters to them that the conclusion they themselves act on is one that would be acknowledged freely and willingly by any rational agent as the right one. If we knew from the beginning that our opponents did not have this view, that they had no respect for the desires or beliefs of agents other than themselves or those committed to their cause, that they did not feel that it was a measure of the rightness of what they wanted to do that other rational people would freely and willingly agree that it was right, then we would regard the whole activity of arguing with them in anything other than coercive terms as a sham.

1.14   Impartialism, Meaning and Objectivity

Besides questions of justification, metaethics also considers questions about the kind of meaning that is possessed by the tenets of an ethical theory, for example, are they expressions of attitude, emotional utterances on a par with 'Footy is great fun!' or 'Pumpkin, yuck!' or are they factual statements, claims about properties of the world that exist independently of what we want and think and each one of which is either true or false? Do we just have intuitions that certain acts are right but no way of showing that some of these intuitions are rationally more defensible than others in the sense that some of them better correspond to an independent moral reality?

As we saw in the section on 'Why Be an Impartialist?', impartialism is ultimately grounded in a 'grand' intuition. In this respect, it fits in with much that is current in metaethical thinking, particularly that elaborated by philosophers with an interest in biology and evolutionary theory. Writers like Michael Ruse and Jeffrey Murphy have suggested that, ultimately, all ethical theories, that is, all theories that advise us on how to live our lives, on which acts are right and which wrong, are grounded in deep preferences.

When a utilitarian (say, a woman), for example, seeks to justify her recommendations on how we should resolve a conflict of desires, she appeals to the principle of maximising happiness, or some such. Such a criterion, however, is not self-justifying. We can ask the utilitarian to offer us reasons as to why this criterion should be preferred to any others. Murphy suggests that there will come a point when the utilitarian says that she can offer no further reasons, that this principle is the one that she feels is correct, that harmonises with her deepest preferences.

It seems to me that this is correct. What impartialism does, however, is to demonstrate to us that there really are only two intuitions that need to be considered, as we saw previously. They are the intuition that conflicts of desires are to be resolved by force or the intuition that they are to be resolved by reason. Which of these intuitions appeals to you is a function of the kind of person you are.

Ultimately, then, you can only be either an impartialist or a partialist. Any other intuition will end up in either of these two categories. I will argue later that utilitarianism is not a theory that would be agreed to in the position of equal power so, ultimately, its advocates - much to their own surprise, I imagine - must be tarred with the partialist brush. If they seek to impose their utilitarian principles on others then they show themselves to be committed to the resolution of conflicts of desire by force and not by argument.

Each of us, then, as a rational agent, is free to choose between impartialism and partialism. There is no higher order of rationality that entails impartialism rather than partialism. The partialist may be many things, including immoral and not the kind of person you might wish to meet in an alley on a dark night, but he or she need not be irrational. In having a deep preference for ultimately deciding conflicts of desire by force, always in their own favour if possible, they are not involved in any contradiction of the will or in any other kind of contradiction that renders their beliefs or practices irrational, internally inconsistent, self-defeating or whatever.

Nor are they in contradiction of the facts, as those who seek to derive 'ought' from 'is' seem to want them to be. There is no empirical state of affairs such that it would be irrational of them not to value it, in the sense that they somehow contradict themselves in not valuing it. It might be thought, for example, that it is prima facie irrational to desire to be in pain. Part of this idea arises from the teaching conditions for the word 'pain', that is, we learn to associate the word with experiences that are caused by states of affairs we wish to avoid. If this is put to one side, however, there is no contradiction in an egoist wanting other people to be in pain, nor is there any contradiction involved in some kinds of sectarians wanting to suffer pain, to be martyrs to a cause. (I will deal with these questions in more detail in Chapter 7.)

In the end, then, impartialism is a form of subjectivism, although it may be better regarded as 'quasi-subjectivist'. There are no claims in ethics that are true or false in the categorical sense that a claim in history or physics is true or false, that is, in the sense that its truth or falsity is as it is regardless of what we want or believe it to be. Ethical claims are all hypothetical imperatives. There are no categorical imperatives.[3] The truth or falsity of an ethical claim is always relative to a want or a goal and that goal can differ from individual to individual, although, if impartialism is correct, ultimately only with reference to either one of the two goals of resolving disputes by argument or by force. Reasoning is always instrumental reasoning, if what this means is that it is reasoning about the means to some end, an end which is not binding on all rational agents - and neither of the two ultimate goals identified by impartialism is binding on rational agents as such.

In spite of this, however, ethical talk behaves as if it is objectivist talk. This is because, as the relations in the real world approximate to a position of equal power, so the judgments that it is rational to make about how conflicts of desire are to be resolved approximate to those of impartialism. While it may rational to be a partialist, in the sense of having partialist deep preferences, it becomes less and less rational to behave as a partialist, or reveal oneself to be a partialist in the attitudes one expresses, as the power between people, or between groups of people, evens out.

In fact, in a position of more or less equal power, ethics has assumed an almost completely objective character. The criteria for rightness and wrongness are relatively straightforward. There are a large number of uncontested cases of right and wrong behaviour, right and wrong principles and rules, just as there are a large number of observations, experimental results and laws of nature that have eventually been accepted as certainly true as far as science is concerned.

All those features of ethics that indicate that we construe it as an objective enterprise, then, can be readily explained, for example, the fact that we regard ourselves as in genuine disagreement in a moral debate such as the debate over the legalisation of abortion. We do not think our views on such a matter are on a par with our taste for chocolate rather than strawberry ice cream.

. Impartialism, then, seems to accommodate all the phenomena that philosophers have identified as needing to be incorporated by any adequate metaethical theory. Is it, however, really an ethical theory or is it just a theory about conflict resolution - perhaps a theory of justice or fairness but not a moral theory? What is the connection between morality on the one hand and the decisions reached by the parties in the position of equal power on the other? I will take up these issues in the next section.

1.15   Impartialism and Morality

What exactly makes an issue a 'moral' issue has been a matter of much debate.[4] I will look at a number of suggestions here in order to show that impartialism is a theory about moral right and wrong as well as about justice.

Geoffrey Warnock (pp.15-26) for example, suggests that the point of morality is to reduce the likelihood of harm arising from our natural inclination to apply our sympathies in a limited way, to favour ourselves and our families over other people. Impartialism fits this criterion. As we have seen, it pushes us away from egoism and sectarianism. It requires us to find the principle that would be most acceptable to both parties given that they cannot assume that they will have superior power in the real world with respect to the matter at issue. This makes an extension of sympathies unavoidable, at least at the imaginative level.

Bernard Gert suggests that morality is a public system governing the behaviour of all rational agents and whose point is the minimisation of evil. Central to it are the moral rules such as 'Don't kill', 'Don't steal' and 'Don't lie.'

Impartialism offers us a public system that applies to all rational persons. Its prime concern is with behaviour affecting others. In fact, it only comes into operation when there is a conflict of desires between people or when the potential for such a conflict is being considered.. Impartialism, however, does not have the minimisation of evil as its end. Rather, it has respect for all parties to a conflict of desires as its end. Nonetheless, the equal power perspective is one whose effect will be to minimise evil to the parties in so far as this is compatible with equal respect for all the parties. When the parties come to choose between various principles each of them will settle on whichever symmetrical principle will bring them the least of what they regard as evil in the real world.

I discussed how impartialism leads to an injunction against murder in the section on 'The Noncoercionist Requirement'. While impartialism also leads to injunctions against stealing and lying, they are not quite as uncomplicated as the versions that Gert offers. As we have seen, when someone in a position of equal power holds an opinion on whether or not an action such as theft should be done, we also have to look for the reason behind their recommendation, that is, the principle from which they derive their conclusion.

In general, the parties in the position of equal power will oppose stealing, if the motive for taking another person's property is laziness or envy or covetness or some such. 'Stealing', here, can be regarded as one person taking what another person has made or acquired as a result of a lot of effort and which that person needs to achieve his or her goals. Rational agents who possess such property would only agree to theft if they knew they had superior power in the real world, that is, they could prevent other people successfully acting on such motives but could get away with acting on such motives themselves. It is ruled out, therefore, by the symmetry requirement.

The above result, however, only applies if the parties under consideration are noncoercionists. It could be the case, however, that Ben, say, is sincerely prepared to risk being stolen from in order to be free to steal, that is, he wants to coerce Ann to surrender her property more than he wants to be protected from being forced by her to relinquish his property. Such a case, however, is ruled out by the noncoercionist requirement. Those who hold such a view show themselves committed to solving conflicts of desires by force and not by reason.

Similar points to those in the previous two paragraphs apply to lying. When the motive for the lie is described more fully, the parties in a position of equal power will allow some kinds of lies and reject others. If the motive is merely to deceive others in order to benefit oneself at their expense, then noncoercionists in the position of equal power will agree that lying of this kind should not be done. The motive, however, may be to benefit other people, for example, to save them embarrassment or some such. In certain circumstances they would agree that such lies are permissible. In fact, they may even agree that, in certain circumstances, lying may be obligatory, but it is not germane to the present topic to develop this in detail now. The points made about the coercionist thief also apply to the coercionist liar.

Another criterion of the moral is that moral claims are 'categorical' claims in the sense that they apply to us regardless of our particular wants or beliefs. Even if we want to steal from someone, or believe that we ought to kill someone, what we want and what we believe may differ from what is actually the case, that is, we may want to steal yet it be wrong for us to steal or we may believe we ought to kill someone yet it be wrong that we do so. Michael Ruse (p.68), for example, offers this kind of 'categoricality' as one of the features of 'the moral'.

If Ruse is right, then impartialism provides the kind of objectivity required. Whether or not an act is right or wrong is not a matter of subjective preference. It is determined by the facts of the matter in exactly the same sense as the truth of a scientific or historical claim is determined by the facts of the matter, although the kind of facts involved will be somewhat unusual in that they are facts about what certain kinds of people (noncoercionists) would agree to when required to reason about conflicts of desire from an equal power perspective. One component of these facts will be facts of a scientific and historical kind but others of these facts are more akin to the kinds of mathematical facts manifested in games-theory.

It might be claimed that a theory about how we ought to act can only be a 'moral' theory if it is a theory about 'the good', about what is worth pursuing, about what we ought to value, that is, if it is a 'teleological' theory. Contractarian theories consciously keep their commitment to any particular content for the notion of 'the good' to a minimum, therefore, it is argued, whatever it is that they are theories of, it is not morality. This, however, excludes contractarian theories by fiat. What contractarian theories do is cover the same ground as teleological theories. They occupy the same domain. In effect, while they do not say that pleasure is good, or obedience to God is good, or the survival of the human species is good, they do say that the question of which of the various candidates for the good is actually the good is to be answered, if at all, within parameters set by contractarianism.

Hare (1952), among others, has claimed that universalisability is a necessary condition for a claim to be a moral one. Wallace and Walker (p.8) describe universalisability as requiring of each of us that, if we think we ought to do some action X, then we must hold that the only reason why other people ought not to do X is that there is some relevant difference between our case or situation and theirs. This condition seems to be equivalent to the symmetry requirement, so impartialism passes as an account of morality on this score.

Wallace and Walker suggest a couple of other criteria I should mention. One is that what makes rules and principles moral ones is that they override other sorts of rules and principles (p.10). The other is that moral rules and principles have an importance not possessed by other rules and principles (p.11). They see the second of these as less open to criticism than the first. However that may be, impartialism meets either criterion. The whole point of impartialism is that the rule or principle favoured by the parties in the position of equal power is to override all of its competitors. Of all the rules or principles that could apply to the given situation, the one selected by impartialism is the most important.

1.16 Objections to Impartiality and Contractarianism

1.16.1 Special Obligations

Recent ethical literature has debated the value of impartiality. It has been claimed, for example, that an emphasis on impartiality ignores much that is important in our moral life such as the special affection we have for our own children and our own friends, that any theory that requires us to be impartial between the needs of our own family and those of other families would be distorting an essential component of moral experience.

This kind of criticism has been well answered by Brian Barry (1995). He shows that many of the criticisms of impartiality have resulted from a failure to distinguish between theories that propose impartiality as a first order value and those that propose it as a second order value. First order impartiality involves such things as not being motivated by private considerations, in the sense that you must not do for one person what you would not do for anybody else unless there is a relevant difference in their situations, and being a friend or relative of one person but not of the other is not allowed to count as a relevant difference (p.11).

Impartialism, however, offers impartiality as a second order value, that is, it says that the principles that we guide our actions by in the real world must meet the impartialist requirements but that it may well be the case that such principles sometimes allow us to do more for a relative or a friend in a particular situation than for a stranger.

For example, impartialism does not require us to be impartial between our own children and the children of strangers. What it requires us to do, instead, is to show that any partiality we have towards our own children is a partiality that would be agreed to in a position of equal power. It rules out our saying that other people should allow us to give special treatment to our own children over their children when they are in a position of superior power but that we will not allow them to give special treatment to their children over our children when we are in a position of superior power. In other words, our principle as to what special treatment parents can give to their own children must be a symmetrical one.

1.16.2 Atomism

An argument offered against contractarian theories is that they have an unrealistic view of the self. It is claimed that the parties who argue as John Rawls (1972) suggests they do, that is, as if they are ignorance of their place in the real world, are impossible creatures. Presumably a similar claim would be made against the parties in a position of equal power. Such creatures are abstracted in a self-defeating way from all that gives them their identity as actual human beings such as their culture, their religion, their period in history, etcetera. The claim is that liberal theories, such as the contractarian theories we are discussing, treat the self as an atom isolated from its social context. Such a self, however, would not have a language, let alone any tradition of argument, criticism and respect for rights. What gives us our humanity is our membership of communities, of collectivities.

This objection has been well answered by Kymlicka (pp.207-215). In essence, he argues that the self is prior to its ends in the sense that it can re-examine its goals and purposes, and it can question and reject the value of a community's way of life. Even if it is the case that the self that engages in either of these activities has largely developed the conceptual scheme that makes this possible from the community into which it was born, it can use that conceptual scheme to challenge what the community has taught or can utilise the aptitudes and abilities it has acquired to critically scrutinise what it has been taught.

Our two protagonists, Ann and Ben, then, need not be regarded as some kinds of ghostly figures unimbedded in a human culture. They are not self-created critical thinkers uninfluenced by their cultural environments. Instead, we should see them as typical representatives of whatever views happen to be in dispute for our purposes, largely moulded by their upbringing. Nonetheless, they are equipped with the standard logical understandings. They recognise contradictions between what they are told and how they perceive the world. They are able to evaluate the conceptual apparatus they have been taught and modify it if necessary.

Another part of the 'atomism' criticism of contractarianism is that it puts the rights of individuals ahead of the rights of communities or collectivities because the contractors are conceptualised as individuals, thereby biasing the outcome of the arguments right from the start. With impartialism, this need not be true, as the parties in the position of equal power can be understood as either individuals or groups.

Nonetheless, impartialism does give priority to individuals in this respect - that arguments can only be conducted by individuals. Groups are not the sorts of entities that can argue. Individuals who see themselves as members of a group can argue on behalf of the group but there is no arguing entity that is the group above and beyond the individual members of the group.

This suggests that individuals who claim that the group has rights above and beyond those of its members are to be regarded with suspicion. What they seem to be saying is that those members of the group who want established arrangements within the group to be continued should be allowed to have their way against any members of the group who wish to change these arrangements. For example, it is sometimes argued by certain individuals in a group that a certain tradition within the group is part of the culture of that group and that it, therefore, should be given special protection, even against members of that group who wish to change it, that is, that all members of the group should be compelled to honour the tradition.

It is highly likely, however, that this tradition advantages some members of the group at the expense of others so this appeal to preservation of the culture can be a disguise for the protection of privilege. What needs to be done is to debate the preservation of the tradition as if both sides were in a position of equal power. It may be that the privilege that the tradition confers upon some members of the group is such that it benefits all members of the group. If so, it will receive equal power support. Alternatively, it may be that the best an equal power argument will allow is that membership of the group be voluntary but that, once one has decided to continue as a member of the group, one is bound by various of its traditions for as long as one chooses to remain in it. There are undoubtedly also other options.

As we shall see, impartialism does not presuppose the value of rational agents as such but merely the value of an 'equal power' resolution of conflicts between rational agents. The same point applies to the value of humans as such, or the value of humans able to talk and offer reasons. Later I will look at what impartialism has to say about the rights of the comatose, the handicapped, etcetera. The point I wish to stress here is that, just because determination of acceptable principles must be the province of those able to reason and to offer reasons to each other, nothing follows in itself about the value of such characteristics. There is no automatic commitment to 'anthropocentricism' or 'sapienism' (that is, favouring rational agents over nonrational ones) or 'sentientism' (that is, favouring sentient beings over non-sentient ones). If impartialism ends up with a commitment in favour of any of these, then it will have to be argued for. It cannot be assumed.

Another objection to contractarian theories is that they mistakenly treat the right as prior to the good. I will look at this objection in detail in the next section.

1.17   Priority of the Right over the Good

Contractarian theories such as impartialism can be described as theories that try to decide which of two acts is the right one, the one we should pursue, before they decide what value or 'good' such actions should serve. In other words they try to decide questions of what is right prior to deciding questions of what is good. In fact, they do not seem to address questions of what is good at all. One criticism made of contractarianism is that such an order of priority is not possible. We are only able to decide which of two acts is the right one, it is claimed, if we first of all know what good it is that the act is supposed to achieve, what value or purpose it is meant to satisfy. If such a claim is correct, then, say the critics, contractarianism must presuppose some good. Hidden away inside the theory must be some assumed value that the theory, almost surreptitiously, seeks to further.

Contractarians, however, are loathe to admit such a possibility. The whole point of a contractarian theory, after all, is to arbitrate between competing values, between incompatible conceptions of the good. To sneak in an unacknowledged conception of the good would be to undermine the entire enterprise. To overcome this problem, the contractarian can adopt one of two approaches. One approach would be to show that contractarianism can operate in a value-free manner. The other approach is to show that it does assume one or more values but that these values are of a special kind that do not bias its application to those value-conflicts that the theory has been designed to resolve. I will take the latter alternative.

Impartialism takes as its starting point a conflict of desires between two parties. It seeks to resolve this conflict by requiring the parties to argue from an equal power perspective. The theory, therefore, treats it as a good thing that conflicts of desire be resolved from an equal power perspective. If the case developed so far in this chapter has been successful, then this amounts to treating it as a good thing that conflicts of desire be resolved by reason and argument and not by force.

Further more, whatever is presupposed by such a form of conflict-resolution will also be a good thing. It might seem, at first, that one such presupposition is that there be rational agents of the kind able to resolve conflicts by reason rather than force. This, however, is not so. The goodness of equal power conflict resolution presupposes the hypothetical that, if there are rational agents in a conflict of desires, then it is good thing that the conflict is resolved by an equal power process, but it does not make the further categorical claim that it is a good thing that there be rational agents capable of equal power conflict-resolution. That it is a good thing for the universe to contain rational agents with such capacities is itself an issue that might well be debated in a position of equal power. Some deep ecologists might well want to argue the contrary.

What, then, is presupposed by an equal power resolution of conflict of desires? As we have seen, one such presupposition is that the parties in the argument be noncoercionists. This is a good that is assumed by the theory. It is a good that is prior to any other specific good that might be derived from the theory. Another presupposition, which will be taken up in more detail later, is that, if there are desires, then it is a prima facie good that they be satisfied rather than frustrated. A general disposition to frustrate desires for its own sake, even nonrational ones, will be treated by impartialism as a bad thing, and will do so prior to the examination of any particular desires. Impartialism also seems to presuppose that it is not a good thing to overcome a conflict of desires by forcing one person into becoming the superfan of another, that is, there does seem to be an assumption in favour of individual autonomy, as expressed by the independence requirement. I will look at such presuppositions in more detail later.

It should be noted that the equal power approach does not come into operation only when there is an actual conflict of desires in the real world. It is a hypothetical approach, that is, it deals as much with hypothetical cases as with actual cases. Were Ann, for example, to be a deep ecologist asking herself whether humanity was a disease on the face of the planet that should be exterminated, the equal power perspective requires her to debate this as if there were two parties to the debate - her own point of view and the contrary one - even if she is totally alone in her reflections on the matter.

1.18   Impartialism and Utilitarianism

Impartialism rules out unqualified utilitarianism.   This is because utilitarianism does not give sufficient significance to consent.   Suppose that Ann is a person with one particular desire that so interferes with her life that it prevents the satisfaction of most of her other desires.   Suppose, for example, that she lives in some country ruled by a totalitarian government where she is a dissident committed to freedom of speech.   As a consequence, she destroys her career, is abandoned by her husband, resented by her children, deserted by her friends and colleagues, jailed, humiliated, tortured.   She is thoroughly miserable.

One way, then, of maximising the preference-satisfaction in the world would be to rid Ann of her commitment to free speech, even if this is the last thing that Ann wants us to do.   In fact, it is precisely her opposition to such a change that stops her living a happier life, regaining her job, her husband, her children and her freedom.   Suppose Ben decided to overrule her own preferences in this matter, using the utilitarian principle that it is acceptable to permanently change a person's desires against her will if this will maximise happiness.

If he did so, Ben would be behaving as a sectarian.   He has this ideal of a world where there is maximum preference-satisfaction regardless of the content of the preferences, and he is prepared to arrange to allow only those preferences that make the biggest amount of preference-satisfaction possible.   Not everyone has such an ideal - Ann, for example. If we symmetrify Ben's principle, then, we find that Ann should be allowed to eliminate any of Ben's goals if this will achieve one or more of her goals.   Ben, then, would only agree to such a principle if he knew that, were the principle to be in operation in the real world, he would be in the position of superior power.   If Ann were to be in the real world position of superior power, it would be self-defeating for him to agree to such a principle.   Utilitarianism, then, does not pass the comparability and symmetry tests and, so, could only be implemented in the real world by those who preferred to resolve conflicts of desires by force rather than by consent reached under fair discussion conditions.

It may seem that Ann, in this case, contradicts the 'nonmonist' requirement set out earlier. In this case, however, there are two explanations available that make her case different from the coercionist monism of the utilitarian. Firstly, she might be a noncoercionist monist, that is, she values free speech above everything else, say, but she is also a noncoercionist, therefore she does not generate mutual destruction problems. Secondly, she may have arrived at her commitment to free speech as a result of impartialist thinking, that is, she did not start as a free speech monist whose values had to be submitted to the test of equal power reasoning. Instead, she concluded from her equal power reasoning that she should have a commitment to free speech. Even here, as I suggested earlier, an impartialist will not be committed to mutual destruction even though she is prepared to die rather than live in a world without free speech.

It may help understand impartialism's rejection of utilitarianism to see how a dialogue might go between a utilitarian and a non-utilitarian. Suppose the utilitarian (Ben) claims that what is good for everyone is the maximisation of preference-satisfaction. Let us imagine that the non-utilitarian is the dissident woman (Ann) we considered earlier. Ann tells Ben she disagrees. He tells her that she has made a number of factual errors. They debate these and, having resolved them, still find Ann unpersuaded of the virtues of utilitarianism. Ben, then, accuses Ann of logical errors. They debate these, resolve them, and still Ann is unpersuaded. All that remains at dispute between them is what is to be valued. Ben values only the maximisation of preference-satisfaction whereas Ann values the preservation of civil liberties such as free speech

Let us suppose further that Ben and Ann are agreed that, if the maximisation of preference-satisfaction is to be achieved, then, Ann must be deprived of her civil liberties, as must many other people. What is it that leads Ben to think that his concept of the good is more likely to be correct than Ann's? He has not been able to convict her of any error of fact or any error of logic. What makes his principle the better principle, especially as it requires a denial of her civil liberties? All that he appears to be left with as an answer is that it is the principle that he, Ben, endorses. But what is it about him that confers superiority on a principle just because he holds it? He is assuming some kind of special insight into the good, some especially penetrating moral vision denied Ann, although he cannot prove that he has it.

Of course, he could offer as evidence that he has such moral insight that he is the one who supports utilitarianism and that utilitarianism is truly what determines the good and the right. But his only evidence that utilitarianism is a reliable guide to the good and the right is that it is what is seen by those like himself who have special moral insight. Per hypothesi, he has failed to convince others equally logical and informed as himself. His evidence, then, and what it is evidence for, are not logically distinct. What we are being offered is a partial definition, not a fact about the world. He is just defining the possession of moral insight in terms of holding utilitarianism to be the good. This kind of stipulative definition is open to anyone. We are still left with the problem of which cases of stipulatively defined moral insight actually identifies the non-circular good.

1.19   Conclusion

At the start of this chapter we set ourselves the task of finding a theory that told us which principles should govern a conflict of desires between two parties. That task has now been accomplished, at least in broad outline. In the remainder of the book I will apply the theory to a number of moral and political issues to see what acts it will judge as right or wrong, what political and social arrangements it will regard as fair or just. The particular items I examine will, of course, only sample the full range of moral, political and social questions but they are intended to cover the most central ones, the ones that have most ramifications for our values.

The conflict between utilitarianism and freedom, discussed above, leads us into the topic of the next chapter. One thing that impartialism seems to regard as a good, once there is an actual or hypothetical conflict of desires, is the fact that the parties in the position of equal power can make an uncoerced decision between principles. They possess a particular kind of freedom, a freedom from manipulation, from being used by other people as a mere means to what those others value. In effect, they can be regarded as self-governing agents, as exercisers of personal autonomy. While there may be other kinds of freedom that also should be valued, this particular freedom is especially important within impartialism.

I want now to look more closely at what such a form of freedom involves and how it is to be distinguished from other kinds of freedom. It is, I wish to suggest, a kind of freedom of especial value to liberals but which is seen as of little or no value by those people who believe that they know best what is good for other people and who are prepared to coerce other people to conform to it, that is, by paternalists. Paternalists, however, are not the only kind of illiberal. We will also see how those who wish to value autonomy can pervert the ideal of freeing others so that it becomes a form of slavery. I will use Sir Isaiah Berlin's distinction between positive and negative liberty as a useful starting point.

Notes

1   Those familiar with John Rawls' notion of 'the original position' and Jurgen Habermas' notion of 'the ideal speech situation' will see some similarities and differences with my notion of the 'position of equal power'. I will give reasons later for preferring my model to theirs.

2   I discuss the question of intuitions, especially in so far as evolutionary theory might be seen to give us a guide to morality, in Woolcock (1995, 1998a, 1998b).

3   See Woolcock (1998b).

4   See the various views in Wallace and Walker. Also Beauchamp, (1991), Chapter 1.

2 Freedom and False Consciousness

2.1   Introduction

As we have seen, impartialism is anxious to separate itself from utilitarianism. In fact, one of the principal motives for developing an impartialist theory is to overcome some of the problems seen as endemic to utilitarianism. One problem especially troublesome for utilitarianism is that it treats justice and freedom as items whose value is a function of the degree to which they serve the maximisation of utility. As a consequence, if utility can be maximised by enslaving people then utilitarianism seems to have no objection in principle to doing so. Likewise for treating people unjustly.

Of course, whether or not utilitarianism is committed in principle to such an extreme denial of freedom as slavery will partly be a function of how 'freedom ' is defined. As we will see later, there are writers who wish to define it in such a way that one group of people is more free than another if they have a greater capacity to satisfy their interests. This account of freedom, however, makes it possible that a slave could have a greater capacity to satisfy his or her interests than someone who is not a slave, thereby making the slave the freer person. If there is such a sense of freedom, then it runs counter to another sense in which a slave is a paradigm example of someone who is not free.

Impartialism is committed to the view that the slave is the paradigm of the unfree person, therefore it needs to identify a sense of freedom other than the capacity to satisfy one's interests. A useful starting point to such an account is Isaiah Berlin's essay 'Two Concepts of Liberty' (1969). He argues there that liberty can take either of two forms, which he labels 'positive' and 'negative' liberty respectively. In essence, the difference between the two is that a person's negative freedom is a function of the degree to which other people actually interfere with what

44

he or she wants to do, whereas positive freedom is a function of the degree
to which other people have the power to interfere in what he or she wants,
even if they do not exercise this power (pp.121-122).

At first sight, there may not seem to be much of a difference
between these two kinds of freedom but the significance of the distinction
can be seen when we return to the case of slavery. There may be many
cases in which a slave has greater negative freedom than someone who is
not a slave. It may be the case, for example, that the slave (say, Ann) is
left largely to her own devices by her master, whereas the non-slave (say,
Ben) constantly has his life controlled by his employer and is unwilling to
leave his job because of high unemployment and the dependence of his
family on his income. In the case of the slave, however, the master always
has the power to interfere, and to interfere to the extent of taking her life,
whereas in the case of the non-slave the employer's powers are much more
circumscribed and, if the opportunity arises, the non-slave can remove
himself from the employer's control, so the non-slave's positive liberty is
greater than that of the slave's.

Berlin's notion of 'positive liberty', however, is more complex
than this example might suggest. In fact, I will argue, it comes in both a
liberal and an illiberal form. The liberal form of positive liberty will be
valued by the parties in a position of equal power whereas the illiberal
form of positive liberty will be one that they will reject as unsuitable to a
society of non-slaves. Exactly which negative liberties are valued will be
determined by which are compatible with the demands of liberal positive
liberty.

2.2   Liberal Positive Liberty

Berlin begins his account of positive liberty with the claim that liberty, in
its positive sense, stems from the wish of a person to be his or her own
master (p.xliii). On this concept of liberty, people will only consider
themselves to be free if decisions about the options available to them are
made in such a way that they regard themselves as each treated as a person,
as a rational agent. This is, Berlin suggests, because their wish is be
somebody, a do-er, a maker of decisions, directing their own lives,
choosing their own goals and putting them into effect. They do not wish to
be nobodies whose lives are determined by the decisions of others, who are
treated as if they are a mere thing, or animal, or slave. In so far as they

feel themselves to be active agents, they feel free. To the extent that they feel themselves to be the mere tools of other people's purposes, they feel enslaved (p.131).

The main point to note here is that, just because I am not the only source of control that determines what I do or am, it does not follow that I thereby lack positive liberty. To lack positive liberty, it must be the case that these sources of control other than myself treat me as a thing, an animal, a slave or, to give another example Berlin could have used, a child.

There are, however, a number of different ways in which I can see myself treated as a slave, etcetera. As a consequence, the concept of 'positive liberty' needs to be understood as having a similar property to a concept like that of squaring a number. Even though squaring the number 2 gives us the product 4 whereas squaring the number 3 gives us the product 9, the concept of 'squaring' is the same in both cases. Both are examples of multiplying a number by itself. Likewise, when the concept of 'positive liberty' is applied from a liberal point of view it has a particular result, but when applied from an illiberal point of view it has a quite different result, yet the same concept is at work in both cases.[1]

In the standard liberal democracy, the parliament and the government are, to a large extent, the source of control that can determine what a person can do or be. However, the liberal (say a woman) does not usually feel that this exercise of power is one that treats her as a slave. She has an equal vote with all the other adult members of the society, including the parliamentarians. In an important sense, she is as self-governing when it comes to the political decisions of the nation as anyone else.

It may well be that the parliament passes laws that amount to obstacles in the way of her felt or conscious or manifest desires, thereby restricting her negative liberty. Nonetheless, she recognises that the requirement on the government to risk rejection from the electorate every few years usually means that the liberties she loses as a result of its laws will be ones that people, in general, are prepared to trade for greater freedoms in other areas of their lives. It still remains possible that the majority elects a government with a mandate to discriminate against certain minorities, that is, that the polity degenerate into a tyranny of the majority. If this occurs, members of these minorities will no longer believe that they are as much a source of control in the political life of the community as any other individual or group. They will feel a loss of political positive liberty, a sense that they have been treated by the majority as things or slaves.

Provided the liberal polity has constitutional devices or appropriate traditions that minimise the likelihood of 'tyranny of the majority' cases, there would seem to be a contingent but reasonably reliable connection between liberal positive liberty and the maximisation of negative liberties with respect to the manifest desires of the electorate, at least as far as legal restrictions on behaviour is concerned.

It should be noted that, recently, Philip Pettit (1997) and Quentin Skinner (1997) have argued that Berlin's distinction between positive and negative liberty fails to capture a third kind of liberty which Pettit labels a 'non-domination' sense and which Skinner calls 'neo-roman'. Pettit understands Berlin to equate 'positive liberty' with 'mastery over the self 'and 'negative liberty' with 'the absence of interference by others'. As a consequence, he thinks, there is room for a concept of freedom which is like negative liberty in being an absence and like positive liberty in focusing on mastery, namely, an absence of mastery by others (pp.21-22). It seems to me that this supposed third sense of liberty is the same as liberal positive liberty, given Berlin's explicit elaboration of the notion of positive liberty as a contrast to slavery.

However, Berlin does not construe this absence of mastery by others as a third kind of liberty but as a variation on positive liberty. This suggests that 'mastery over the self' is too narrow an interpretation of what he means by 'positive liberty'. Rather, he conceives of it as the absence of unwanted control over one's life, whether by others or by elements within one's self. As we have seen, one can feel the absence of such control in a number of ways, one of which is that others treat one as an equal in the political process. One is not being treated as a slave or, as we shall see, as someone whose conscious preferences are merely those of his or her lower self and, therefore, to be dismissed. Berlin's account of liberty does connect it with equality but points out that such a connection can sometimes, but not always, take a pathological form. He, therefore, is not an appropriate stalking horse for those who wish to defend liberty as 'non-domination'. He is on their side. Political equality does not need to treated as prior to the account of liberty that is central to liberalism, either in the sense of being more valuable than liberalism's conception of liberty or in the sense of having a prior historical occurrence. 17th century arguments in favour of political equality are part of the first awakenings of liberalism.

So what exactly is this 'illiberal positive liberty' that is to be contrasted with its liberal variant? In order to answer this question it will be helpful to distinguish between 'personal' and 'political' positive liberty.

2.3   'Personal' versus 'Political' Positive Liberty[2]

'Political' positive liberty concerns the degree to which one person, (say, Ben), is the source of control over what another person, (say, Ann), is or does. It is important to note, as we shall see later, that Ben and Ann only count as different persons if they are bodily distinct from each other.

'Personal' positive freedom, by contrast, occurs in those cases where the issue is the degree to which Ann is the source of control over what she herself is or does. To use an example from Taylor (pp.152-153), she may recognise that she has an irrational fear of public speaking that prevents her from doing something she very much wants to do. She may see this desire as coming from an inferior self and her wish to change as coming from a higher self. However, only if the decision comes from within herself is this a case of her being the source of control as to which self has its way. If Ben, for example, decides to surreptitiously feed her a drug that gives her loads of self-confidence, then it is Ben who is the source of control of what she is or does, not Ann herself, so the case is not one of her personal liberty but of her political liberty.

Questions about the degree to which Ann has either political and personal positive liberty are also questions about the degree to which she is self-governing, but the kind of self-government involved in each case is different. In the first case, the question of her self-government is about the extent to which what she does is limited by other people whereas, in the second case, the question of her self-government involves the extent to which who she is or what she does is limited by features of Ann herself.

Even if Ben's compelling Ann to behave in a particular way is, in a sense, done with her concurrence, as it could be said to be when the government enforces democratically enacted laws in a liberal society, what is at issue is her 'political' liberty. In order for something to count as an exercise of her 'personal' liberty, the person who instigates it has to be Ann herself. If she does not realise that the source of control over what she does or is lies outside her in a particular case, then this means that what she thinks is a matter of her personal liberty is actually a matter of her political liberty.[3]

2.4   Political Illiberal Positive Liberty

What content, then, does the concept of positive liberty have for someone who is not a liberal? I will focus first on political illiberal positive liberty. The kind of person that Berlin calls a 'hedgehog' (1978, p.22) will serve as an example of an illiberal. There could be purely egoistic illiberals but our concern will be with an illiberal (Ben once more) who identifies with some nonegoistic cause, say a religious or political cause. He does not see himself as having a meaningful existence independently of such a cause. Its goals are his goals. If it suffers, he suffers. If it rejoices, so does he. His life is committed to this one overriding value. No other goals in his life genuinely conflict with his desire to see it triumph. Nonetheless, he may sometimes feel tempted to do things that will entice him away from his cause, or that lessen his contribution to it or reduce the likelihood that it will succeed.

Such a person will only feel that he is free, in the sense of being a source of control, when his cause is being furthered. If it is not dominant, then he feels that he is a slave to forces outside himself. He can only be himself, only realise himself - given the monolithic role his cause plays in his life - if his cause is victorious.

Note that the concept of positive liberty at work here is the same concept as it is for the liberal, even though it is a different outcome,[4] because the notion of what it is to feel that one is treated as a thing is applied to a different set of values or to a personality type or some such. In the liberal case, it is applied to people who do not identify themselves with any single cause but who see themselves as having a range of goals which compete with each other for priority. In the illiberal case, it is applied to people who see themselves as intimately bound up with a cause.

This is not to say that all people who refuse to identify themselves with a single cause are liberals or, even, that no liberals have a single cause to which they devote their lives. People can be illiberals in the sense that they do not value liberal democracy, say, yet still not identify themselves with a single cause. They might be egoists, for example.

Likewise, people could devote themselves to a single cause yet be committed to pursuing it in a way consistent with liberal democracy, forgoing pursuit of their cause if its success required the overthrow of liberal democracy, not identifying themselves with their cause in the obsessive manner of the illiberal. An example of such a person would be a man who believes that his religion is the only one that will bring people salvation and who devotes his life to convincing them of this. However, as long as he values their freedom of conscience more than he values their making what he thinks is the right choice, then his commitment to his cause is compatible with liberalism.

However, if you are like Ben, you will feel any defeat of your cause as a personal defeat in a way a liberal will not, because the liberal values the kind of negotiation between the conflicting interests of people that Ben rejects. The only way in which you, as a nonegoistical illiberal, will feel that you are the source of control of what you do is if your cause is in control. Liberal positive freedom is not the kind of self-government you want, even though it is a way in which people can feel that they are the source of control over what they do. You will not accept that you are treated as a subject, as a person, even when you are given the same control over your life at the fundamental political level as anyone else. Instead you will only feel in control when society as a whole is working towards the achievement of your cause's goals.

2.5 The Relation between the Personal and the Political for the Illiberal

The nonegoistic illiberal, as we have seen, identifies himself with a cause as embodied in some group such as a nation, religion, class, race, gender, or whatever. As a consequence, he will see any inclination he has that distracts him from his cause as a desire he is better off without. He will want to abolish all those options that might attract him away from the true path. He will see his own political negative liberty - in so far as this means that he is free to do what does not further the cause and may even hinder it - as a bad thing, something to be reduced. He will happily accept laws that keep him on the straight and narrow. In this situation, loss of negative liberty does not conflict with his positive liberty as he sees it. Moreover, he will see anyone who opposes his cause as a threat to his very survival, to the continuance of himself as a self. He will regard defeat of his cause as a kind of psychological death.

One way in which he can regard those who oppose, or are indifferent to, his cause is to treat them as really wanting what he wants, but unconsciously in some way. He can see them on analogy with his higher and lower self - as people who also have a higher self of whose desires they are unconscious. Their higher selves, he believes, also want the success of his cause but are prevented from doing so - as he would be if he did not have a strong will - by the manifest desires of their lower selves. Their true selves would be realised best, however, if they were denied the same negative freedoms that he believes he should be denied.

In fact, he will think, their true selves would be even better realised if they are denied the kind of positive freedom that liberals value. The clash is not just between positive freedom and negative freedom but between positive freedom as it turns out when a liberal applies it to her own case and positive freedom as it turns out when an illiberal applies it to his own case. It is the very opportunity for people to reject his cause that he will wish to deny them. Allowing them to vote on whether or not his cause should triumph is too risky. They might take advantage of this electoral opportunity to put his party out of office thereby rejecting all that he is, all that gives his life meaning.

If he adopts this approach to those who oppose his cause, he will regard his use of force to make these people conform to the dictates of his cause - which is his will or self externalised - as a case of making them free in the same sense that he is free, namely, *positively* free. He will be helping their true selves be the source of control of what they do. Admittedly, they may be less free in a negative freedom sense, with the options open to them almost certainly less than under a liberal order.

Ben does not favour less negative liberty merely because he has a fear of freedom, wanting to hand control of his life over to others because he is afraid of exercising choice. Rather, he sees himself as most a person, as most himself, when the cause's good and his own good are inseparable He is not in the cause in order to be happy, although it may be that this is the only way in which he can be happy. Moreover, he thinks that others also are most themselves when they conform to the requirements of his cause.

2.6   The Liberal Attitude to Negative Freedom

Unlike the illiberal, the liberal will want as few options closed to her as possible but will recognise that the limitations on negative freedom to be achieved by a collection of independent agents with diverse goals will be a compromise. She will argue that others should not lessen the number of her negative liberties unless some communal good or, indeed, her personal good, is achieved to a significant level.[5] In particular, she will want those negative freedoms that are essential to equal political participation such as freedom of speech, freedom of assembly, the vote, the right to stand for parliament, to form a political party, etcetera. She will not see the removal of negative liberties as protecting her sense of identity but, if anything, the opposite. The liberal, in effect, is likely to be one of those people that Berlin calls a 'fox' (1978, p.22). She does not see her existence as a self, her very concept of who she is, as inextricably bound up with some cause. Rather, she has a diversity of personal goals. In the terms introduced in the first chapter, she is a nonmonist whereas the illiberal, as we have described him, is a monist.[6]

2.7   The Liberal Account of Personal Positive Liberty

The liberal, like the illiberal, might well conceptualise her internal conflicts in terms of a higher and lower self. As a liberal, however, she does not externalise these selves onto society so that the group whose political views she favours represents her higher self and the groups whose views she opposes represent her lower self.[7] She does not regard her higher self as triumphant over her lower self only when her cause is politically triumphant over its opponents.

However, were she to be denied equal political rights and civil liberties, she would regard herself as being treated as a slave or as a child, but she would not explain this in terms of society succumbing to its lower self (unbeknownst to itself) but, rather, would explain it in terms of either a case of people knowingly behaving unfairly or else a case of their having an illiberal conception of positive liberty.

2.8   Paternalism versus Arrogationism

Berlin describes the person who is committed to illiberal positive freedom as engaging in a 'monstrous impersonation'(1969, p.13). This is because the illiberal person Ben arrogates to himself the determination of what it is that some other person Ann desires, a prerogative that would normally seem to belong to Ann herself. For this reason, I will label the illiberal Ben an 'arrogationist'.

Berlin contrasts arrogationism with paternalism. The paternalist is someone who coerces others for their own good and who may, on occasion, be right. The arrogationist, however, believes that, if what he is doing for you is for your own good, then you are not being coerced at all because, whether you realise it or not, this is what you truly want, even if you struggle desperately against it (1969, p.134).

The arrogationist and the paternalist have in common a belief that there are one or more things G that constitutes Ann's good, say, (although they may disagree with each other or, as we shall see, even with liberals, as to what it is). This good G, is conceived by them as something objective in the sense that it can be true of Ann that G is her good, or in her interests, or constitutes her flourishing, or similar notions, regardless of what Ann herself is conscious of wanting or might ever be conscious of wanting. They regard it as objective in the same way that the shape of the earth is an objective matter, namely, in that the earth's shape is not a function merely of what any human, now or at any time, thinks it is. It will be useful to have a technical term for this position about what things constitute the good for a person, or all persons, or what their interests are. I will call it 'interests-objectivism'.

Paternalists and arrogationists, then, are both interests-objectivists. It may even be the case that some liberals are interests-objectivists. Kymlicka, (pp.133-134, 141-145) for example, would seem to fall into this category, as does Hunt (1991, 1995) and, probably, Taylor. In order to count as liberals, however, interests-objectivists must treat political liberal positive liberty as either an independent value that trumps any inclination on the part of governments or others to act paternalistically (in the strong sense) in a person's interests or else as an interest a person has that forbids paternalistically imposing on her a regime that achieves her other interests at the cost of her political liberal self-governance.

At first sight, the fact that the paternalist and the arrogationist have in common their illiberalism and their interests-objectivism might seem of greater significance than their differences. However, their disagreement over whether or not Ann can genuinely choose to reject G rests on a fundamental difference over the nature of freedom, as we will now see.

2.9   Interests-Freedom and Person-Freedom

For the paternalist, whether or not Ann's freedom increases or decreases is a function of the degree to which she is able to further her interests, where the term 'interests' is to be understood widely to cover what is in her 'true' interests, that is, what is her 'true' good or what constitutes her wellbeing. If a humanly preventable change in circumstances means that she is less able to further such interests then she is less free, and if it means that she is more able then she is more free. Whether or not Ann herself was, in any way, the source of control over these changes is irrelevant to the paternalist unless her active involvement would have made a genuine difference to the degree to which her good was able to be satisfied. If it were objectively to be the case that her good was better able to be satisfied in a condition of slavery than as a non-slave, then the paternalist would see slavery as a liberating condition.[8] If she insisted that she did not regard herself as free, this would be seen as evidence that she did not understand what her true good was.

From the viewpoint of this account of freedom, there is also no significant difference between removing obstacles to the achievement of a person's good and supplying her with the means to achieve it. Her capacity to pursue her good can be increased either by eliminating those barriers that block it or by providing the material or other resources needed. The paternalist, therefore, will be puzzled by those like Berlin who want to make a distinction between freedom as the removal of obstacles to what one might desire, that is, negative freedom, and some other kind of freedom called 'positive freedom'. The paternalist will be inclined to think that Berlin must have the remedying of deprivation in mind by the term 'positive' liberty and will be perplexed as to why this is seen as radically different to the notion of 'negative' liberty. The paternalist will see them as merely different sides of the same coin.

This lacuna on the part of the paternalist occurs because he has no room in his conceptual scheme for self-government as a kind of freedom. At the most it may be an instrument for increasing Ann's capacity to pursue her good but he does not see it either as an important part of her good or as a separate value to be weighed up against her good. Nonetheless, there is a perfectly familiar sense of 'free' in which I am said to be less free the less I have a say in what I shall do or be, as is illustrated by the previously mentioned example of slavery.

On an account of freedom which acknowledges that there is such a thing as positive freedom in Berlin's sense, the mere fact that my good has been met will not lead me to regard myself as free, unless I also feel myself to be the source of control of my actions.[9] Of course, Berlin's focus is on writers who accept the existence of positive freedom or who see it as a competing value with negative freedom and a person's good. They realise that there is a problem with paternalism. It is paternalism they wish to reject - the idea that there is someone else who knows better than I do what is good for me and who takes this as a warrant to coerce me contrary to my will. They are offended by the thought that there are people who have no respect for my desire to be the source of control in my own life. These anti-paternalist writers see that there is a crucial conflict of values between being the source of control on the one hand and achieving my good on the other. It may well be, as Hunt suggests (1995, p.468), that a paternalist can try to justify the suppression of freedoms on the grounds that suppression of people's freedom in one respect can increase their freedom overall, but what has happened here is that it is the paternalist's judgement of what is important that has carried the day, not the person whose freedom has been reduced. The person (say, Ann), therefore, may well say that, even though her capacity to pursue her good has been increased in some sense (that is, she has greater 'interests-freedom') she still has missed out on a freedom, or has less of it, that is of equal if not greater importance to her, which I will call her 'person-freedom'.

Such a person will not see herself as free, no matter how greater is her capacity to pursue her good, because she will see herself as treated as a thing. It may well be the case that there is an incompatibility between her interests-freedom, as determined by the paternalist, and her person-freedom. The paternalist may want to resolve this conflict in favour of Ann's interests-freedom but Ann herself may give far greater weight to the preservation of her person-freedom than to the satisfaction of all her other interests or to any other account of her good, that is, she may regard her person-freedom as having lexical priority over her interests-freedom.

2.10 Liberalism Perverted

Once we accept that there is such a thing as positive political freedom in Berlin's sense, we need to recognise that it can go wrong, which is the central point of Berlin's paper. Arrogationism is, in effect, liberalism gone wrong. It is liberalism perverted. It is the liberal motive turning itself into what it is fighting against. If one doesn't care about positive political liberty, about whether or not people are slaves, then one will be a paternalist. One can happily live with a purely interests-based or wellbeing-based account of freedom. However, if one does care about people not being slaves, then one will see oneself, and others, as unfree when they are treated as slaves even though there may be no question that this slavery brings them a much greater capacity to pursue their good (other than that aspect of their good that involves not being a slave.)

So, the arrogationist will want people not to be slaves, to be no more under the control of what someone else thinks is important in their lives than he is. However, he also wants his cause to triumph. He wants people to conform to its demands, even against their will. This is necessary for his self-realisation, for him to see himself as 'self-governing'. How can he do this and still oppose slavery and paternalism? He can do so by claiming that the freedom he wants for himself is the same freedom he wants for others, that he wants them to be as much the source of control in their lives as he is in his, while yet limiting their negative liberty in illiberal ways. How is this possible? Only if the selves that are to be free are the higher selves of other people, selves who want what he wants, whose self-realisation (which he equates with self-government) comes from restraining their other desires in the way he wants his to be restrained.

One example of how we might not want to be treated as slaves is if we wish to throw off the yoke of a foreign tyranny, insisting that we should be governed only by our own fellow citizens. We may so identify with this cause that its fulfilment is what constitutes our self-realisation, our concept of what it is to be self-governing. We will see those of our desires that would undermine the cause as part of our lower self, as something that the higher part of ourselves that is committed to the cause must resist. By analogy, we will see those of our country's men and women who oppose our cause as themselves at the mercy of their lower selves, too cowardly to throw off their foreign masters, or seduced by the benefits of colonialism or lacking the passion for national independence that we know they really feel, even if unconsciously, in their heart of hearts.

As a consequence, we will feel ourselves entitled to impose a highly restrictive and coercive regime on them in order to ensure that they make their contribution to freeing our nation. Moreover, we will feel entitled to continue this discipline even after the foreign tyrant has been defeated, just in case there are elements of counter-revolution or a third force left in our midst. In doing all this, we will be acting in the name of our positive political freedom as a nation, so that our fellow nationals can be the source of control, not treated as slaves by a foreign power . At the same time, however, we deny them all kinds of liberty, effectively depriving them as citizens of positive liberty at the level of their manifest desires. We do this by claiming that they have it at the non-manifest level, that each of them has a self that really is not a slave and is really not being treated as a child by this procedure. Similar temptations exist for those who would give people positive freedom at the level of a social class or a particular religion or a particular sex.

Byron, in his poem 'The Isles of Greece' provides us with a nice illustration of how even tyranny can be regarded as liberating as long as it serves our patriotic, or whatever, cause. He appears to excuse the behaviour of the ancient Greek poet Anacreon in courting the patronage of tyrants on the grounds that:-

> *He served - but served Polycrates -*
> *A tyrant: but our masters then*
> *Were still, at least, our countrymen.*

He proceeds to develop the point with reference to Miltiades, the tyrant who advised the Greeks to fight the Persians at Marathon. While one may wish to honour Miltiades for his military foresight, the praise in the second line is surely excessive, as are the sentiments in the final one. Byron writes:-

> *The tyrant of the Cheronese*
> *Was freedom's best and bravest friend;*
> *That tyrant was Miltiades!*
> *Oh! That the present hour would lend*
> *Another despot of the kind!*
> *Such chains as his were sure to bind.*

It should be noted that Kymlicka (pp.203-294) offers what I will call the 'internal perspective' argument against paternalism (including slavery, presumably). In his view, interest-objectivists who are liberals will oppose paternalism because no life goes better if the values it is lived by are imposed on an agent by someone else. Lives go best when they are led from the inside, according to the agent's own values. Even if it is the case that the paternalist (say, Ben) is correct about what activities are valuable to pursue, another person (say, Ann) will gain nothing from being forced to do them. She must first endorse them, see the point of them, otherwise her performing them will not work from the point of view of improving her life.

This, however, is hardly an argument against paternalism or slavery *in principle*. It will only appeal as an argument against paternalism or slavery to those people who already think that what is most valuable about a life, what makes a life worthwhile, is that it is lived from the inside, that it is an arena of personal choice, commitment and responsibility, that is, that what matters most is person-freedom or autonomy. For such people what is most in Ann's interests is the preservation of her independence as an agent or, at least, her being as much an independent agent as any person who might be seeking to coerce her. Ben, however, may well believe that the maximum value that Ann can get out of her life, whether she chooses to do so or not, is if she makes her contribution to the achievement of God's purpose for the universe, or some such. She may resent this at the time but she will come to see that this was the most valuable thing she could have done. In fact, the 'internal perspective' argument, although offered as a defence of liberalism, teeters on the edge of arrogationism. Ben might well come to convince himself that Ann's 'real' self, her fully rational, enlightened self, actually has chosen the path that her manifest self has had imposed on it.

Moreover, the internal perspective argument hardly constitutes an refutation of those who, like the elite in Aldous Huxley's *Brave New World*, wish to genetically engineer humans into biological castes, each with its own unique set of interests. Such humans have been designed by the elite to have their lives go well from the inside when they play whatever role in society that the elite has determined for them. They may even have their capacity to satisfy their interests met to a maximum extent by the elite, and so be as 'free' as possible in an 'interests' sense, while being unfree indeed in the 'person' sense by comparison with members of the elite.

I will now look at some of the recent controversies that 'Two Concepts of Liberty' has generated. I will begin with the claim that Berlin's analysis commits him to a preference for negative liberty over positive liberty.

2.11   Berlin's Supposed Preference for Negative Liberty

Many commentators on Berlin have thought that he preferred negative to positive liberty.[10] This is understandable if some of his remarks are not interpreted in terms of the account I have given above. For example, he says, that the ideal of a pluralist society, with its attendant negative liberty, is a more humane ideal than the ideal of positive self-mastery for a class or a people, or even for humanity as a whole which is found in the disciplined structures of authoritarian societies (1969, p.171).

Berlin is saying here that, when a choice is to be made between a pluralist dictatorship which gives you no liberal positive liberty but plenty of negative liberty and a society which gives you plenty of illiberal positive liberty but little negative liberty, then the more pluralist of the two illiberal societies being compared is to be preferred.

This does raise the question of what if there is more pluralism in a dictatorship than in a society with liberal positive freedom - that is, more negative liberty in the former?   Such a situation faces one with an incompatible set of values here, which is part of Berlin's point - the positive liberty does not reduce to the negative liberty. They are distinct and you have to choose between them. I suspect he would choose the society with the greater liberal positive liberty because it has within itself the seeds for a peaceful transition to a state of greater negative liberty or pluralism.

In particular, liberal positive liberty does not involve any commitment to the ideal of 'positive' self-mastery by classes or peoples or the whole of mankind. Instead, we have the idea of compromises between the competing preferences of individuals. It is this that Berlin sees as the more humane and true ideal.

How, then, can negative liberty come into conflict with positive political liberty as just described or be the 'opposite' of liberal positive political liberty? To see how this can be so, suppose that Ann is offered a choice between two societies, or two political arrangements within the one society, where the choice is between greater negative liberty in exchange for less liberal positive political liberty. It may be, for example, that the liberal democratic society she lives in (let's call it 'First Society'), does not allow her to smoke marijuana, or bans euthanasia, or bans cigarette smoking in public buildings, or requires environmental impact statements before it allows her to build a factory or a marina etcetera. It may well be the case that there is another society ('Second Society') that does not have all these restrictions on her negative liberty, but which operates under the control of a benevolent dictator. She can exchange her current situation of less negative liberty and more liberal positive liberty for less liberal positive liberty and more negative liberty. She has to make a decision here - which matters to her more?[11]

Of course, she may not always be faced by such a choice, but she can be. It is a meaningful case where she can have more negative liberty at the cost of less liberal positive liberty or more liberal positive liberty at the cost of less negative liberty. What should be noted here is that Berlin, like the woman in the example, is most likely to prefer the greater positive liberty in this case to the greater negative liberty. His distinction between positive and negative liberty is not such that he has built in a preference for negative freedom.[12]

Moreover, while there is clearly a distinction between negative liberty and liberal positive political liberty - that is, Ann has a genuine choice between First Society and Second Society - the distinction between higher selves and lower selves has no relevance here. If Ann were to choose one kind of society over the other, this choice can be accounted for without any need to invoke her having two selves.[13]

2.12 Positive Liberty versus Empowerment

Nor is the distinction between liberal positive liberty and negative liberty the distinction between 'freedom' in the sense of empowerment for action and 'freedom' in the sense of the absence of obstacles or constraints in the way of action (Hunt, 1991, p.288). That this is so can be seen by looking at a case where Ann has to make a choice between liberal positive freedom and empowerment for action. Consider the situation where she has a choice between a liberal democratic society (First Society again) and another society (Third Society) where there is greater empowerment for action than in First Society but less liberal positive liberty. It may have been the case, for example, that First Society contains a political party such as a communist party which has as part of its platform a commitment to equalise wealth in a way which empowers the majority of the population in an economic sense in comparison to their previous condition.

Let us suppose, however, that when the people in First Society go to the polls they exercise their liberal positive liberty to choose another political party which has little commitment to an empowering re-distribution of wealth. Liberal positive political liberty here is quite distinct from empowerment. It has to do with the fact that each citizen has an equal vote in determining who shall represent them in parliament, that is, it has to do with being someone whose interests are given equal weight in the basic decision-making system as opposed to a slave or a lower self whose interests are given no weight. It does not have to do with what resources are available to an individual such as Ann to enable her to pursue the goals she is permitted to pursue by the laws made by her elected law-makers.

In Third Society, by contrast, the citizens do not have the option of choosing between a communist party on the one hand and parties that give greater priority to matters other than equalisation of wealth or 'empowerment' in whatever form proposed. Instead, its citizens are required to live in accordance with the 'empowerment' ideal of the single political party in power. Our person, Ann, then has a choice between a society that gives greater value to positive political freedom of the liberal kind and a society which gives greater priority to empowerment. (Or between parties within one society where some parties will respect the liberal conventions but others will abolish all their competitors once power is achieved.)[14]

Of course, it may have turned out in First Society that the people voted in a political party that was committed to the same kind of empowerment as the Third Society communist party. However, the values of First Society are such that they still value liberal positive political liberty more than empowerment. They are not prepared to sacrifice their equal vote, their right to choose between political parties, just to gain greater empowerment. By contrast, the people in Third Society have lost their liberal positive freedom, either voluntarily or by force. What they have lost, in addition, is the right to remove the Third Society communist party if it fails to deliver on greater empowerment.

Ann, then, can be faced with a choice between positive political freedom and empowerment where these are not the same things. There is a clear distinction between them. Berlin has not confused them, even though he regards positive political freedom in such a situation as something quite different from negative freedom. It could be the case, for example, that the Third Society communist party is successful in empowering people and is able to have less obstacles in the way of what people want to do than First

Society, even though such a possibility may not have much historical plausibility.[15]

We have, then, seen how positive political liberty can be the opposite of negative political liberty yet the distinction not be confused with either the higher/lower self distinction or the empowerment/no obstacles distinction.

2.13 Positive Freedom, One Ideal and the Concentration of Power

According to Hunt (1995, pp.468-469), Berlin thinks that, in order to for self-government to be effective, it requires a concentration of political power or an adherence to one true ideal but, Hunt argues, this is to conflate freedom as a capacity for self-government with freedom as empowerment for action. Berlin, however, does not conflate these two things because it is not his own view that a concentration of power or adherence to one true ideal is required for self-government as such, therefore he does not suppose that both are necessary to make self-government effective, regardless of what form it takes.

He does not think that a concentration of power or adherence to one true ideal is necessary for self-government, where what is meant is political self-government, because he accepts the existence of liberal positive freedom. In societies where the liberal application of positive freedom is at work, there will be a tendency to pluralism, to a diffusion of power, to checks and balances to prevent the domination of one ideal or the concentration of power, that is, there will be liberal democratic self-government.

Where what is meant is personal self-government, the existence of concentrated political power or the national adherence to one ideal will be seen as irrelevant. What the liberal sees as personal positive freedom has to do with clashes of desires that are regarded as internal to the person herself, not as interior reflections of clashes of causes in society at large. Personal self-government in the liberal case, as opposed to political self-government, has to do with adhering to the goals that one has decided are of most value in one's life. Berlin does not see concentrated political power or adherence to one true ideal as essential for self-government if what is meant is personal self-government. What is needed in these cases, presumably, are strength of will, perseverance, etcetera.

It may be that certain factors external to the individual may assist in personal self-government, for example, living in a stable society, being in a loving relationship, having been brought up by parents who encouraged some degree of self-denial and the development of a certain kind of character in us, but the existence in the society of a single ideal or the concentration of political power are not the relevant factors. Nonetheless, Berlin may still be opposed to a concentration of political power but because it is more likely to put liberal positive political freedom at risk and, thereby, threaten restrictions on negative liberties so that one section of society treats the rest as slaves or as lower selves.

2.14   Theories of Political Self-Realisation

Hunt (1995, p.468) also argues that Berlin can only sustain the claim that a monstrous impersonation is at the heart of all theories of political self-realisation by conflating freedom taken as a capacity for self-government with freedom for the 'higher', 'true' self.

This is not so. On the account of the distinction between positive and negative liberty given here, Berlin can distinguish cases of freedom as the capacity for self-government that are quite distinct from freedom for the 'higher', 'true' self. These are the cases of what I have called 'liberal' positive political freedom. The citizens in a liberal society are free in the sense that they exercise their capacity for self-government. However, it is not self-government construed on the model of personal positive freedom, that is, personal psychological self-government where a single agent suppresses some of her desires in order to act on others and where she is the only meaningful chooser. Rather, the liberal citizen is self-governing in the sense that she is as much the source of control over what she is or does as other people are over what they are or do, at least at the level of basic political institutions like the vote.

The crucial point about liberal positive political freedom and the political theories that advocate it is that they are not theories of political self-realisation in terms of higher and lower selves at all. Liberal positive freedom is not the kind of political freedom you need for realising yourself, except in the sense that it provides you with the negative freedom (the range of options, the lack of interference from others) that you need to realise yourself in your own individual terms. It does not help you realise yourself, and is not intended to, in terms of some grand cause embodied in organisations outside yourself. Certainly, it is not to do with self-realisation in the sense of higher and lower selves that can be arrogated by others. It is, instead, designed to reconcile conflicts between people who are seen by others, and see themselves, as distinct persons, not manifestations, in a sense, of one giant self scattered over a multitude of different bodily locations. (For, on this collective model, Ann's true self is, so to speak, no different from Alice's, or Angie's true self)

It is only illiberal theories that are theories of political self-realisation in terms of higher and lower selves. Not only that but, once one enters into the game of seeing the political structure of society as representing those who are higher selves on the one hand and those who are lower selves on the other, then monstrous impersonation is unavoidable. However, one does not have to see the representative structure of society in these terms. Liberals, for example, do not.

2.15   The Contemporary Relevance of Berlin's Distinction

Hunt suggests that, even if Berlin is right about the existence of a genuine distinction between positive and negative liberty, the kinds of worries he has about illiberal positive liberty as a force in politics is now outdated (1995, p.469). My own view matches that of Ronald Dworkin who sees illiberal positive freedom as a matter of contemporary concern. It is too easy to underestimate the degree to which there are still people like the arrogationist Ben who see their identity as inextricably involved in the success of a particular cause, who see themselves as somehow psychically at risk if their particular version of the women's movement or the working class movement or a nationalistic or racial or religious movement is not triumphant.

In particular, such a person may find himself impatient with the speed at which liberal democracies accommodate his particular conception of the good, seeking an explanation for the recalcitrance of the electorate in terms of each recalcitrant citizen having a higher self that shares this conception but whose lower self is a mere tool of manipulatory forces in society. Such impatience can easily lead to a denigration of liberal democracy, to a model where he or his party arrogates to themselves the right to represent the true will of the people without a vote, rejecting the mechanism of the vote because, in their view, it has been irredeemably corrupted by the gullibility or weakness of the electorate's malleability.

As a recent example of arrogationism at work I would like to consider Bronwyn Davies' 1991 paper 'The Concept of Agency: a Feminist Poststructural Analysis. She claims there that poststructuralist thought differs from liberal thought in that it understands the concepts of the individual and the collective in non-dualist terms. Dualism is overcome in poststructuralism because it treats both the individual and the collective as constituted through the discourses of a number of collectives. It is these various discourses that make possible who one is. The nature of who one is, one's being, changes with the various discourses through which one is 'spoken into existence' (p.43).

What Davies is saying here is that poststructuralism does not think that there is a meaningful distinction ('dualism') between the individual and society. Who you are, your identity as a person, is a function of what concepts are built into the language of your culture or sub-group about who you can be. Now, the liberal does not disagree that how we think of ourselves will largely depend on the roles and positions that are 'given' to us by society. However, each of us is able to go beyond what society makes available to us. We can see contradictions between how society conceptualises the world and our own experience of the world. We can invent new concepts or new theories that are more reliable predictors of how the world behaves than the ones we were taught.

Why, then, does Davies wish to deny this 'dualism' between the individual and society? Davies herself presents the matter as if it is a factual dispute, that is, a dispute about whether there can be individuals who do not accept poststructuralist theory yet whose picture of the world is not entirely determined by the concepts society has provided. If so, then surely only poststructuralists will be convinced that poststructuralists alone have escaped the webs of social determinism. How could they have arrived at so solipsistic a view? One likely explanation is that the poststructuralist has disguised a value issue as a factual issue. It is not that there is no dualism. Rather, the poststructuralist does not think that there 'ought' to be one. She wants the individual to be defined in terms of some collective or the other, rather than being able to stand apart from any collective whatsoever. As a consequence, her political aim is not to get people to be able to criticise the world picture of any collective whatsoever but, rather, to get people to move out of their current collective's world picture into the poststructuralist collective's world picture or, even more narrowly in Davies' case, into the poststructuralist feminist collective's world picture. In fact, Davies seems to go so far as to say that it is only when a person is able to criticise other world pictures from within the poststructuralist feminist collective that a person counts as an 'agent', as someone who speaks with 'authority'.

If, however, people are not agents until they are converts to poststructuralism, then this strongly suggests that their opinions on such matters as who should govern them lack 'authority'. Their votes in a liberal democracy can be treated as the manifestation of false consciousness in their lower selves. Depriving them of the vote and forcing them to obey the dictates of those whose views do have 'authority' is merely to put them into contact with what they would truly want, what their real 'poststructuralist' selves would believe to be in their best interests, regardless of whether or not their foolish manifest selves struggle against this. All this talk of 'constructed' selves just seems to be a way of denying people the right to live their lives according to what they themselves regard as their wants on the grounds that their wants are merely an artefact of any one of a number 'unauthoritative' collectives, while claiming some special status for the authority of the collective that the poststructuralists happen to favour, an authority presumably derived from some special insight into the truth that poststructuralists have that is denied the rest of us. This, surely, is arrogationism in all its finery, and an arrogationism undiluted.

2.16   Conclusion

Central to a correct understanding of Berlin in 'Two Concepts of Liberty' is the idea that self-government for the arrogationist inextricably links the personal and the political in a way that is not true of the liberal. Once Berlin is understood in this way, it becomes clear that, when negative liberty and positive liberty are construed as opposites, he does not favour the former over the latter regardless of whether the positive liberty at issue is liberal or illiberal. It also becomes clear that positive freedom, as Berlin understands it, does not require either a concentration of political power or adherence to one true ideal. Each of these is only required if it is illiberal positive liberty at issue. Nor does he see all political theories that advocate positive freedom as theories of political self-realisation, as freedom for the 'higher' 'true' self and, thereby, as all committed to 'monstrous impersonation.' This is only true of political theories that advocate illiberal positive liberty.

Further, he has not confused positive liberty with empowerment. This confusion is more the prerogative of those who, like paternalists, see interests-freedom as the only kind of freedom. Once we recognise the distinction between liberal and illiberal positive liberty, however, we see that there is another kind of freedom, namely 'person-freedom', that is valued by both liberals and arrogationists. Unlike the paternalist, both of these reject as inadequate any account of freedom that allows slaves to be free, even if only in principle. In operational terms, however, the arrogationist's political practice is possibly even more enslaving than that of the paternalist because he perverts the notion of person-freedom into freedom only for the higher self, a freedom that he recognises in others only when they act in accord with the requirements of whatever cause he endorses, turning the lower self, which is regarded by the individual as his or her real self, into a slave. When we interpret Berlin in this way, then, we see that he has mounted a powerful case about the danger posed to both our negative liberty and our liberal positive liberty by the arrogationist's commitment to illiberal positive liberty.

In the next chapter I wish to apply the impartialist methodology developed in Chapter 1 to an issue of contemporary interest. Exactly what are the rights of the indigenous people of a nation vis a vis the majority of its citizens who are descendants of colonial powers? Some of the issues raised by such a question are to be found in the case of the conflict in South Australia over whether or not a bridge should be built from the mainland to Hindmarsh Island at Goolwa near the mouth of the Murray, Australia's longest and largest river. A number of Aboriginal women claimed that this site was sacred to the women of their group, the Ngarrendjeri people. The situation was complicated by the fact that another group of Aboriginal women, also of the Ngarrendjeri people, claimed that they were unaware of any tradition that made Hindmarsh Island a special place. I will, however, ignore this particular complication and treat the claim about the sacredness of the site as a given. In effect, then, what we shall be considering is - were this place to be a sacred site to the Ngarrendjeri women, what would follow as to their right to veto any development in the area? What grounds, reasons, principles might they be able to offer for veto powers that would meet impartialist criteria?[16]

Notes

1   In correspondence (1996) Berlin says 'this is exactly right'. The example is borrowed from Geach (p.69). Rawls appears to express a similar idea in his distinction between a 'concept' and a 'conception' (1972, p.5).

2   See Woolcock, (1995). In that article, and in Chapter 1 of this book, 'personal' liberty is referred to as 'internal liberty' and 'political liberty' as 'external liberty.' In correspondence (1995) Berlin says that this article 'had me absolutely right.'

3   In correspondence (1996) Berlin says this point has 'got me completely right.'

4   See Note 3.

5   In correspondence (1996) Berlin recommended the addition of the reference to her 'personal good' here.

6   In correspondence (1996) Berlin says that this point 'is excellent.'

7   See Note 3.

8   For a discussion of how slavery might be regarded as compatible with freedom, see D.B. Martin, *Slavery as Salvation*. Also see P. Garnsey, *Ideas of Slavery from Aristotle to Augustine.*

9   In correspondence (1996) Berlin says that 'this is particularily right.'

10   See G. C. McCallum, T. Gray, J. Gray , I. Hunt (1991, 1995).

11   As for Note 3.

12   As for Note 3.

13   As for Note 3.

14   As for Note 3.

15   As for Note 3.

16   The main purpose of this chapter has been to demonstrate that there is a sense of freedom in which the slave is the very opposite of the free person, that is, that the paternalistic concept of freedom as the capacity to satisfy one's interest is not the only contender in the game. It seems to me that it is a demonstration that is necessary only because there are writers who appear to have denied it. Be that as it may, a secondary aim of the chapter has to been to provide an interpretation of Sir Isaiah Berlin's account of 'positive liberty'. While Sir Isaiah's views on how he is to be interpreted are not necessarily the final word on the matter, it is useful to know what he understood his concept of 'positive liberty' to entail. In correspondence with me (29 September, 1995) Berlin said, of the article mentioned in Note 2 above that it was a 'very effective, intelligent and, to me, extremely gratifying defence of my position on "Two Concepts of Liberty". You have, if I may say so, grasped the central doctrine which I wish to put forward more accurately, and expounded it better, than anyone else who has dealt with it in the considerable literature which this essay has stirred up.' In correspondence (19 March, 1996), in addition to the

other comments noted about the points made in this chapter, he wrote 'that it is an extremely accurate interpretation of my position - perhaps the best that I have seen so far. ... It is wonderful to find people who, after all these years, understand not only oneself, but the fallacies of one's critics'.

3   Indigenous Rights

3.1   Introduction

In May 1994 Robert Tickner, the Australian Federal Minister for Aboriginal Affairs, used his powers under The Aboriginal and Torres Strait Islander Heritage Act 1984 to place a ban on the building of a bridge over the Murray River between Goolwa and Hindmarsh Island in South Australia. He did so because he accepted the claim that building such a bridge would contravene sacred beliefs of the Aboriginal women of the tribe from that area, the Ngarrindjeri.

Exactly what these beliefs were was a matter to which he was not privy, as they were 'women's secret business'. Nonetheless, after advice from a white woman anthropologist and a white woman lawyer, both of whom were given access to the women's secrets, he concluded that the secret matters were serious enough to justify banning the bridge for twenty five years. As we will see, however, enough of the general nature of these beliefs has been made public by the women themselves to give us some idea of their concerns. Our focus will be on what they believed the consequences to themselves and to the environment would be if the bridge went ahead.

3.2   The Consequences for the Ngarrindjeri Women

The anthropologists, Ronald and Catherine Berndt, were told by the Ngarrindjeri that they regarded the River Murray as a kind of lifeline, a huge artery of a living body made up of the lakes and the bush of the southern plains. One of the legs of this body included the stretch of water known as the Coorong towards the south-east and the other leg went south-west towards Encounter Bay. The body, which symbolised a significant male mythological figure called Ngurunderi, covered five different kinds of intermingling environment, from salt-water country, to riverine, lakes,scrubby bush and desert plains - this combination of environment types being of especial relevance for the socio-economic life of the Ngarrindjeri.

Doreen Kartinyeri, the leader of the Aboriginal woman, told Professor Saunders, the lawyer whom Tickner employed to investigate the significance of the site, that the Ngarrindjeri regarded Hindmarsh Island and the waters separating it from the mainland as especially important for the reproduction of the Ngarrindjeri people and their survival (p.33).

Doreen Kartinyeri further told Professor Saunders that building a bridge between the island and the mainland would result in the destruction of 'all the mothers that was, all the mothers that is and all the mothers that is to come' (p.40). She explained that the already existing barrages and ferry would not have a similar effect because they aided the proper functioning of the Lower Murray in much the same way as a pacemaker assists the proper functioning of the heart (p.41). Saunders was told by the Aboriginal women that a bridge would make the estuary system sterile because it went above the waters from shore to shore, creating a direct and permanent link (p.42). Dr Fergie, the anthropologist consulted by Saunders, suggested that an appropriate interpretation of what the women believed was that Hindmarsh Island and another crucial island could only perform their life-generating function when linked by the life-supporting waters of the Goolwa Channel (p.42). In essence, then, it seems that the Ngarrindjeri women's case is that a bridge from the mainland to Hindmarsh Island will cause a loss of fertility in Ngarrindjeri women. This is what they believe will be the cost of building the bridge.

3.3   The Consequences for the Developers and Others

Geoffrey Partington, in his Current Affairs Bulletin article, claimed that the loss to the local community of not building the bridge would be a reduction in potential jobs of 300 whose total multiplier effect would be 1,200 jobs, as well as a loss of identified future income within the Fleurieu Region of $172.8 million, and the loss of $120,000 in annual rates revenue from a potential increase in rateable assets of $40 million (p.10).

Partington also points out that a number of people have spent their life-savings setting up businesses in the area on the assumption the bridge would be built, an investment which will presumably now produce little or no return. Another cost he does not discuss is the cost to South Australian tax-payers for any compensation pay-out, unless this can be anchored back to the Federal Government and the Australian tax-payer.

How, then, is this conflict of interests to be resolved? Does moral philosophy have anything useful to say about how the law might deal with the matter ? I will try to show that impartialism enables us to narrow down the considerations that are relevant to resolving the problem.

I will now look at a possible principle that might be supplied to resolve the dispute between the Ngarrindjeri and the developers namely, the suggestion that the dispute should be resolved in favour of the Ngarrindjeri women because building the bridge is contrary to their religion. In the course of doing so I will spell out the ethical model in more detail.

3.4   The 'Contrary to Ngarrindjeri Religion' Principle

The principle proposed is that some action X should be banned by law because it is contrary to the Ngarrindjeri religion. Let's suppose that Ann is a member of the Ngarrindjeri or someone who has taken their cause to heart. The principle proposed has all the signs of a sectarian principle, one that Ann would only propose if she were a particularist sectarian. There is little point, however, in her offering such a principle to the other parties in the position of equal power (Ben, say) because his role in the position of equal power is to represent those people whose values are such that they are opposed to the building of the bridge unless it can be shown that, at some deeper level of their values, one they have not yet appreciated and will not appreciate until it is drawn to their attention, their values will be served by building the bridge or, at least, by a principle that favours the building of the bridge.

As it stands, the principle that the bridge should not be built because it is contrary to the Ngarrindjeri religion invites Ben to ask Ann to tell him either what is special about the Ngarrindjeri or what is special about their religion that warrants his reducing the satisfaction of what he values on its behalf? Ann will be wasting her time giving any answer that amounts to the claim that what is valuable about these things are that they are things that she values, or that Ngarrindjeri value. She needs to extend her claim beyond those who are the obvious beneficiaries of the principle to those who do not seem to benefit but who need to be convinced to allow it.

To do otherwise is to be secretly wedded to the solution of disputes by power but only if we have the power. It is treating our ideal as superior to those of other people merely because it is our ideal. It is treating ourselves as more worthy of respect than other people.

As a consequence, she might propose a universalist sectarian version of the principle, for example, that 'Any action X should be banned by law if it is against the religious beliefs (or equivalent) of any members of the community.'

3.5   The 'Contrary to Some Religion' Principle

While Ann would accept this principle if the Ngarrindjeri and their supporters are in a position of superior power in society, she should be reluctant to accept if they are in a position of inferior power, that is, she might accept it when she is in the winner scenario but reject it when she is in the loser scenario. The principle makes it possible for Group A to gain some benefit at the expense of some or all of the Ngarrindjeri, Group B to gain a benefit at the expense of some or all of the Ngarrendjeri, and so on for Group C, Group D, etcetera.

It is, for example, against the tenets of some religions that people work on Sundays, so this is a loss to those Ngarrindjeri who wish to work on Sundays. It is against other people's religion that people drink, or gamble, or dance, or have pre-marital sex, or engage in homosexual acts, or use contraception, or have abortions, and so on. (Of course, it may not matter to Ngarrindjeris as such that people have each of these rights but it may matter to some Ngarrindjeris as individuals that they have one or more of them. Each of them, then, will have to decide whether the benefit that this principle gives them - namely, the bridge - is worth the loss of whichever of these other rights they value.)

The potential costs of this principle, then, for Ann and the members of her cause when it is looked at from a universalist sectarian point of view would seem to outweigh its potential benefits. As such, it can be rejected without looking at the winner and loser scenarios from the developers', or anyone else's, point of view, although they, too, will have the same problems with such a principle. This is so because it would only seem to be worth Ann's while to accept this principle if she and her group were in a position of superior power, so she would have to be proposing it as a pseudo-universalist sectarian. This, however, puts her back with the particularist sectarian problems outlined earlier.

3.6   The 'Monism' Problem

Suppose, however, that Ann cares more about banning the bridge than she does about all the possible losses she might suffer if she were not the winner under this principle. If this is her attitude, then she seems to be a monist. She seems to be indifferent to all her potential losses under the loser scenario of this 'religious harm' principle because she would rather take the chance that she has superior power and can ban the bridge, even at the risk that the other side might end up with the superior power and build the bridge, rather than agree to reject this principle. If she went this way, however, she clearly has abandoned the effort to settle the dispute by means other than force. In fact, she is committed to force as the only means of solution, and so seems open to be dealt with only in terms of force.

If we are not universalist sectarians or monists, then, we will seek to modify the principle once again, perhaps to read something like 'Any action X should be banned by law if it will harm some community C according to that community's religious beliefs or equivalent.'

3.7   The 'Harmful According to Some Religion' Principle

The Ngarrindjeri women, as we have seen, believe that some harm will befall them if the bridge is built. This harm is a loss of fertility and the basis for this belief is their religion. Banning the bridge on the basis of such a principle, though, has the same problems as the previous principle. While there will be a gain when we look at the winner scenario from the viewpoint of Ann and the Ngarrindjeri supporters, it will be outweighed by the multiple losses of interest they could suffer in the loser scenario. In the loser scenario, Ann could find herself banned from all the things listed above for the previous principle if the adherents of those religions believe themselves harmed by them. Consider the case of the Christian sect that thought Adelaide would be wiped out by a tidal wave because the parliament under the premiership of Don Dunstan looked like passing a bill legalising homosexuality. They sold their houses, probably at less than maximum value, gave up their jobs, etcetera, and headed for 'them thar hills'.

Moreover, it is not beyond the scope of imagination that a religion come into existence whose adherents believed they would be harmed if the bridge was not built. Perhaps, the Saviour is going to appear on Hindmarsh Island and there is a prophecy that he must cross a bridge if he is to save us.

The point here is that the invocation of harms whose likelihood is not testable in the public arena is not a general principle that we would adopt, even when viewing the case from the viewpoint of the Ngarrindjeri. Even if it helped us in this particular example, its universal adoption would put at risk other interests we hold dear when other people invoke the same principle.

3.8   Sacred Sites

The point of this section is to look at whether there is a principle that sites or things or items that are sacred to a group should get special protection at the tax-payers', or the rest of the community's, expense? Should a Jewish Torah manuscript, or the holy objects in a church, or a section of the church that is a holy of holies where no-one but a priest may enter, get special protection? There does appear to be a principle of private property protection here, regardless of whether it is a religious matter or not. Also, in the case of individuals, it does appear that there is a principle of voluntary membership. Whether you belong to a group with unorthodox beliefs and practices is a matter of consenting adults in private to a large degree. The law should not protect holy of holies as such, but protect private property as such or, at least, those kinds of private property (if any) that would be agreed to in a position of equal power.

3.9   Heritage

It begins to look as if no reason on the basis of religion can justify banning the bridge, so what alternative reasons might there be that take special account of the significance to the Ngarrindjeri of the bridge site?

An alterative kind of reason might be found in the notion of 'heritage'. The Australian national parliament and various state parliaments have passed various heritage acts which empower governments to give special protection to places deemed to be 'heritage'. The Australian Heritage Commission Act 1975 defines 'heritage' as 'those places, being components of the natural environment of Australia, or the cultural environment of Australia, that have aesthetic, historic, scientific or social significance or other special value for future generations as well as the present community.'

Australia is also party to the World Heritage Convention which gives special protection to items or areas 'of cultural heritage and natural heritage which it considers as having outstanding universal value.' There is also the Aboriginal and Torres Strait Islander Heritage Protection Act 1984 which says that 'the purposes of this act are the preservation and protection from injury or desecration of areas and objects in Australia and in Australian waters, being areas and objects that are of particular significance to Aboriginals in accordance with Aboriginal tradition.'

However, the Minister is required by section 10 (1) (c) of the Commonwealth Heritage Act to have 'considered the report and any representations attached to the report'. The report referred to here is a report by a person the Minister commissions. This report has to deal with 'the effects the making of a declaration may have on the proprietary or pecuniary interests of persons other than the Aboriginal or Aboriginals referred to in paragraph (1) (a)'as well as 'the extent to which the area is or may be protected by or under a law of a State or Territory, and the effectiveness of any remedies available under such law.'

It should be noted that the Full Court of the Federal Court in Tickner v Bropho (1993) 40 FCR 183 had ruled that the Minister was not required to make an s9 declaration in respect of an area in Perth known as the Old Swan Brewery site. In effect, this ruling indicates that the Minister can refuse to list an area if he or she believes that there is some competing interest that outweighs the Aboriginal interest, although as French J. of the court said, the Act 'accords a high value to such protection for heritage areas   threatened with injury and desecration' (224). Lockhart in Wamba Wamba Local Aboriginal Land Council v Minister administering the Aboriginal and Torres Strait Islander Heritage Protection Act 1984 (1989 - 1990) 23 FCR 239 at 247 makes the point that 'the purpose of a s9 declaration is to preserve the status quo of a significant Aboriginal area which is under immediate threat of injury or desecration until the

(Minister) decides whether to make a more permanent declaration under s10.'

So much, then, for the background that the acts supply. The issue to be taken up here is whether 'heritage' supplies a non-religious reason as such for special protection of an area, such as the banning of the bridge. In other words, could the Ngarrindjeri appeal to heritage as a sound reason for banning the bridge in such a way that did not constitute mere special pleading? It may well be the case that lots of places on a heritage list are religious places but do they receive this special protection because they are special to a particular religion or do they get it for some other reason? In 1993 there were 705 churches on the Register of the Australian National Estate compared with 82 sites of mythological or spiritual significance. As Deane Fergie (p.18) points out 76 per cent of the places on the register of the National Estate in June 1993 were historic places, 7 per cent were Aboriginal places and 16 per cent were natural places. This does not indicate the comparative amounts of land or monetary value of each. Fergie (p.18) also points out that, in South Australia, the Register of State heritage items includes a bakery, numerous banks, breweries, cinemas, conservatories, a fort, dwellings, hospitals, precincts, a walkway, an incinerator and even a sewerage works.

So, when is it justifiable to declare an item a 'heritage' item? Is it a ground for making something 'heritage' that it is specially significant to a particular group? If so, this suggests a principle that some action X should be banned by law if it destroys something that any group regards as significant to its traditions. While we may well support such a principle if we were in the winner scenario for the Ngarrindjeri, we would not be so keen on the principle if we were in the loser scenario where we might be taxed to support everyone else's heritage claims or we might be banned from actions that we wanted to perform with respect to certain objects or places because these were significant to some group. To give examples - would all mosques be heritage because they have special significance to Moslems? all Australian League Football grounds ? all spots where people played as children, all lovers' lanes, and so on? The point is that any place you want treated as special to you is not special to some other group and banning any acts that change it will affect their interests.

It would appear that the principle that will apply in general is that something of special significance to a private interest or minority group is to be preserved only if that group can raise the private capital to buy it. Its preservation is part of the activities of civil society, not part of the political realm.

So, when does it become part of the political realm? The case, surely, has to be that the place is significant to the nation, the State or society, as a whole in some way. In such a situation, an argument needs to be offered indicating that we will all be harmed if this place does not remain available to us all. This is the kind of argument offered with respect to natural places when it is suggested that there is something unique about this particular environment that gives it special value in terms of anyone, either in Australia or the world.

So, at the level of human artefacts, or items valuable because of the role they play in a history or a culture, there would need to be something that relates this item to the development of the society as a whole, or the nation, or events significant in the formation of the nation. (Eureka Stockade, Sovereign Hill, the tree where the Australian Labor Party began, Burke and Wills' 'DIG' tree, the Aboriginal 'ramshackle shed embassy', and so on.)

In other words, places that played an important role in making this country the place it is in the sense that people who see these places are encouraged to think to themselves 'It was this struggle, or this event, or events in this place, that made us as we are now in religion, or how we are now in literature or art - for example, such places as the first school run by Mary McKillop (the first Australian to be beatified); the locations where the Heidelberg artists lived while they painted their famous landscapes; places important in the life of the writers Patrick White or Henry Lawson; the place where the stump jump plough was developed, etcetera. Provided you can show that this field of endeavour is important in the Australian context (literature, music, Stockman's Hall of Fame, and so on), then something significant in making that field how it is now is also going to run a good chance of significance.

However, and this is the crucial point, not everything that belongs to that field can be equally important. It cannot all be preserved.

Clearly, Aboriginal culture is important as part of the development of Australia as a nation. Any appreciation of how the nation is now must involve an appreciation of how it was, and in some cases still is, in non-tribal and tribal aboriginal communities. But it is not clear why everything of aboriginal significance should be preserved unchanged any more than everything of colonial English significance should, or Irish convict significance, or Malay pearl divers, or Italian canecutters, or Cornish or Chinese miners or Barossa Valley Germans or whatever.

What we have as a principle here is that the interests of those who wish to change a site loses out to the interests of those who wish to preserve a site, at least in terms of government intervention, only when there is something of community significance in that site in the field the site instantiates. 'Community' here must mean some group larger than the group directly associated with the site (or object). Otherwise, its preservation or change is a matter of civil society. The argument here would have to be that the harm done is the loss of a sense of community, of a sense of common striving and endeavour to produce institutions or whatever. Moreover, it would need to be shown that the loss of such a sense of identity loosens the bonds that unify us as a nation, significantly increasing the risk of social instability in a degree that those who wish not to be coerced by others will find threatening.

3.10 Does the Women's Secret Business Qualify as Heritage?

The banning of the bridge was done as an exercise of federal power. It over-ruled a decision by the South Australian Minister for Aboriginal Affairs Dr Michael Armitage on 3 May 1994 to allow the bridge to go ahead. Dr Armitage, presumably, had decided that the benefits to the local Goolwa community, or to the South Australian community as a whole, of building the bridge outweighed the benefits of protecting the area as a heritage site.

This raises the issue of proper domains of federal versus state power. It is likely that the parties in the position of equal power will prefer decisions that affect only local people to be made by local people, or the State by the State. The issue, then, becomes whether this is a matter that only affects the local community or the State community or is it a matter that affects the nation as a whole. Is it a heritage site of 'national significance'?

. Fergie (p.14) quotes ASTIC (the Aboriginal and Torres Strait Islander Commission) as saying that the Act 'exists essentially to ensure that areas of significance to Aboriginal and Torres Strait Islander people are not under threat of injury or desecration as a result of deficiencies in State or territory legislation for the protection of such sites and objects, or from a failure by State or Territory administration to apply for protections available to them.'

However, as I pointed out earlier, the principle should seem to be that national governments ought only over-rule the decision of local or State governments when it is a matter of national significance or when it is an infringement of basic human rights or civil liberties. The latter has not been argued, nor, for that matter, has the former as far as I know. As it happens, the federal act does not make this distinction although it does specify that the purpose of the act is 'the preservation and protection from injury or desecration of areas and objects in Australia and Australian waters, being areas and objects that are of *particular* significance to Aboriginals in accordance with Aboriginal tradition.'

The basis of any decision, then, seems to be one of whether the site is of significance to Aboriginals, not whether it is an Aboriginal site of national significance. The way the Act is worded is subject to the problems raised earlier about religions unless some extra argument can be offered that shows why sites of significance to Aboriginals get this kind of priority treatment. In fact, the way the Act is worded it strongly suggests that the Minister cannot but protect such sites no matter what other interests are at stake. Again, it is difficult to see how anything other than a partialist perspective can insist on such a principle.

What is needed, then, is some process by which the federal Minister can halt change to a heritage site while it is determined whether or not it is of national significance. If it is determined not to be, then its fate is properly a matter of State or local considerations. This would mean changing the current federal act.

It would also mean setting up a procedure for determining national significance that is less susceptible to misuse for political advantage than the current system. No doubt it is the case that Tickner banned the bridge out of a genuine concern for Aboriginal heritage but the current act makes it too easy for a federal Minister of one political party to try to gain political advantage over a State Government of a different political party or to gain kudos from special interest groups that the Minister, or the Minister's party, think will be especially influential in the next election.

3.11   Compensation for Disadvantage

There could be a principle that disadvantaged groups be compensated in ways that they themselves see as significant, even if this is at the expense of the rest of the community. Something like this would be acceptable in a position of equal power because, while I might wish to avoid personal loss to compensate some group of which I am not a member, I would wish others to incur losses to compensate me if I am a member of a disadvantaged group. Furthermore, I would want the compensation to be something that I, as a member of that particular group, regarded as truly compensatory.

Exactly what limits should be placed on the amount that I may have to pay should I not be the relevant disadvantaged group will be difficult to determine. Clearly it cannot be open-ended or the two scenario model will lead me to reject the principle. Suppose, for example, first that I am in the winner scenario for a disadvantaged group. I receive $1000 compensation and paying for this is shared among the nondisadvantaged group. Suppose, second, that I am in the loser scenario for this disadvantaged group, that is, some other group or lots of groups claim disadvantage compensation from the rest of the community, which includes me and this amounts to more than $1000, then the principle isn't one I will accept.

Perhaps the solution here is some variation of Ronald Dworkin's suggestion (1981), namely, to ask what insurance would we be prepared to take out in the position of equal power to cover compensation should we be in a disadvantaged group, yet be prepared to pay if we are not. This parallels the kind of reasoning involved in how much we should be taxed to compensate for physical or mental disabilities. If we were not disabled, we would not want to pay out what is necessary to cover the full cost of enabling a handicapped individual to do all, or most, of what a non-handicapped person could do, so we would have to balance the costs of paying the relevant insurance against the other things we could do with our money. Such speculations indicate the kind of path the 'equal power' model draws us down. It should be kept in mind here that we are talking about compensation coming from people who are not themselves the causes of this disadvantage in any obvious sense.

Could this argument justify the banning of the bridge? It certainly would be an argument to be weighed if the Ngarrindjeri were seeking compensation for disadvantage. However, this was not the case with the

Hindmarsh Island bridge, although the flyer from the anti-bridge Kumarangk Coalition does claim that the Government has no right to investigate the spiritual or religious beliefs of anyone in our society and least of all those who have been treated so unjustly.

If it had been the case, then some procedure other than a unilateral decision by a federal Minister would seem appropriate. There would, for example, need to be an inquiry into what exactly the Ngarrindjeri wanted in the way of compensation, with the implication that compensation is not an open-ended matter. Once it has been given it is not open to ask for it again unless there has been a new set of disadvantages created since the compensation.

In deciding what the Ngarrindjeri wanted in the way of compensation, the issue of the bridge would be considered, but, clearly, there is not unanimous agreement among the Ngarrindjeri that the site is significant to them and, therefore, is the appropriate compensatory vehicle. They themselves would need to resolve this matter - perhaps preferring financial compensation or the grant of workable land somewhere to protection of the bridge site.

3.12   Conclusion

We have given close attention to the various principles that might be offered to justify why the building of the Hindmarsh Island should be banned, given the concerns of the Ngarrindjeri women. As we have seen, most of the arguments actually offered are not successful - for example, that the area is sacred to the Ngarrindjeri, or that the Ngarrindjeri women believe they will be harmed if it is built, or even that they actually will be harmed. An argument in terms of heritage does seem to at least be the kind of argument that would pass the scrutiny of the vigilators in the position of equal power but the factual case needs to be made out both that this area is really sacred to Ngarrindjeri women (contrary to the claims of the dissident women) and that what is sacred to the Ngarrindjeri women is something of either state or national heritage interest, that is, something of significance to groups other than the Ngarrindjeri themselves.

In the course of this discussion, it became clear that the various Commonwealth heritage acts are not sufficiently precise on when a matter ceases to a heritage issue for a State Government and becomes one for the Federal Government. A brief answer to this was offered in terms of when the matter is such that people other than those in the state itself see it as affecting their understanding of their history as a nation. Compensation did see to offer one avenue, although it was threatened by the dissension within the Ngarrindjeri women.

In the end, then, my discussion has not demonstrated what justice requires as to whether the bridge should be built or not, but, hopefully, it has illustrated how impartialist reasoning can be used to rule out certain principles as acceptable bases for a decision.

In the next chapter I will begin the task of spelling out in more detail the actual principles on which I think that the parties in a position of equal power will agree. I will do so by comparing the impartialist form of contractarianism with that offered by John Rawls, whose book *A Theory of Justice* offers the most developed form of contractarianism available.

4   The Scope of Impartialism

4.1   Introduction

In this chapter I will compare impartialism with the contractarian theory that Rawls develops in his book *A Theory of Justice*. Although he published the book in 1972, it remains the most thorough account yet produced of a contractarian derivation of claims about how we should structure the basic institutions of society. As such, it is a theory about the principles that make a society a just one rather than a general theory of the principles that make acts right or wrong. Nonetheless, as Farrell notes (p.188), Rawls accepts the idea that his theory can be extended to a general theory of normative ethics which Rawls (p.17) calls 'rightness as fairness', even though Rawls himself has not proceeded to develop it in this way.

Since writing *A Theory of Justice* Rawls has modified his account in various ways but the features I describe below remain central to his theory. They articulate the plausible components of a contractarian theory and challenge competing contractarian theories to show either that such a component is unnecessary or can be better achieved by an alternative means. I will, however, utilise his later explications of his ideas if they enrich the account he provided in *A Theory of Justice*, provided they remain consistent with it. I will now turn to a brief exposition of those elements of Rawls' theory on which I wish to focus for the purpose of comparison with the position of equal power.

4.2   Rawls' Theory

Rawls suggests that a proposed arrangement for the basic structure of society will only be just if it would be agreed to by people of a certain kind who are located in a certain kind of decision-making situation. The decision-making situation, which he calls the 'original position', must be one that prevents the parties to the discussion arranging the basic structure of society to benefit themselves and their values to the disadvantage of other people.

In order to avoid this kind of bias, Rawls believes that the people in the decision-making situation should be conceived of as behind what he calls a 'veil of ignorance', that is, they are to reason about the basic structure of society as if they do not know who they will be in the society that eventually has whatever structure they agree on. They are to treat their current talents, intelligence, strength, conception of the good, character, disposition to risk-taking, as irrelevant to any conclusion they reach because they are to argue as if there is no guarantee that they will have these features when they emerge from behind the veil (p.12).

Rawls requires the kind of people to be found behind the veil of ignorance to be free, equal, rational and reasonable. To meet the first of these requirements, which I will call the 'free-will' requirement, people need to have the capacity to form, revise and rationally pursue a conception of the good, to be self-authenticating sources of rational claims and capable of taking responsibility for their own ends (p.11; 1993, p.72).

To meet the equality requirement people must meet three criteria. Firstly, they must the capacity for a sense of justice. Secondly, they must have the capacity for a conception of the good. Rawls calls these two criteria the 'moral powers'. Thirdly, they must have the powers of reason in the sense that they are able to participate equally in the debate, having the necessary ability to understand arguments and to act on whatever is concluded. They must, in fact, meet all three of these criteria to an extent sufficient to ensure that they can be fully cooperating members of society (p.19; 1993, p.19).

People will meet the rationality requirement to the extent that they choose a course of action on the basis that it will satisfy more of their desires rather than less and has the best chance of being successful. They must, in effect, act so as to do what is best for their essential interests (p.143; 1993, p.19).

The reasonableness requirement involves meeting two criteria. The first I will call the 'fair terms of cooperation' criterion. It requires the parties behind the veil to be willing to propose fair terms of cooperation and abide by them provided others do. The second I will call the 'burdens of judgement' criterion. It requires them to be willing to bear the consequences of their decisions and to accept these consequences for the purposes of public reason in directing the legitimate exercise of political power in a constitutional polity (1993, p.54).

In addition, Rawls places what I will call the 'mutual disinterestedness' requirement on the parties behind the veil, that is, they do not seek to benefit or harm each other or gain by comparison with each other, nor do they wish to impose their conceptions of the good onto other people, nor are they envious of others' good fortune (p.144). He also invokes what I will call the acceptability' requirement, that is, that they realise that they can only offer reasons licensed by the veil of ignorance.

In addition to these features of the original position itself and of the people in it, Rawls also places a number of conditions on the conduct of the argument behind the veil. One of these is that the kinds of cases they deal with must lie within what he calls 'the circumstances of justice'. Another is that the principles arrived at must meet what he calls 'the formal constraints of the concept of right'. I will look at these in more detail later in the chapter. Before I do that, however, I wish to compare the other requirements just listed with what would be required of the parties in the position of equal power.

4.3   Comparing Contracting Positions

Rawls introduces the veil of ignorance into his theory in order to ensure that the parties debating over what principles should govern a society do not choose principles for either egoistic or sectarian reasons. If they must argue as if they do not know which role they will occupy in the world to which the agreed-upon principles apply, then they will not be able to suggest principles that favour themselves as individuals or as members of some particular group. They will, in effect, have impartiality between the interests of different individuals, and between different conceptions of the good, forced upon them. The same result is achieved within impartialism by the impartialist axioms, especially the symmetry and noncoercionist requirements. The symmetry requirement rules out particularist egoists and particularist sectarians. People who offer such principles show themselves to be partialists, that is, people who would use a position of superior power to break any agreement reached under equal power if it conflicted with their self-interest or their ideal. Such people are not suitable members of the contracting position if it is to produce agreement under conditions of equal power. The noncoercionist requirement rules out universalist egoists and sectarians for the same reason.

It seems, then, that the veil of ignorance ought to produce exactly the same normative proposals as impartialism, but there is often a divergence between what Rawls derives from the veil and the conclusions that I believe that the parties would reach in a position of equal power. While there is agreement on such matters as the desirability of constitutional democratic government, religious tolerance, tolerance for sexual diversity and ways of life, anti-paternalism, anti-racism and anti-sexism, I think that the parties in a position of equal power would reject his position on the distribution of opportunities (his 'Difference Principle'), and his position on how liberal nations should relate to illiberal nations. While impartialism agrees with him on the importance of freedom of religion and conscience, it disagrees with him over why these freedoms are important. If the veil of ignorance, then, is normatively equivalent to the symmetry and noncoercionist requirements, then either Rawls or I have made an error in our deductions from our respective starting points.

As we just saw, Rawls thinks that the parties behind the veil of ignorance are to argue as if they are ignorant of what talents, intelligence, strength, conception of the good, character and disposition to risk-taking they have in the real world. It would appear to be straight forward enough that the parties in the position of equal power, too, cannot take such factors into consideration. They cannot use such factors to give themselves an advantage in the position of equal power itself because, if the characteristic truly constitutes an advantage, then they are to be conceived as having it in equal amounts. In considering a rule to cover the real world, they are further to be conceived as divided into two parties, one of whom proposes arrangements that favour the more intelligent, say, and the other which proposes arrangements that do not. Unless the former group can show that it is the interests of all, from a noncoercionist perspective, to have arrangements that favour the more intelligent in some way, then the latter party will not agree in a position of equal power. The former group must be able to offer reasons for privileging the more intelligent person that do not amount to their knowing that they themselves are among the more intelligent in the real world. To do this is to suggest that they would have proposed arrangements favouring the less intelligent if they had thought that was the group in which they were to be found in the real world, and this further suggests that they want superior power for whatever group they belong to regardless of what properties it possesses.

While the above points cover some aspects of the 'risk-taking' case, it is a case that does raise further issues. Ethical dilemmas will arise in which some lives will have to be sacrificed in order to save others. Any adequate ethical theory needs to be able to accommodate such cases. What, for example, is to be done in a situation where only twelve people can fit safely into a lifeboat, but there are fifteen people to be rescued? Or a case where the twelve people in the lifeboat have eaten all their rations and one of them has to be killed and eaten if the rest are to survive, and so on? At first sight, it might appear as if the ban on counting a person's propensity to risk-taking rules out the obvious kinds of solutions to these problems, such as drawing straws, or some other randomised procedure. However, such solutions are not problematic from an equal power perspective. In fact, they are precisely the ones we would expect the parties in the position of equal power to propose. Such a solution is precisely the kind of solution where the proposer shows a willingness to be in the position of inferior power, that is, that he or she turns out to be one of those that draws the short straw. Likewise, they seem to fit Rawls' veil of ignorance because the parties there must reason as if they do not know whether or not they will be in the rescued or the abandoned group. Both procedures enforce the requisite impartiality on the reasoners.

A more difficult case is the one where someone in the position of equal power (say, Ben) puts forward a principle such as 'The religion of the majority is to be free to suppress the views of minorities'. This kind of a case is a problem because Ben is acting on his personal disposition as a risk-taker in the position of equal power, not in the real world, and is prepared to lose his freedom of religion as a member of the minority in the real world in order to suppress what he regards as heresies if he turns out to be in the majority which, of course, he has the greater chance of doing. This kind of case could be generalised to any majoritarian suppression of any minority, religious or cultural or whatever. Ben, however, is not permitted to propose such a principle just because he thinks that the majority will have superior power. If some minority has superior power he cannot abandon his majoritarian principles just to improve his own situation.

In effect, then, if he is not being a partialist, he is proposing the deeper principle that conflicts of interests always be settled by unlimited majoritarian decision-making procedures. This, however, puts him into a two-party conflict with Ann, say, who rejects such a decision-procedure. His propensity as a risk-taker, then, becomes irrelevant as such in that it translates into an inter-party dispute. As we have seen, and will spell out in more detail later, the parties in the position of equal power, who must be noncoercionists, will not accept such unlimited majoritarian decision making power, although they will accept constitutional (that is, limited) liberal democracy with majoritarian decision-making as a central component but with the powers of majority-elected governments limited by majority-determined (either directly or indirectly) constitutional restrictions.

The parties in the position of equal power will have to meet the 'free-will', equality' and 'rationality' requirements that Rawls specifies for the parties behind the veil of ignorance, otherwise they will not be the kind of being that can enter into conflicts of desires and debate them rationally. They will also need to meet the reasonableness requirement if they are to be the kind of person who can honour any agreement they negotiate, otherwise they would not be the kind of person able to reach agreement in a position of equal power. They will also need to meet the acceptability requirement in that they are motivated to propose principles that they know they must follow in the real world.

The disinterestedness requirement needs a somewhat fuller treatment than these other requirements. It is equivalent in Rawls' theory to the noncoercionist and nonmonism requirements of impartialism. What is to be stressed about it is that the parties in the position of equal power, or behind the veil for that matter, can be conceived of as caring about other people, as loving them and committed to them but not in a way that impinges on the autonomy of other people. Ann may well believe that Ben's good requires him to worship a particular god or endorse a particular politics, and her love for him may lead her to do whatever she can to convert him, but the noncoercionism and nonmonism requirements mean that she cannot use methods of conversion that amount to the exercise of superior power.

A number of writers such as Scanlon (1982) and Barry(1995) have developed post-Rawlsian versions of contract theory. According to the Scanlon-Barry theory, in order for a political arrangement to be a just one, the situation which produces it must be one in which well-informed people who are motivated to reach agreement with others negotiate in a situation of equal power (in the sense that each has a veto) about the arrangements to apply in the real world, the basis of the negotiation being that they try to offer each other terms that cannot reasonably be rejected (Barry, 1995, p.10).

While there is much to recommend the Scanlon-Barry approach, it seems to me that it is not specific enough on what makes a term one that cannot reasonably be rejected. I believe that this weakness can be remedied if we develop the notion of 'equal power' that both they and Rawls invoke at various times but which all three of them leave largely unexplored.

4.4   The Circumstances of Justice

One of the conditions that Rawls places on the conduct of the argument behind the veil is that the kinds of cases they deal with must lie within what he calls the 'circumstances of justice'.[1] My concern is whether or not there is any good reason to limit the scope of impartialism to only those conflicts of desires that fall within Rawls' 'circumstances of justice'. He divides the circumstances of justice into two categories, namely, (1) objective circumstances and (2) subjective circumstances (pp.126-130). I will look at the objective circumstances first.

I wish to consider three of the objective circumstances of justice that Rawls proposes. I will call them (1) the Robinson Crusoe circumstance (2) the humanhood circumstance and (3) the moderate scarcity circumstance. I will look at each in turn to see whether there is any good reason why impartialism should not be used to resolve conflicts of desire that lie outside these circumstances.

4.4.1   Objective Circumstances: The Robinson Crusoe Circumstance

The circumstances of justice, according to Rawls, are the standard circumstances of human life which make cooperation both possible and desirable (p.126). This would appear to exclude those cases of what humans do in situations where cooperation is neither possible nor necessary. One of these is the Robinson Crusoe case of someone marooned alone and incommunicado from the rest of the world on a desert island. It is only when Man Friday turns up that the possibility of cooperation or not arises.

Nonetheless, people do disagree about how a person should behave when alone, even on a desert island. For example, many people would think that Robinson Crusoe should not masturbate on his desert island, whereas others would think that there is nothing wrong with his doing so. Is this conflict one in whose resolution a contractarian theory has no role to play due to the fact that human cooperation in such a case is neither possible nor necessary?

Suppose, then, that Robinson Crusoe wants to masturbate on his desert island. His situation, as it stands, does not constitute a conflict of desires, as there are not two parties involved. However, we can readily imagine a conflict of desires between Ann and Ben, say, that bears on this case. Ann, for example, may want Crusoe, or anyone in his situation, to do whatever he feels like doing, provided he isn't unknowingly harming himself physically, say, whereas Ben wants him not to do so.

We see, then, that contractarianism, at least in its impartialist form, can be used to produce principles concerning cases like the Robinson Crusoe one which lie outside the circumstances of justice. What Ann and Ben have to resolve is which of their competing desires about how Robinson Crusoe should behave is to be satisfied. The Robinson Crusoe circumstance, then, is not a restriction on the application of the position of equal power.

4.4.2 Objective Circumstances: The 'Humanhood' Circumstance

Rawls does not regard the circumstances of justice as covering cases of what humans do to non-humans. As he only applies the veil to cases that fall within the circumstances of justice, this means that he does not think that the veil provides principles about how humans should treat animals. Is the same true of impartialism?

As the only beings capable of Rawlsian-type contractarian argument appear to be humans, this may suggest that a device such as the veil or the position of equal power only applies to cases of how humans treat humans. This is not so. One set of humans may want humans to exploit animals regardless of the suffering to the animals this causes. Another group of humans may want to stop this kind of exploitation. There is a clear case of a conflict of desire here. Ann and Ben, for example, can employ the impartialist apparatus to try to resolve this conflict of desires.

In deciding whose desire is to be satisfied, they will be coming up with principles about how humans should treat animals, even though the animals themselves were not, and were incapable of being, parties to the generation of these principles. Once again, a distinction needs to be drawn between what the principles are that the procedure can be about, on the one hand, and the conditions that need to be met before there is an argument at all, on the other hand. There will only be an argument if the parties to it are persons, just as there will only be an argument if there is a conflict of desires.

What this discussion of the humanhood circumstance shows us is that principles need not be only about the relationships between rational agents even though the parties who develop these principles must themselves be rational agents. The veil, and the position of equal power, can be used to arrive at principles that constrain how rational agents treat non-rational agents such as animals or, possibly, even such things as trees, rocks and eco-systems.

While Rawls may be right that principles about the relationships between humans and non-humans cannot be principles of justice, nonetheless they are principles that resolve conflicts of desire between humans as to how non-humans should be treated. Rawls has concerned himself only with principles that fall within the circumstances of justice. His doing so, however, does not show that conflicts of desires about matters lying outside these circumstances do not also merit resolution or that the veil, or the position of equal power, cannot be used in producing resolutions.

4.4.3   Objective Circumstances: The 'Moderate Scarcity' Circumstance

Rawls believes that questions of justice only arise in conditions of moderate scarcity. Conditions of moderate scarcity are to be contrasted with what I will call conditions of 'extreme scarcity' on the one hand and conditions of 'superfluity' on the other. Conditions of extreme scarcity occur when circumstances so harsh that cooperation must inevitably breakdown. Conditions of superfluity are those where an abundance of natural and other resources makes schemes of co-operation superfluous (p.127).

Rawls may well be correct in his view that questions of justice do not arise in conditions of extreme scarcity or of superfluity. It may still be the case, however, that conflicts of desires can occur about what happens in these circumstances, as they did about what happens in Robinson Crusoe-type situations and in situations involving the treatment of non-humans by humans.

Superfluity   As an example of a dispute that might arise in conditions of superfluity, consider the case where one set of people wants to engage in the mindless destruction of an endless supply of plant life, whereas others do not want them to. Let us suppose that Ben agrees with the first group and Ann with the second. The position of equal power will provide the appropriate framework within which they should try to settle this dispute. It does not seem to follow, therefore, that conflicts of desires cannot be about states of affairs that occur in conditions of superfluity.

However, there seems to be no reason why Ann and Ben could not themselves be located in a situation of superfluity and be in conflict with each other over whether or not acts of mindless destruction should be allowed there. Ben might not need Ann's cooperation to engage in such an act, in the sense that he could annihilate plenty of vegetation by himself, but he may well need her cooperation in the sense that she does not actively seek to suppress his behaviour.

Extreme Scarcity Similar points apply in the case of extreme scarcity. No matter how extreme the scarcity, it is difficult to see that cooperation is not possible, even in cases where people's lives are at stake. Consider the case of people adrift in a lifeboat faced with the decision of throwing one or more overboard in order to save the rest. It seems that, even in such a case, there are fair and unfair ways of deciding who has to die.

Two historical cases bear witness to how the legal system, at least, regarded the obligations of the parties in such a situation. In the case of U.S. v Holmes (1842) the judge directed the jury to convict Holmes of manslaughter. Holmes was a crewman in an overcrowded lifeboat who obeyed the orders of the ship's mate and helped throw sixteen male passengers overboard. However, no fair procedure had been followed by the mate or Holmes in choosing who should die. According to the judge, who went should have been chosen by lot (Glover, p.204).

In the second case, R v Dudley (1884), a group of shipwrecked sailors killed and ate a cabin boy. They were found guilty of murder even though their belief was reasonable that cannibalism was the only way they would survive and the already weakened cabin boy would probably have died first anyway (Glover, p.204).

As I said earlier, however, it is not my purpose here to dispute Rawls' account of justice. I am interested, instead, in whether there is any good reason why the veil of ignorance, or the position of equal power, could not be used to resolve conflicts of desires in such cases. If Ann wants to decide who should be thrown off the overcrowded lifeboat in terms of who is the least popular whereas Ben wants to use some alternative method such as drawing straws, then there is a conflict of desires here that can be debated in a position of equal power or even behind the veil of ignorance. The extreme scarcity involved does not seem to present an obstacle to the use of such procedures.

Admittedly, the two cases described are cases where human cooperation is possible, in that the people on the boat could agree that some of them have to be thrown overboard and that these be the ones who draw the short straws or whatever. As a consequence Rawls might argue that this isn't a situation of extreme scarcity. Such a move, however, runs the risk of making the notion of 'extreme scarcity' an empty one.

Likewise, even in a situation of superfluity, cooperation may be necessary for cases like the mindless destruction of abundant plant life. To say that the mere fact that cooperation is necessary for this kind of case means that the situation is not one of superfluity also runs the risk of rendering the notion of 'superfluity' empty.

So far, then, we have seen that there are no good reasons to restrict the use of contractarian devices such as the veil or the position of equal power to resolving only those conflicts of desires that fall within the objective circumstances of justice, as Rawls specifies them. Our discussion of the objective circumstances of justice has, however, shown us (i) the position of equal power is an appropriate device to use to arrive at principles about how humans should treat non-humans provided the parties who agree on the principles are beings of a kind capable of arriving at, and living in accord with, the principles they determine (ii) that the position of equal power can be used to arrive at principles about how people should behave in conditions of superfluity and extreme scarcity provided the notions of 'superfluity' and 'extreme scarcity' are not defined in such a way as to make cooperation in such conditions logically impossible.

4.5   The Subjective Conditions of Justice

In Rawls' view, not only do certain objective circumstances have to exist before questions of justice arise but also certain subjective conditions have to be met. I will be interested in three of these, which I will call the 'dissensus' circumstance, the 'mutual disinterest' circumstance, and the 'fallibility' circumstance. Like the objective circumstances, these are circumstances that Rawls believes have to apply to people in ordinary life before their situation is one that is properly the subject of questions of justice. I will now look at Rawls' subjective circumstances of justice in order to see whether two parties, Ann and Ben say, can try to resolve conflicts outside these circumstances by using the position of equal power, or, for that matter, the veil of ignorance.

4.5.1 The 'Dissensus' Circumstance

I borrow the word 'dissensus' from Alasdair MacIntyre (p.590) where he says that dissensus is the obstacle to meaningful conversation between the various groups in society because of an excess of rival conventions, conflicting anecdotes; and the repetition of assertions and denials. It is precisely this kind of dissensus that the impartialist conditions of argument are intended to overcome. In Rawls' view, the disputes between people that the veil of ignorance resolves arise because each person has his or her own plan, or conception of the good, that leads people to develop different goals and to be in competition with each other for the natural and social resources available (p.127). This raises the question of whether the veil of ignorance, or the position of equal power, has a role to play only if there is actual conflict between Ann and Ben, say, or whether it also applies to hypothetical conflicts of desire.

I can see no reason why the position of equal power cannot be used to anticipate the principles that will be needed to resolve conflicts of desires that might happen. Also, it is possible that the agreement reached by Ann and Ben when they are not in a position of equal power is a case of forced consent, as discussed in the first chapter. It is, therefore, not even the case that consensus between Ann and Ben in the real world obviates the need for devices such as the position of equal power or the veil of ignorance. It may well be that there is only a lack of dissensus between Ann and Ben in a position of uncertain power because at least one of them has acted contrary to the principles that they would have agreed to in a position of equal power.

4.5.2 The 'Mutual Disinterest' Circumstance

In proposing the 'mutual disinterest' condition Rawls (p.144) is proposing that the parties behind the veil of ignorance do not wish to benefit or injure each other. They are moved by neither 'affection or rancour'. They are out to maximise the degree to which their own conception of the good is satisfied but they are not out to gain relative to other people. If the achievement of their conception of the good imposes a cost on others then this will not dissuade them from that course of action but neither will they gain pleasure from the inconvenience it causes others.

The effect of this condition is that it limits the application of the veil to only those conflicts of desires between Ann and Ben that are not due to the vanity of either nor due to their envy or vindictiveness or beneficence. Conflicts of desires with these causes, however, continue to exist. While Rawls might be right in thinking that such conflicts do not involve questions of justice, there still seems to be a role for the veil of ignorance, or the position of equal power, to find principles that resolve conflicts of desire between Ann and Ben caused by envy, vanity etcetera.

It could be argued, however, that unless the veil's application is restricted to conflicts of desire that fall within the mutual disinterestedness circumstance, then the veil cannot produce a principle that yields a determinate result as to whose desire is to be satisfied. It is not necessary, however, for impartialism to impose the mutual disinterest condition on the parties in the position of equal power, even if Rawls has to do so for the parties behind the veil. The same result can be derived from the impartialist axioms. This can be seen by an examination of the case of envy.

4.5.3 The 'Envy' Principle

Suppose there is a conflict of desires between Ann and Ben where Ann wants Ben not to receive an award because Ann envies him. Ann, then, seems to be prescribing the principle that Ben is not to receive a benefit whenever Ann envies him. Symmetrified into a form that is not self-defeating this becomes, 'Ben is to be stopped from gaining a benefit because Ann envies him and Ann is to be stopped from gaining a benefit because Ben envies her.'

They will reject this principle, however, in a position of equal power because it fails to pass the noncoercionist axiom. If Ann wants not to be coerced more than she wants to coerce, then she will not agree to this principle. Likewise for Ben. It appears, then, that neither of them in a position of equal power will accept it as a reason for a person being stopped from receiving a benefit that the other is envious.

It is a principle, then, that is deducible from the impartialist axioms that envy is not to be a reason for coercion. I will call this principle the 'nonenvy' principle.

4.5.4 The 'Fallibility' Circumstance

Another circumstance of justice is human fallibility. Rawls' idea here is that one of the factors involved in people making conflicting claims to the division of social advantages is their liability to shortcomings of knowledge, reasoning, memory, attention, anxiety, bias and an excessive concern with their own affairs (p.127). It is not clear whether Rawls understands this as necessary factor in there being conflicting claims or merely a compounding factor. If the latter then it is not really a fully-fledged circumstance of justice as there would still be conflicting claims even if people were infallible, unbiased, etcetera.

I shall treat fallibility as a compounding factor in the generation of conflicts of desire rather than a pre-condition for the existence of such conflicts. Even humans with complete knowledge, unlimited and unerring powers of reasoning, memory, attention and undistorted judgment, might still be in conflict over values, over what they want in the world. The position of equal power, therefore, and the veil of ignorance too for that matter, may still have a role to perform in settling conflicts between infallible, as well as fallible, agents. In effect, then, there are no conflicts of desires that need to be excluded in advance from the scrutiny of impartialism. In so far as any are to be excluded, it is only because the retention of such a conflict shows a commitment to resolution of conflicts of desires by force and not by reasoning and argument.

Rawls also wishes the parties behind the veil of ignorance to limit their reasoning so that it only results in principles that meet what he calls the 'formal constraints of the concept of right'. I will now turn to an examination of whether or not there is any good reason to limit impartialism's application in this way.

4.6   The Formal Constraints of the Concept of Right

Rawls puts certain restrictions on the way in which the parties behind the veil can reason, not only about justice but about the choice of all ethical principles. In his view, these constraints would apply even if the parties were to acknowledge principles, not just for justice, but for the other virtues as well (p.130). These constraints are such things as the requirement that all principles be general; that they all apply universally;

that the principles be widely known and explicitly recognised (that is, public); that they be ordered; and that they be treated as the final court of appeal. He calls these restrictions the 'formal constraints of the concept of right'.

What is interesting about these constraints is that Rawls does not wish to derive them from the veil but to impose them onto the reasoning that occurs behind the veil, as if the veil itself is insufficient to generate them. I will look at each of them briefly to see if they can be generated by the position of equal power rather than laid down by fiat. Certainly, if they can be shown to be conditions required by the possibility of unforced agreement their status as constraints on the reasoning of the parties in the position of equal power becomes uncontentious. If, however, they only apply because of some intuitions about the nature of morality then they will only be found acceptable by those who share the intuitions that ground them.

4.6.1 Generality

Rawls (p.131) requires that the parties behind the veil adopt principles that are 'general', that is, that can be formulated without using what we would intuitively recognise as proper names or rigged definite descriptions. (A 'rigged definite description' occurs when Ann, say, tries to gain an advantage over Ben by proposing a principle to that does not mention her as such but, instead, says something to the effect that decisions favour all people who are female and whose names start with the letter A and a list of other characteristics whose import is to pick her out uniquely.) However, it is conceivable that there is a conflict of desires over whether the principles that govern interpersonal relations should be general (Group A) or can include proper names and rigged definite descriptions (Group B). What we would then have is a conflict of desires over how to settle conflicts of desires. Rawls states that generality rules out egoism. Stipulating generality as a formal constraint on the concept of right, then, has given him an easy victory over the egoist. It does not, however, throw any light on what is wrong with egoism.

As I have shown earlier, the position of equal power does rule out egoism. Particularist egoism is ruled out by the symmetry requirement and universalist egoism is ruled out by the noncoercionist requirement. Its dismissal from our calculations is not a matter of fiat but a consequence of what makes an unforced agreement possible.

4.6.2   Universality

Rawls (p.132) requires that the principles governing the behaviour of people in the real world be 'universal in application'. This places a restriction on the kind of reasoning that can be done by the parties behind the veil. They must reason only in those ways that lead to universal principles.

To be universal, principles need to meet a number of criteria. The first criterion, which I will call the 'moral persons' criterion, says that a principle must hold for any being merely because that being is a moral person. The second criterion, which I will call the 'complexity criterion', says that the principles must be such that all moral persons can understand them and use them in their deliberations. They cannot be too complex or draw too many kinds and numbers of distinctions. The third criterion, the 'self-defeatingness' criterion, states that a principle must not be self-contradictory or self-defeating if everyone acts on it and the fourth criterion, the 'exemption' criterion, rules out principles which it would be reasonable for a person to follow only if everyone else follows some other principle.

Katzner (p.50), argues that what I have called the 'self-defeatingness' and the 'exemption' criteria are not formal constraints on the concept of the right but a substantive moral principle that tells us that it is more reasonable to base our ethical decisions on hypothetical consequences than on actual ones. To see how this is so I shall look firstly at the self-defeatingness criterion.

The Self-Defeatingness Criterion   The self-defeatingness constraint is only applicable if principles can be divided into two kinds, namely, those that have self-defeating consequences if everyone follows them and those that don't. What, however, is it for everyone to follow a principle? Suppose we have a principle such as 'Break a promise whenever doing so is profitable'. This has the form, 'Do an action of class X under circumstances C'. To whom is it addressed? Presumably to anyone, or everyone, in circumstances C. The form of the principle then, can be expressed as 'For all js (individuals), if j is in C, then j is to do X', that is, for all js, if j is in a situation where breaking a promise is profitable, then he or she is to break the promise.

This particular principle is, presumably, one of those that Rawls, along with Kant, regards as self-defeating if everyone follows it. It is self-defeating because, in Kant's words, 'it would make promising, and the very purpose of promising itself impossible, since no one would believe he was being promised anything, but would laugh at utterances of this kind as empty shams' (1948, p. 90) Assuming Kant's argument to be correct, then Rawls would not let the parties behind the veil consider such a principle. If only some people, however, up to a threshold figure, followed this principle, its consequences might not be self-defeating. Why should Rawls want to prevent the parties behind the veil taking this into account?

Katzner (p.50) suggests that doing so thereby enables Rawls to ensure that the parties behind the veil do not adopt any act-utilitarian principles because it elevates the hypothetical consequences of everyone's performing some action over the actual consequences of some people doing it. This rules out grounding morality in what will actually happen. While it may be reasonable to do this, it cannot be a formal constraint of the concept of right because it would thereby rule out major alternatives to Rawls' contractarianism by definition. In Katzner's view, this means that Rawls is committed to saying that act-utilitarianism is a non-moral theory.

If Katzner is right about the effects of the self-defeatingness constraint, then it is a constraint that prevents the parties behind the veil resolving a particular conflict of desires, namely, the conflict of desires between Group A who wants to resolve other conflicts of desire by taking into account the actual consequences of doing X rather than Y and Group B who wants to take into account only the consequences of doing X rather than Y under hypothetical conditions. Rawls wants to commit the parties behind the veil to siding with Group B. If he does so, then the effect of this is to make any conclusions they reach unacceptable to members of Group A. This kind of strategy, then, fails to get the agreement of all rational persons. Rawls has to come up with reasons convincing to Group A why their position is excluded. He cannot appeal to the impartiality of the veil because he has ensured by fiat that the veil is not impartial between Group A and Group B.

How does impartialism stand on the issue? As it happens impartialism would reject the position of group A because it transgresses the symmetry requirement, that is, anyone who advanced such a principle in a position of equal power would only do so because they thought they would not be a member of the group that would be disadvantaged by it. The position of group A, then, is excluded because people who would advocate it are the kinds of people who cannot be party to an unforced agreement. They are partialists and have committed themselves, in advance of any debate, to the resolution of conflicts of desire by force. Excluding them, then, is not a condition imposed on them by factors extrinsic to impartialism. It is not a fiat independent of the basic purposes of the impartialist enterprise but arises intrinsically. I will now turn to the exemption criterion.

The 'Exemption' Criterion The 'exemption' criterion is the reverse of the 'self-defeatingness' constraint in that it rules out considering principles in terms of the consequences of only some people following them if you are not one of those who follow it, whereas the self-defeatingness constraint is concerned with the consequences if you do follow the principle. The same points as were made for the 'self-defeatingness' constraint apply for the exemption constraint. It rules out taking actual consequences of adopting the principle into account and allows only the hypothetical consequences of everyone following it, even if some people actually don't. This means that it rules out act-utilitarianism for the reasons Katzner gives.

Impartialism, however, does not need to impose an exemption constraint on its reasoning. Such a restraint is a consequence of the impartialist axioms. Anyone in a position of equal power who advocated a principle which he knew most people would follow but he would not would be contravening the symmetry requirement. He would only recommend such a principle if he believed that, in the real world, he would be in the group who could get away with benefiting themselves at other people's expense.

As we have seen, Katzner thinks that the various constraints that we have considered so far rule out act-utilitarianism. In his view, act-utilitarianism cannot be ruled out by the formal constraints of the concept of the right because act-utilitarianism is a moral theory if anything is. In this I think he is correct. Act-utilitarianism cannot be excluded from consideration as a moral theory by definition, and impartialism does not do so. However, impartialism does conclude that act-utilitarianism is an unacceptable moral theory - although a moral theory for all that. It is unacceptable because, as we saw in the first chapter, it would not be agreed to by the parties in a position of equal power. Anyone who acted on it would, ultimately, be committed to resolving conflicts of desires by force rather than by reason.

4.6.3 The 'Publicity' Constraint

Rawls (p.133) requires that the parties behind the veil choose between principles on the assumption that the principle that Ann, say, chooses will be known by people in the real world to be the one on which she bases her actions. The 'publicity' condition, however, has the same problems as the generality and universality conditions. It excludes by fiat a range of positions actually held in the real world, rather than demonstrating that these positions would be rejected by the parties behind the veil. There is nothing in the requirement that we reason as if we didn't know whether we were A or B that imposes the publicity condition on our reasoning, although once we begin reasoning as if behind a veil of ignorance we may conclude that the only principles that should govern the actions of people in the real world are principles about which everyone in the real world is fully informed.

Katzner, however, claims that the presence of the publicity condition is what distinguishes contractarian from non-contractarian theories. Rawls (p.16) makes remarks that support this view. Katzner (p.52) concludes that the publicity condition as a formal constraint of the concept of right arbitrarily excludes all non-contractarian theories of right, including act-utilitarianism. As a consequence, he thinks that Rawls must accept that publicity, as such, is not a constraint which applies to all moral principles in so far as they are moral.

While Katzner's criticisms are correct, a few comments need to be made to put them into context for our discussions concerning impartialism. Rawls may wish to insist that the proponents of utilitarianism are not presenting moral theories. If he does, this is merely because he has given the word 'moral' a stipulative definition that excludes theories that don't conform to the publicity condition. He can use the word 'moral' this way if he wishes, but this kind of philosophical legerdemain merely leaves us with the problem of why we should prefer moral theories (ones that meet the publicity condition, etcetera) about what we should do to non-moral ones such as utilitarianism? In the real world, there may be group A that supports only those principles that meet the publicity condition, and group B that does not. All that the veil requires of someone behind it (Ben, for example) is that he reasons as if he doesn't know whether he is a member of A or B. If the publicity condition is included as a constraint on how he reasons, then he reasons as if he knows that he is a member of A, which contravenes this requirement.

Nonetheless, it may be the case that, even without the publicity constraint, any person behind the veil will conclude that people in the real world should only act in accord with those principles about which everyone in the real world is, or could be, fully informed. If Ben does reach this conclusion it should only be as a consequence of the constraints imposed on him by the veil itself.

A rather intriguing consequence of defining contract theories so that they conform to the publicity constraint in advance of the outcome of the discussion behind the veil is that my impartialist theory fails to be a contract theory. It is a contract theory, however, if contract theories include those theories that conclude that the publicity constraint should apply to the principles to be followed in the real world.

The force of Katzner's criticism of the publicity constraint can be seen from an example given by Haksar (pp.168-170) who points out a paradox that applies to both contractarianism and utilitarianism. Situations can be imagined in which the contractarian cause is harmed by preaching and implementing contractarianism, as could be the case in a happy hierarchical society than in an unhappy contractarian one.

Haksar's criticisms of the publicity constraint occur as part of his attack on the unargued-for value that Rawls gives to autonomy as a feature of real world people that must be preserved. In the real world, however, there may be Group A that supports only those principles that preserve the autonomy of people in the real world and Group B that supports principles that don't. All that the veil requires of Ben, say, is that he reasons as if he doesn't know whether he is a member of A or B. If he reasons as if there is an autonomy constraint on the principles that the people in the real world must follow, then he reasons as if he knows that he is a member of A, which contravenes the impartiality of the veil. This means that the kind of conclusion that Haksar sketches as a possible outcome of impartialist reasoning is not excluded. In my view it needs to be excluded, but it cannot be excluded by fiat.

As we have noted, making publicity a requirement of a theory's being a moral theory has the effect of ruling out all non-contractarian theories as candidates for moral theories. This, presumably, is not Rawls' intention, that is, while he wants to show that contractarianism is superior as a moral theory to non-contractarian theories, he does not want to do this by the linguistic fiat of excluding non-contractarian theories from the domain of the moral.

What he does want to do, however, is rule out the situation where the parties behind the veil agree that a principle such as the principle of utility is to be used to resolve conflicts of desires while all or most people in the real world do not know that it is, following instead some lower level principles such as 'Keep your promises' rather than the real principle 'Keep your promises if this maximises utility in this case (or whatever)'. Without the publicity constraint, the parties behind the veil would, it seems, be able to adopt utilitarianism of the kind just described where all, or most people in the real world think they are acting on the basis of one kind of principle when the principle they are unwittingly following is quite different.

A moral theory which does not meet the publicity constraint does raise interesting problems from a contractarian point of view. It would be less question-begging, however, if these questions could be answered by applying the contractarian machinery rather than by an ad hoc restriction of its application. What Rawls effectively does is to say that the conflict of desires between those people in the real world who want to resolve other conflicts of desires by use of public principles (Group A) as opposed to those who allow some non-public principles (Group B) is not itself to be a conflict of desires resolved by the veil. It is to be resolved in favour of Group A prior to the use of the veil. While this gives Rawls the answer he wants it does so at the cost of his answer being unconvincing to members of Group B.

Impartialism, then, if it is to escape this kind of criticism, has to be able to deal with the 'publicity' issue from within the impartialist axioms. One approach that the impartialist might take is to see what a party in the position of equal power (say, Ann) would think about a proposal by another party (say, Ben) that not everyone in the real world be informed of the principles behind the laws or rules they are all required to obey. What kinds of grounds could Ben offer Ann to change her mind, given that she is to be conceived as opposed to such a strategy? The suggestion is that there be people in the real world, presumably those in power, who know what the real point is of the constraints placed on them all but that there are large sections of society who are to be kept in ignorance of the truth. Now, Ben cannot propose this because he suspects that he will be in the power group and such an arrangement will benefit either his self-interest or further his cause at others' expense. Ann will know this is his intention in a position of equal power and, not being his superfan, will not accept it, having the power in their contracting situation to prevent herself being compelled to adopt it. Moreover, in having such a reason for making the proposal, Ben shows himself to be committed to force rather than reason for settling disputes. Ben, then, needs to offer some genuinely universalist reason, for example, that, if some people know the true principle, then this will prevent the achievement of what is best for everyone, including those kept in ignorance. Those in power have special qualities that enable them to resist whatever forces would seduce the rest of society. We end up, then, with a society ruled by people very like Plato's philosopher-kings. Will Ann, however, accept the principle that Ben, say, is to make decisions on the basis of principles of which she is unaware on the grounds that he thinks he has special qualities? This would be a dangerous principle for her to accept. She must, at least, be convinced herself that he has these qualities and that she has the power to eject him from office if she, or sufficient of her community, decides that he has lost them. It is possible, then, that Ann may agree to some secret decision-making by her rulers, provided she has an equal say with anyone else in determining what the limits of such decisions will be and an equal say in how the propriety of such decision-making is monitored. She would not be prepared to give *carte blanche* authority in this matter. It does seem, however, that, even here, she will insist on the general principles on which such a delegated power is given to be completely open.

4.6.4   Ordering

Rawls (p.134) requires that a moral theory be able to order all the claims that are likely to arise in practice. Katzner (p.52) criticises this requirement on the grounds that it is too strong. It rules out as a moral theory any theory, for example, that lets us decide which of utility or justice is to take precedence in a particular case on the basis of intuition.

While Katzner's criticism is well-taken, it is not the one of central concern to those interested in the impartiality of Rawls' candidates for formal constraints of the concept of right. As I indicated earlier, for any definition of what it is to be moral, there can be disagreements in the real world as to whether or not one ought to do what morality requires rather than what it forbids, in whichever sense of 'morality' has been offered. In the real world, therefore, there may be group A that supports only those principles that are required by 'morality' in the sense that some speaker has offered, and group B that supports principles regardless of whether they are 'moral' in this sense.

From an impartialist point of view, however, no one in a position of equal power is allowed to argue on the assumption that he or she will be in whichever of group A or B has the advantage over the other. If he reasons as if there is a constraint on him to reach conclusions consistent with the principles of group A, then he is arguing as if he knows he is a member of A rather than B. This contravenes the symmetry requirement. In particular, if group A believes that principles must be ordered, and group B does not, then Ann, say is not to argue as if she already knew she is a member of A. The conditions inherent in the axioms of impartialism, in so far as they capture what is crucial to achieve unforced agreement, must be sufficient to lead her to require ordering or else ordering is not required.

Rawls (p.134) requires that the ordering between principles be transitive, that is, we rank the institutions generated by Principle P as more just than those generated by Principle Q, and those of Q as more just than those of R, then we must rank those of P as more just than those of R. This eliminates the use of 'intuition', which cannot guarantee transitivity. Transitivity, therefore, cannot be a prior condition on the reasoning of the parties behind the veil unless it can be shown to be required by whatever is entailed by the parties being rational agents able to discuss what acts should be done.

Rawls (p.134) adds a further requirement to ordering, namely, that not any old way of arriving at an ordering is good enough. In his view, it is a formal constraint of the concept of right that an ordering cannot be determined by an appeal to force and cunning. He rules out, therefore, operating according to the dictum 'to each according to his threat advantage'. This is, in his opinion, not a relevant sense of ordering. A relevant ordering should be independent of social position or capacity to intimidate and coerce.

Now, it is precisely this latter that impartialism is meant to eliminate. Nonetheless, coercion may still be required, as we have seen, but it is coercion that the parties in a situation of total noncoercion agree should be applied in the real world. While it is hoped that the equal power conditions will result in the parties agreeing to use methods in the real world other than the resort to arms or its equivalent, this cannot be a prior requirement on the argument there. Even so, as we have seen, agreement in a position of equal power is only possible if the parties there are noncoercionists. Impartialism, then, rules out ordering principles on the basis of the proposer's threat advantage. It is, however, ruled out for reasons to do with what is necessary to reach unforced agreement at all.

4.6.5 The 'Completeness' Requirement

It is possible that the parties behind the veil conclude that there are two or more principles that are equally important determinants of actions. This means that two groups of people in the real world, Group A and Group B, could want to do incompatible actions X and Y, where X is required by one principle P and Y by another principle Q. If this situation arose, the parties behind the veil would have no way of deciding with action should be done. Rawls requires that the parties behind the veil do not treat all principles as equally important. They must rank principles. Furthermore, they cannot rank principles by some arbitrary means, such as flipping a coin, in order to determine which one to give priority to. At least, they cannot do so if this does not produce a transitive relation.

Clearly, the people in the real world can't be left in a situation where the rules they follow permit them to do either X or Y where these are incompatible actions. This puts them in a situation of deciding which shall be done by force. It is this that the veil is supposed to avoid. However, just because the rules that the people in the real world follow must be ordered in a complete and transitive manner, it does not follow in Rawls' system that the parties behind the veil arrive at principles that are ordered in a complete and transitive manner, as long as they decide which of X or Y is to be done. They could do it on intuition, or by flipping a coin, or whatever, and it could be that the relationships between their decisions are not transitive. Of course, this couldn't occur in too many cases otherwise the people in the real world would never know what to do (this harks back to the complexity component of the universality constraint).

Given, however, that the people behind the veil are, in fact, just people in the real world constrained in how they argue, the fact that P and Q are equally important does lead to the situation where there is no solution as to which of X or Y is to be done. This is not solved by their relying on their intuitions because, even if they try to think as if they were behind the veil, there is nothing available to them that gives them any guidance as to which intuitions are right and which wrong. This means that members of Group A will have intuitions favouring X when they try to think as if behind the veil, and there is no reason why they shouldn't, whereas members of Group B will have intuitions favouring Y when they try to think as if behind the veil, and there is no reason why they shouldn't. They are still no closer to a solution as to which of X or Y should be done.

If Group A has superior power, it could resolve the situation by forcing Group B to follow A's preference but then A's members are behaving as if they know whose desires were furthered by X's being done rather than Y. If they reason as if they could be in either group, then they might have opted to force Y rather than X, that is, they would have chosen as a random procedure such as coin-flipping would have chosen. Their bona fides in this direction is best demonstrated by their actually choosing such a random procedure. This eliminates intuition as an acceptable procedure.

4.6.6   Finality

Rawls (p.135) puts forward as a formal constraint of the concept of right that the parties are to treat the system of principles as the final court of appeal in practical reasoning. If one has reasoned successfully from these principles, then one's reasoning is conclusive. This is meant to be a constraint on the parties in the original position, that is, behind the veil of ignorance. Does it also apply to the parties in a position of equal power?

In one respect the constraint of finality is redundant from the viewpoint of impartialism. There may be people in the real world who do not regard the decisions of the parties in the position of equal power as final. They constitute Group A, as opposed to Group B, who do treat these decisions as final. According to impartialism, a person's moral rightness in real-world decision-making is a function of the degree to which he or she acts in accord with the principles chosen in a position of equal power, consequently what the parties there would do is final from the viewpoint of impartialism. There is no higher court of appeal, assuming that the equal power axioms have correctly operationalised the concept of unforced agreement. If what we are trying to decide is whether or not an act or institution is the one that uncoerced people would prefer, then the decisions of the parties in the position of equal power is final.

What is of interest is whether the finality of these decisions is something the parties in the position of equal power accept prior to arriving at them, or whether it is one of the conclusions they reach there? It is, presumably, an assumption they have prior to discussion. This does not render its impartiality suspect, however, because, even if the parties were to come to the (self-referentially) paradoxical conclusion that people in the real world shouldn't act in accord with the principles agreed to by the parties in the position of equal power, it would be their coming to this conclusion that rendered it right for people not to follow the conclusions reached by the parties in the position of equal power.

As it is, of course, people cannot (logically) follow this advice because, if they followed it, they wouldn't be following it, and if they didn't follow it, then they would be following it. This means that the parties in the position of equal power, if they are rational agents, cannot offer this advice as a serious guide to actions. It needs to be an assumption, therefore, of the parties that their advice is final, that is, they argue as if they knew that their advice is the ultimate court of appeal. It is not a question that it is meaningful for them to discuss, in that their function would be rendered futile were they to conclude their decisions weren't overriding. Were, for example, they to conclude that their advice isn't final, this conclusion would itself be final from the viewpoint of impartialism, thereby generating the same kind of paradox previously discussed.

4.6.7 *Finality as a Necessary Condition of Morality*

Rawls' inclusion of finality as a formal constraint of the concept of right could be interpreted as the claim that a system of principles is not a moral one unless it constitutes the final court of appeal. Now, there are people in the real world who believe that the requirements of liberty are sometimes incompatible with those of happiness, for example, but that there is no system of principles that properly captures the proper demands of both values. If happiness is made overriding, as in utilitarianism, it leads to unacceptable infringements of liberty. If liberty is made overriding, as in a theory such as Nozick's, then some people's happiness is unacceptably frustrated, or the proper demands of a value such as justice are ignored. They believe that a balance between these competing values can only be achieved by intuition, that is, they do not believe that we act on a system of principles that is final or overriding but rather that we test the conclusions of various systems of principles against our intuitions, sometimes doing as one system requires, sometimes as another does, but letting no single system be final.

One can refuse to call such an intuitionist process a 'moral' one but this merely means, as we have seen earlier, that the parties behind the veil have to decide whether to act morally, as someone such as Rawls defines it, or non-morally. If they are required in advance of arguments behind the veil to argue morally in the sense of only following a system of principles that they regard as final and not using intuition to choose between systems of principles, then they are arguing as if they know in the real world that they favour 'moral' systems of principles, that is, that they are the kind of people who require the acts they perform to be derivable from a system of principles regarded as final. This however, is contrary to the requirements of impartiality.

Rawls' requirement that systems of principles be final or overriding might be a consequence of his rule-contractarianism (Farrell, pp.193-9). He wants the finality of the decisions of the parties behind the veil to be applied only to the choice of the system of principles. Once the system is chosen, Rawls wants it to be final. This means that the system has to be such that it settles all disputes between principles within itself. It doesn't generate any conflict of principles that amounts to a conflict of systems between which the parties behind the veil have to arbitrate.

Rawls, then, insists that the parties behind the veil be moral monists. They must have one overriding value, not two or three equally important ones, with intuition as the arbiter. The parties behind the veil choose as if they know they are rule-theorists rather than act-theorists in real life when they are required prior to their arguments behind the veil, to reach only rule-contractarian conclusions. This means that those people in real life who are act-theorists will not regard the veil as a neutral device for arbitrating between them and rule-theorists.

As we saw in Chapter 1, however, nonmonism is a requirement that arises directly from the conditions that need to be placed on the parties in the position of equal power in order for any agreement they might reach to be an unforced one. Impartialism, therefore, favours rule-theories and oppose intuition. Its lack of neutrality, here, however, is something that anyone must accept who is committed to resolving conflicts of desires by reason and argument rather than by force.

4.7   Reasonableness versus Morality

Katzner (p.51) claims that Rawls' list of formal constraints of the concept of right confuses two distinct elements:- (1) constraints that select some principles rather than others because these principles fit our concept of what a principle has to be in order to be a moral one, and (2) constraints that select some principles rather than others because these principles fit our concept of what a principle has to be to be a reasonable principle of action. He claims that Rawls' arguments for generality, universality and finality as constraints of the concept of right are really arguments about the nature of morality and moral principles rather than arguments about the reasonableness of the theory that proposes these constraints

This, however, is contrary to Rawls' own declared view (pp.130-131). According to him, these conditions do not follow from either the concept of right or the meaning of morality although they do exclude egoism. This means that they are not purely formal but do have substantive force. As a consequence, they have to be justified by the reasonableness of the theory that contains them. Katzner (p.52), however, remains unconvinced. He accepts the idea that generality, universality in the weak sense (that is, that a principle must hold for all moral people), and finality, do seem to apply to all moral principles, but he rejects the notion that we can determine that they so hold by an assessment of the reasonableness of the theory they belong to.

Katzner (p.51) earlier points out that the other constraints on the concept of right such as publicity, ordering and universality in the strong sense (that is, principles must be judged in terms of the effects of everyone's complying with them) are not to be regarded as constraints which apply to the choice of all moral principles yet should be assessed in terms of the reasonableness of the theory in which they are found.

So, if Katzner is correct, publicity, ordering and strong universalizability are not formal constraints on the concept of right, that is, a theory can still be a theory about what is and isn't morally right yet not meet these three criteria. Alternatively, a theory of what is morally right that doesn't meet these criteria, while still a moral theory, is not a reasonable one. On the other hand, generality, weak universalisability and ordering are formal constraints on a theory's being a moral theory, yet a moral theory can meet these and still be unreasonable. In Katzner's view, Rawls has confused these two quite distinct issues. Katzner appears to accept that the formal constraints do apply to the reasoning of the parties behind the veil, that is, their reasoning must be general, weakly universal and final if it is to be moral. As we have seen, however, this merely causes the parties to reason as if they know they are in the Group A that prefers moral theories of how to act rather than members of Group B who don't. This contravenes the requirements of neutrality, which means the parties behind the veil must debate whether the principles they should follow should be general, weakly universalizable and final. They may well so conclude, but they cannot, in all neutrality, be required to so conclude before they argue behind the veil.

Rawls (p.130) claims that his six constraints are justified as constraints on the conceptions of justice that are to be allowed on the list to be presented to the parties. This seems to suggest that there are candidates for conceptions of justice that are not on the list. It entails the further strange notion that someone has censored this list. In particular, any egoistical theory that poses as a theory of justice is excluded. Also, any tyrannical candidate for a theory of justice is excluded (by the generality constraint). Any theory of justice that only works if it is kept secret from some of the people is excluded. Any theory of justice that settles disputes by appeal to force and cunning is excluded, and so on. Now, Rawls might be able to exclude these on the grounds that such candidates for theories of justice are charlatans, false pretenders who are not theories of justice at all. He can exclude them by linguistic fiat. But this doesn't show that they are not theories about which actions we should prefer to do, so they all remain candidates for a theory of right.

Hare (1975, pp.89-90) has similar misgivings about Rawls' methodology here. If, as Rawls admits, the formal constraints rule out egoism, then what is the veil of ignorance left to do? Abandoning egoism is, in Hare's view, paramount to being impartial. He accepts that the veil can perform a function in eliminating 'rigged' principles that are formally general or universal but, if these are ruled out by the formal constraints of the concept of right, then why also appeal to the veil?

Even if Hare is right about the role that Rawls has left the veil in his theory, the same ad hominem does not apply to impartialism. As we have seen, non-general principles are ruled out by the position of equal power and the requirement of noncoercionism, not because of any ad hoc constraint. On my account, the mere fact that Ann and Ben are in a position of equal power does not prevent them choosing between general and non-general principles. It is only the addition of the symmetry and noncoercionist requirements that leads them to always choose general principles. On Rawls' account, the mere fact that they were behind the veil meant that they were not free to consider non-general principles in the first place.

Rawls justifies his appeal to these constraints on the grounds that they are 'reasonable'. This raises the question of 'reasonable for what?'

The kinds of things that are said to be reasonable are not so described because of some innate property of reasonableness but because they are appropriate to some purpose. A constraint is reasonable if there is some purpose that is better fulfilled with the constraint imposed. Rawls (p.731) indicates that he wishes the reasonableness of these constraints to be judged in terms of how well they enable us to adjust the claims that persons make on their institutions and one another. He sees these constraints as 'natural' in terms of the principles of justice playing the role of assigning basic rights and duties and determining the division of advantages.

The problem here is that there are many 'reasonable' ways of assigning basic rights and duties and determining the division of advantages. The word 'reasonable' can only do the job that Rawls wants it to if the constraints we place on the principles by which these things are assigned are reasonable from the point of view of 'justice'. After all, we can assign basic rights and duties and divide advantages from other points of view, for example, from that of a particular egoist or in terms of a particular ideal. It would be reasonable, then, to put in other constraints. In particular, as Katzner has pointed out, not all of Rawls' constraints on principles assigning rights, duties and division of advantages are reasonable from the utilitarian point of view.

Rawls, then, appears to be constraining these principles in ways that are reasonable from the viewpoint of a just distribution. He is, therefore, appealing to us to agree with him that, if we want the principles contracted behind the veil to produce a just distribution, then it is reasonable to place his constraints on them. Why would it be reasonable? Because the principles the parties behind the veil could produce without these constraints might not be just, that is, they might not match with (in fact, Rawls can see that they will not match with) his intuitions of which distributions were just.

Rawls (p.130) does not think of the constraints as following from the concept of right or the meaning of morality. Rather, they follow from his concept of justice. They derive from what he feels is meant by the word 'justice'. He has not avoided basing his theory on a definition. He has merely avoided explicating the definition that he has based his theory on, leaving the reader to piece it together from the various constraints and other restrictions he places on the parties behind the veil. Hare (1972, p.88) comments, in his review of a Theory of Justice, that Rawls as usual says that 'it seems reasonable' to impose the constraints on the principles.

He then rather tartly adds that Rawls fails to tell us what he would say to somebody to whom they did not 'seem reasonable'.

The answer to Hare's point, however, is clear enough. Rawls must say that his concept of what justice is differs from that of anyone who does not find the constraints reasonable. It is possible, therefore, for people to find different constraints reasonable, and still see their own constraints as appropriate for justice, because they have different concepts of justice. Rawls is, then, faced with the problem of either showing that his is the correct concept of justice, or else of showing that his distribution is better (from an agreed upon point of view) than the ones that come from different concepts of justice, even though his meaning for the word 'justice' is no more correct than anyone else's. Even if he can show that his meaning for the word 'justice', as embodied in his selection of constraints, is more correct (closer to common usage or whatever) he would still have to show why this makes it the one to choose. He cannot say that it is more reasonable, if he means by this that it is more reasonable from the viewpoint of justice as he defines it, because this merely begs the question. Rawls, then, needs to define justice independently of the veil, the constraints, etcetera. He can then use this definition to identify those features of the veil that are consistent with, or required by, this definition, then use the veil to judge principles. He will still need to show however, why his sense of justice is to be the standard by which he determines that a principle or institution is to be preferred.

4.8   Conclusion

The scope of impartialism, then, as the above discussion indicates, is intended to be far wider than the scope Rawls intends for his theory. Conflicts of desires between people are to be resolved by the application of equal power methodology, not by any prior rulings in favour of one side of the conflict rather than the other, even where the conflict might appear to be one over formal matters. What appear to be formal matters can often turn out to disguise a conflict over a substantive issue. so there needs to be unanimous agreement that the matter is purely formal, otherwise it should be subjected to impartialist debate.

In the next chapter I will apply the impartialist axioms to substantive questions about the kinds of political arrangements that the parties in the position of equal power would agree to. Once again, I will use the arrangements that Rawls derives from the parties behind the veil of ignorance as a point of comparison.

Note

1   Rawls, like a number of other contemporary political philosophers such as Lucas and Richards, has developed his account of the circumstances of justice from that first presented by Hume (1978). The problems with both Hume's and Rawls' account of the circumstances of justice as limitations of the application of the concept of justice are discussed in detail by Hubin.

5 The Enabling Liberties

5.1   Introduction

What I wish to look at in this chapter are the most fundamental or basic freedoms that the parties in the position of equal power will agree to. As I said at the end of the previous chapter, I will do this by first examining what freedoms Rawls thinks his parties behind the veil of ignorance will regard as most important and why, then see in what ways, if any, impartialism would vary them or justify them differently.

According to Rawls (p.42), the parties behind the veil will choose as their highest principle what he calls 'the First Principle of Justice'. This principle has what he calls 'lexical' priority over any other principles in the sense that we must satisfy all the requirements of this principle before we can move on to satisfy the requirements of the next principle. Once the requirements of the First Principle of Justice have been met we can proceed to implement the requirements of the Second Principle of Justice which, in its turn, is superior to the other principles in his system. The First Principle of Justice says that freedom is to be distributed among people so that each person has an equal right to the most extensive total system of equal basic liberties compatible with a similar system of liberty for all (p.302). The Second Principle of Justice, which is also called the 'Difference Principle', says that social and economic inequalities are to be distributed to meet two conditions. The first, which I will call the 'least advantaged' condition, is that they must be of the greatest benefit of the least advantaged, consistent with just savings for future generations. The second, which I will call the 'equal opportunity' condition, requires social and economic inequalities to be arranged so that offices and positions are open to all under conditions of fair equality of opportunity (p.302).

Rawls (p.61) believes that his model enables him to derive what he calls the 'basic liberties' from the first of these principles of justice. There are four basic liberties, namely, (1) political liberty, that is, freedom of speech and assembly and the right to vote and to be eligible for public

116

office (2) liberty of conscience and freedom of thought (3) freedom of the person and the right to hold personal property (4) freedom from arbitrary arrest and seizure as defined by the concept of the rule of law.

I will now see whether impartialism would produce the same basic liberties, beginning with 'equal liberty of conscience'.

5.2   Basic Liberties and Equal Liberty of Conscience

Rawls (p.450) talks as if he has shown that, not only does the first principle of justice enjoin freedom of conscience, it also enjoins freedom of action in sexual and other matters where these affect the state's interest in public order and community. Barry (1973), however, sees Rawls' arguments as only concerned with 'conscience', with your freedom to do what you believe in, rather than with your being free to do other things that matter to you but for reasons other than conscientious ones, such as engaging in certain kinds of sexual practices, or wearing certain kinds of clothes or hairstyles, tattoos or body-piercing jewellery, or whatever.

In fact, Barry thinks that Rawls' arguments for freedom of conscience can't be generalised to non-conscientious cases precisely because they rest on the conscientiousness of the act. Rawls, however, is concerned to accommodate these freedoms because this is where his theory triumphs over utilitarianism. Utilitarianism may deny the right to sexual preferences for reasons other than state security if enough people are offended by a preference. Rawls does not want to allow this.

Barry (p.39) thinks that Rawls can only extend his argument for liberty of conscience to other liberties such as sexual liberty if the parties behind the veil assume it to be irrational to prevent the fulfilment of a desire that was strongly felt by some people and which did no harm to others just because enough of these other people felt strongly that the fulfilment of such a desire should be suppressed. In other words, the parties behind the veil would regard it as irrational to allow the possibility that homosexuality, for example, be banned even though homosexuals strongly wanted to engage in it, and (let us suppose) their doing so did not harm other people, just because enough non-homosexuals might find the thought of homosexual activities abhorrent and wish them banned.

Barry has two objections to Rawls assuming this. They are (1) that it is factually implausible that the strength of feeling of those in favour of some sexual or whatever practice is sufficiently great to make it irrational in this way, and (2) that we do allow desires to be fulfilled that cause injury to others if those who desire it do so strongly enough and those who are injured are only mildly injured.

The crux of this second point is that Rawls wants to rule out the possibility that the strength of Ann's desire, say, that Ben not engage in his preferred sexual practices, is greater than the strength of Ben's desire to engage in them. Barry thinks that this makes the detailed adjustment of conflicting demands impossible and, therefore, rational people will not agree with Rawls in ruling it out.

Let's look at this from an impartialist perspective. We need to look first at Rawls' reasons for liberty of conscience. His argument (p.207) is that the parties behind the veil of ignorance would regard one as not taking one's religious and moral values seriously, and not showing sufficient concern for the freedom to examine one's beliefs, if one left open the possibility that one could be persecuted or one's beliefs suppressed by the dominant religious or moral authority if it wished.

Rawls' account of this is oddly put. The liberal conclusion is reached in a more straightforward manner by impartialism. First, however, it is necessary to recognise that a person's religious beliefs and practices (say Ben's) can be divided into two parts. The first part is the one consisting of the beliefs and practices that he wishes to be free to perform himself. For example, he will want to be free to attend his own church, participate in its services and ceremonies, engage in prayer either privately or communally, read whatever book or books he regards to be holy scripture, debate and discuss his beliefs and so on, without any of these activities intruding on what another person (say, Ann) does.

The second part consists in what Ben thinks are the freedoms that his religion requires other people be denied. He may believe, for example, that his religion requires that other people be denied the freedom to work on a Sunday, to wear clothes of a certain kind, to be taught doctrines other than his own in schools, and so on.

Ben's sexual practices can similarly be divided into these two groups. He may believe that the only morally acceptable kind of sexual intercourse is heterosexual intercourse between consenting adults in a marriage. In so far as he follows these dictums himself, his sexual morality is quite independent of Ann's. However, he may also believe that his religion demands that people not be free to engage in any other forms of sexual activity. If Ann is a lesbian, or someone who does not see marriage as a prerequisite to sexual activity, then his beliefs will impinge upon her if the advocates of his religion are able to gain control of the state.

As people in the position of equal power, however, both Ben and Ann are noncoercionists. As such, each of them wants to not to be coerced by the other more than they want to be free to coerce the other. Both, therefore, will agree that the polity create a system which has sufficient power to prevent either of them forcing their religion or morality on the other - where 'morality' here means a code of conduct other than the one imposed by impartialism itself. The fact that one is a matter of conscience and the other is not does not seem to affect the situation.

Rawls is forced into his particular argument by his failure to recognise the difference between noncoercionists and coercionists. Were Ann and Ben coercionists instead then, even if neither of them knows their religion or their morality (for whatever reason), they both know that they will want to coerce the other more than they will want not to be coerced. Ann, therefore, will prepared to take the risk that she is coerced into Ben's religion, whatever it may be, just so that she has the chance to coerce him into hers, whatever it may be. The same applies to her morality, whatever it turns out to be.

Now, Rawls wants to argue that such a coercionist attitude amounts to neither Ann nor Ben taking their religious or moral convictions seriously. The problem is that he has not analysed closely enough what such a conviction involves. If my conviction is that I should practise my own religion and make others follow it, too, even though they would not agree to this limitation on their freedom in a position of equal power, then my being serious about this means my rejecting the position of equal power as a decision-procedure. In effect, it means that I have to be a coercionist. I have to want to be free to coerce others so strongly that I am prepared to risk living in a situation where they are free to coerce me, that is, a situation where whoever coerces whom is entirely dependent on who is the stronger. It's only if I'm serious about practising my religion and not serious about suppressing others that I will agree to religious tolerance. But there is nothing special about the religious case here. The same logic would apply if I was more serious about suppressing other people's sexual practices than I was about being guaranteed the freedom to indulge in my own. What we have here is a generalised finding of impartialism that I will call the 'degustibus' principle. It is as follows:-

The Degustibus Principle:- *No one has the right to stop others from performing some action just because he or she does not want those others to perform it, or because he or she does not like it, does not approve of it or do not think it right.*

Let's now return to Barry's specific criticism of Rawls. Barry thinks that Rawls can only get equal liberty of sexual preference along the same lines as used for equal liberty of conscience if people wanted to engage in their own sexual preferences (without injury to others) so strongly that they wouldn't allow it to be restricted no matter how strongly other people abhorred it.

As we have seen, however, Ann and Ben would agree to equal liberty of sexual preference because, as noncoercionists, each of them will want to be free to practice his or her own sexual preferences more than he or she will want to stop the other from doing so. Not everyone in the real world, however, is a noncoercionist. This is undoubtedly a problem for impartialism if Barry is right that tolerance of sexual lifestyles requires that the desire to suppress in real life is weaker than the desire not to be suppressed. It could well be the case that puritanism in some communities is stronger than hedonism.

Impartialism, however, does not rest on any factual findings that people actually are noncoercionists. Many undoubtedly are not. In fact, as far as impartialism is concerned, they may all be coercionists. If this is the case then they can only settle their conflicts by force. Being a noncoercionist is a prerequisite to settling disputes by noncoercive means. Barry's point, then, can not be used as a criticism of impartialism even if it is effective against Rawls.

Barry also comments that, just because a desire is of central importance in a person's life, it doesn't follow that it won't cause harm and injury to other people. As we have seen, however, what matters for impartialism is not so much that the desire be one whose fulfilment causes no injuries to others but, rather, that the desire be such that, if one wants not to be coerced more than one wants to coerce others, then one will not agree to this kind of desire as such being suppressed. If one wants not to be coerced more than one wants to coerce, then one will not want to have others restrict one's sexual preferences more than one will want to restrict other people's sexual preferences.

This conclusion doesn't depend on it being the case that the sexual preferences one has do not harm others. Admittedly, if I am a sadist whose sexual pleasures involves killing people, then I clearly harm them, but my freedom to do this is ruled out by principles dealing with killing others, or physically mutilating others or deliberately causing others bodily pain, not by the principle of free sexual choice.

Nonetheless, there is a lexical relationship between the principle of freedom of sexual preference and principles outlawing murder, torture etcetera. This means that the principle of sexual preference does not have to be explicit about the kinds of injuries it allows. It allows none that are ruled out by other principles higher than it in the total system of liberties. This finding, too, can be generalised. Any 'equal liberty of conscience' principle or 'no injury type of desire' freedom will be restricted by the limits placed on coercing others. The noncoercionist Ben will agree to freedom of conscience for Ann provided her freedom of conscience is not itself a coercion of Ben, and likewise with Ben's sexual preferences.

Of course, some coercion of Ann is allowed, for example, Ben's freedom of conscience can entail the coercion of Ann's freedom of conscience if hers is such as to coerce his, and so on, although the appropriate coercing agency here will normally be the state, not Ben himself. In other words, if Ben wants to coerce Ann into a religion or a sexual preference, but this is ruled out by the position of equal power, that is, it is only possible in a coercionist world, then, as a noncoercionist, Ben will agree that, even if he wants to coerce Ann, he not be free to do so - and likewise for Ann. (The coercionist world, it should be noted, has many similarities to Hobbes' state of nature.)

It is worthwhile exploring here in some detail the rest of Barry's remarks on this matter because they reveal very well how easy it is to misunderstand what the liberal is doing. Barry says, with respect to his two objections to Rawls' 'equal liberty of conscience', that rational people will not rule out a priori the relevance of the strength of person A's desire to do something and the strength of another person B's desire that A stopped from doing it. He thinks that Rawls is going to be stuck with the parties behind the veil having to use 'a calculus of social interests'. It cannot, in his view, be avoided by including heroic assumptions into the original position about a universally valid ranking of human goals.

Now, there are a number of ways of making detailed adjustments of conflicting demands. One is by force. Barry presumably does not mean this. As we have seen, however, if Ben wants to coerce Ann with respect to some action X more than he wants not to be coerced by her with respect to X (or some action Y that plays the same role in his system of desires as X does in Ann's), then force is the only way of adjusting conflicting demands that can be used with Ben. One, therefore, has to take into account the degree to which he wants to do something and the degree to which Ann wants to stop him doing it. Once, however, we are within the impartialist framework, what is relevant is not how much Ben wants to do X or how much Ann wants to stop him doing X. The relationship between the strength of Ben's desire and the strength of Ann's desire is not the issue at all. The issue is whether Ann wants to stop Ben's doing X more than she wants to be free to do X herself.

Let us put numbers to these strengths of desires, just to illustrate the point. It's not a question of Ben's desire to do X being 1000 units whereas Ann's desire to stop him doing X is 2000 units. If it were merely this relative strength of desire then, whether or not Ben is free to do X, depends on whether he or Ann has the stronger desire. It is, instead, a question of Ann's desire to stop Ben from doing X being 2000 but her desire that Ben (or anyone else) not stop her from doing X is 4000. If it is, then the fact that her desire to stop Ben is twice the strength of his desire to do X is not germane to whether or not she be free to stop his doing X.

Hare illustrates how a utilitarian concerned with impartiality can reason in a similar manner to the impartialist and yet still miss the boat. He says (1981, pp.128-129):-

> I have to give a bun either to Jones or to Smith, and Jones wants it more bun J2, and Smith with-bun S2. Jones prefers J1 to J2 more than Smith outcomes, four positions in all. My choice is going to be between J1 plus S1 (Jones-with-bun plus Smith-without-bun) and J2 plus S2 (Jones - without-bun plus Smith-with-bun). It is not necessary to imagine myself occupying the four positions simultaneously; that would be asking too much. We might follow a suggestion of C.I. Lewis (1946, 546f) and suppose that I have a choice between occupying J1 and S1 in random order and occupying J2 and S2 in random order. Clearly, given the assumed strengths of Smith's and Jones' preferences, my own preference will be for the first of these alternatives.

The first thing to note about Hare's example is that it is not about coercion but merely about distribution. Suppose that Smith actually has the bun. Jones prefers J1 to J2 by a margin of 1000, say, whereas Smith prefers S2 to S1 by 500. However, Jones can only get the bun by taking it from Smith by force for, whereas Smith prefers S2 to S1 less than Jones prefers J1 to J2, it is still the case that Smith prefers S2 to S1. He is not going to give Jones the bun. In this situation, the fact that Jones prefers J1 to J2 more than Smith prefers S2 to S1 is irrelevant, morally. It is only relevant in Hare's example because Hare is playing God, or Father Christmas. While such situations do arise in real life, they are not usually the morally interesting ones. Moral interest tends to be in cases where something is taken from one group and given to another. Now it may be the case that Jones' desire to take the bun from Smith is 1000 units but his desire not to have Smith take things from him is 2000. The fact that he prefers J1 to J2 twice as much as Smith prefers S2 to S1 no longer matters.

A related point can be made with respect to Barry's discussion of a case proposed by Braithwaite (Barry, 1989, pp.31-49). Suppose Luke the pianist and Matthew the trumpeter live in adjacent rooms without soundproofing and each, for various reasons, can only practise at the same hour of the day. Suppose further that the greatest preference of each of them is to practise when the other doesn't and their next greatest preference is to be silent while the other practises. Their third preferences, however, diverge. Matthew prefers they both play together while Luke would rather neither of them played, that is, cacophony is Matthew's third choice whereas silence is Luke's. Their fourth preference reverses this - Matthew hates silence most but Luke hates cacophony most. This means that Matthew has a greater threat advantage over Luke because, if Luke tries to bring about the silence that Matthew hates most, Matthew can use this silence to practise by himself, which is what he likes most whereas , if Luke causes cacophony, he is causing something that he dislikes more than Matthew does.

For reasons that we need not go into here, Braithwaite thinks that the fair distribution of playing time, given Matthew's threat advantage over Luke, is that Matthew practise 27 hours to every 16 that Luke practises. Barry argues that the proportion suggested by what is known as the Nash solution is a fairer one, namely, that Matthew get 73 hours of practice for every 33 that Luke gets (that is, were we to compare this with Matthew's 27 hours, then Luke would only get a little over 12 hours - less than Braithwaite's proposal). I suspect, however, that most of us would regard either of these solutions as unfair, that Matthew's greater threat advantage is irrelevant to the fairness of the time division between them. In the position of equal power, this kind of threat advantage would be cancelled out and Ben, say, would only propose a principle that gave one of the parties in the real world the kind of advantage that Matthew has over Luke on either Braithwaite's or Barry's scenarios if he had reason to believe he would be in Matthew's situation, that is, if he contradicted the symmetry requirement. What would appear to be fair here is that they get equal time each, which seems the plausible solution if each has equal power. It is also the solution one would assume would be reached by the parties behind Rawls' veil of ignorance.

This discussion of the Braithwaite-Barry case is related to the Hare case in that it is not the inter-personal comparison between Matthew and Luke that is central to determining what the fair distribution between them would be. It is not how much more Luke hates cacophony than Matthew that is the relevant factor. Rather, what is to be compared, for either of Matthew or Luke individually, is the strength of the *intra*-personal desire not to be coerced as opposed to wanting to coerce. If they are both noncoercionists, then they will not agree to settle the dispute over practice time in terms of the degree to which one of them has a greater threat advantage over the other.

5.3 Equality

Barry (1973, p.41) raises the question of what Rawls means by 'equal' in the statement of the first principle of justice. He concludes that Rawls' first principle of justice is really a maximin principle rather than a truly egalitarian one. To be 'truly egalitarian', in Barry's view, the first principle would have to require that Ann and Ben get exactly equal amounts so that it would be better that each got less rather than that the distribution was unequal, for example, if a freedom is such that Ben can only have it at all if Ann has more of it then it is better that neither of them have it because neither having it is more equal, although less free, than Ann's having slightly more freedom than Ben.

Rawls, however, is concerned that Ben can get as much freedom as he can, and that this is distributed as equally as is possible for Ben to get as much as possible even if this means that Ann gets more. What is crucial is that Ben doesn't get less freedom in order that Ann may get more. Rawls is not out to increase the total amount of freedom as such but, rather, to give both Ben and Ann as much freedom as possible as is compatible with not decreasing the freedom of the other. In Rawls' view this is only possible if Ben and Ann are not envious.

How does impartialism deal with this? Each of Ben and Ann will want to have as much freedom as possible with respect to the implementation of their own particular values. There is only a problem between them when Ben's freedom to do what he wants is incompatible with Ann's freedom to do what she wants. Given that they each want not to be coerced more than they want to coerce, then they will each agree that their freedom be curtailed, by force if necessary. It would appear that the symmetry of this argument must ensure that their freedoms are equal. Ben will not agree to any arrangement where Ann is free to coerce him for her betterment but he is not free to coerce her. Admittedly, if he granted her such a freedom then he would be agreeing to there being actual inequalities in the real world.

What would be such an inequality with respect to freedom to get what you want? It could only be a freedom which Ben is prepared to concede to Ann but deny to himself because he thereby gains a more important freedom. Nearly all the cases I can think of are cases where both Ben and Ann would be prepared to allow a third party Colin, say, to have a certain freedom denied both of them in order to ensure that they had more important freedoms, that is, it is essential that someone have this freedom whereas everyone else is denied it.

Consider, for example, the freedom of police officers to carry guns, or of the taxation department to have access to bank records, and so on. Now, in none of these cases would Ben and Ann agree that Colin be allowed these freedoms in order to pursue ends other than the preservation of freedoms that Colin has in common with Ben and Ann, nor would they agree to Colin's using this freedom to advance his private interests as a citizen by employing his freedom to carry guns (or make arrests, or drive over the speed limit) when this freedom was given to him solely to further public ends.

5.4   The Total System of Equal Basic Liberties

Rawls' principle requires that each person have an equal right to the most extensive total system of equal basic liberties compatible with everyone having such a system of liberty. (1972, p. 302). This is oddly worded. Why is it an equal *right* rather than an equal *freedom*? Why is it 'the most extensive total *system* of equal basic liberties' rather than 'equal liberties' Why are the equal liberties the *basic* ones? What makes a liberty basic?

Barry's answer (1973, p.34) to some of these questions is that Rawls conceives of the different liberties as able to have an existence independent of each other such that, should maximising one be incompatible with maximising the others, then bits of them can be combined to make the 'total system' one of as much liberty, equally distributed, as possible.

Rawls (p.203) himself gives the example of freedom of speech. If genuine discussion is to occur, then people need to be restrained by appropriate procedures of inquiry and debate. These rules of order, however, are not to be confused with rules that actually restrict the content of what is said. If freedom of speech is to be effective, then we cannot speak whenever we please.

It is to be noted here that it is not that Ben has one system of liberty and Ann has another. This is contrary to the impression that Rawls gives when he puts his first principle in terms of each person is having an equal right to the most extensive total system of equal basic liberties that is compatible with a similar system for all. Putting it this way makes it sound as though Ben has system of liberties S whereas Ann has system of liberties T. It could be, then, that S is similar to T in either of two ways:- (1) it has the *same* liberties as T, but with reference to Ann rather than Ben, or (2) it may have quite different liberties but makes Ann as free as Ben.

Now, Rawls' freedom of speech example makes it sound like (1). If Ben is the chair of the meeting, and Ann a speaker, then Ben's freedom to choose the next speaker, to rule when a speaker has spoken enough etcetera, does not constitute a system of freedom that Ben has but which Ann lacks and for which she is compensated by having the freedom to speak. All that the principle requires is that freedom be organised into a system which is, essentially, the same system for all, not that there are lots of different systems all of which give different people equal totals of different freedoms. The only variation between Ben and Ann may be that he, say, has certain allowed powers that Ann lacks but which enable both their freedoms to be enhanced.

What the parties in a position of equal power are faced with, then, is to decide whether or not the freedom to be heard is more important than the freedom to speak whenever you feel like it, and they have to rank these two freedoms so that this ranking applies to them both. It will not be the case that they rank being heard as high for Ben but low for Ann, making other adjustments within the systems of freedom S and T so that these give Ben and Ann equal freedom respectively. Rather, they have to decide between the freedom to be heard and the freedom to speak when you feel like it in the context of both Ben and Ann wanting not to be coerced more than they want to coerce.

If this is so, then neither Ben nor Ann will risk not being heard just for the chance to prevent the other being heard. Nonetheless, it could be the case that Ben ranks speaking at will more highly than being heard, whereas Ann ranks them in the reverse order. Rawls treats it as unproblematic that the parties behind the veil will agree to give being heard priority over speaking at will. This is, presumably, because he regards it as the more important.

What needs to be established, however, is that the freedom to be heard contributes more to the preservation of other freedoms than the freedom to speak at will, even for those who want to speak at will more than they want to be heard, that is, that even those who want to speak at will more than they want others to listen to them will find that there is more freedom for them overall in all the areas of their lives that matter to them if they live in a system of freedom which ranks the freedom to be heard higher than the freedom to speak at will.

We cannot just assume that this is easily shown, but it is the kind of thing that does need to be shown. Impartialism gives the framework in which this is possible, that is, it has eliminated a lot of argumentative options that would have made agreement impossible. Nonetheless, the hard, normative, nitty gritty of showing that the freedom to be heard is more important than the freedom to speak at will is yet to be done. While Rawls is right that freedom of speech loses its value for those who see its prime function as the freedom to be heard if there are no rules of order or debate it may still have other values that do not require these rules, values to be found in the freedom to speak at will. The case needs to be made that the freedom to be heard is more important.

The point, however, has been established that what is under discussion here is the ranking of freedoms in a system that is common to all members of the community, not different, but equally free, systems of freedom for different members of the community. This is not to deny that the use people make of the common system of freedom will be such as each appears to have a different system. How the novelist and the politician use freedom of speech is quite different but they may still be part of a system that ranks the freedom to be heard higher than the freedom to speak at will.

The system, however, will give some people freedoms that are denied to others, for the express purpose of making the system work. In effect, the people who have these freedoms also have special powers that are consequential on these freedoms, for example, not every citizen is free under the law to defect unroadworthy vehicles. Only police officers are free to do so. As a result, they have a power under the law that other citizens lack which I will call 'delegated powers'. Some people, then, will have powers denied to others in order to maximise the overall system of freedoms. As the parties in the position of equal power want not to be coerced more than they want to coerce, they will insist that these delegated powers are both minimal and not open to abuse. It is possible, for example, that police may use their powers of faulting vehicles or arresting drunk drivers to persecute their personal enemies, and so forth.

Suppose that the parties in the position of equal power rank the freedom to be heard higher than the freedom to speak at will. This will then become the system of freedom (say, S) which will apply to Ben and Ann and whoever in the real world. If they had ranked these freedoms in the reverse order, then this would have been a different system (say T). S is to be preferred to T if its ranking of freedoms actually gives more freedom to Ben, Ann, etcetera, than T does.

In order for S to work, someone will have to police situations where the freedom to be heard can be frustrated by those who want to speak at will more than they want to be heard. If this task is given to Ben (say), then he does not thereby gain a greater right to be heard in his capacity as a private citizen. His greater right to be heard, if any, must be only with respect to what he needs to do to facilitate everyone's (his included) equal right to be heard. To do otherwise is to abuse his power as chair (for example) and is grounds for the invocation of removal procedures. It may even be that he has a lesser right to be heard when he acts as chair. If he wishes to be heard as an equal with others, he must relinquish the chair. This suggests that there needs to be further procedures to ensure the chair has an equal right to be heard, that is, that the selection of a chair cannot be used to gag a troublesome individual. There would need to be 'fair' selection procedures, and so on.

To return to the dispute between those who value the freedom to be heard (say, freedom H) higher than the freedom to speak at will (say, freedom W), H can only be ranked higher than W if those who prefer W can see that the system S which ranks H higher gives them more freedom overall than T which ranks W higher. This parallels the kind of case where those who wish to kill other people surrender this freedom because they prefer not to be killed, and therefore are prepared to give someone the power to prevent them killing others even when they want to do so. Those who want W, then, have to be persuaded that they should give someone the power to prevent them speaking at will, even though they want this more at the time than they want to be heard.

This can only be done if it is the case that it is more important to them in their lives overall to be heard at various times than it is to speak at will. This is a different case from the one in which they want to prevent others being heard more than they want to be heard themselves. This has already been ruled out as coercionist. What we have instead is a conflict within the individual, (say, Ben) over what matters to him most - being heard but at the cost of sometimes not speaking or speaking but sometimes at the cost of not being heard. In fact, the situation is more complex than this as there is a continuum of cases. If Ben prefers to speak at the cost of sometimes not being heard, then he might never be heard. This is a risk he takes. Ann, say, who prefers to be heard at the cost of sometimes not speaking does not run the same kind of risk. She can only sometimes be heard if it is the case that she sometimes speaks.

Whichever is chosen, symmetrification still applies. If the parties are both ones who prefer to be heard at the cost of sometimes not being able to speak when they want to, then they will be prepared to empower someone to act as a chair in the manner that Rawls describes, that is, if the parties in the position of equal power consider the case of people who want to be heard more than they want to speak at will then they will not risk Ben's speaking at will when Ann wants to be heard (under specified conditions). On the other hand, if they consider the case of people who want to speak at will more than they want to be heard, then they will risk Ben's speaking at will when Ann wants to be heard (even under the specified conditions).

The parties in the position of equal power, then, have no problem with rules of order and debate when both of them prefer H to W. When they both prefer W to H or one prefers W to H, then further argument is necessary to show that ranking W higher puts a whole range of freedoms at risk which, either individually or together, are more important than W and can only be protected if H is ranked higher. Part of this may involve an appeal to majoritarian decision-making as a device for conflict-resolution.

They still have problems, however, when either Ben or Ann prefers W to H, and prefers W to any other freedom, individually or as a total. There appears to be little profit, however, in argument with someone like this. We have here what appears to be a recurrence of the 'sectarian' case in a new guise. Resolution of an argument between Ben and Ann over whether X is to be done is only possible without recourse to force if neither party places an absolute value on doing X, that is, if neither are monists. The upshot of all this is that Rawls' first principle would be one adopted by an impartialist, at least with respect to each person having the same freedoms as any other person in a system of freedoms which ordered all freedoms so as to achieve the maximum freedom possible when everyone has the same freedom.

If Barry is right, and Rawls' first principle chooses between systems of freedoms on a maximin basis rather than on a strict egalitarian basis, then it is in accord with impartialism in this respect, too. The impartialist will not reject a system which gave police, or chairs, or politicians (parliamentary privilege, for example) freedoms not possessed by the rest of society merely because this meant freedoms were unequal. Provided these freedoms are really delegated powers, there can be an inequality of freedoms. Nonetheless, the parties in the position of equal power will choose that system which maximises freedoms with minimum delegated powers. However, even if S has more delegated powers than T but more freedom overall, they will still choose S, provided its delegated powers can operate in such a way as to ensure that the freedoms in S remain greater than those in T.

Political freedom, however, is not a delegated power. It is, rather, what I will call an 'enabling freedom'. Within impartialism, a freedom will only be a 'basic' freedom if it is an enabling freedom. A freedom is basic only if it is inalienable. No matter who you are, you will need the freedom to form political parties, to publicise political views, to put up candidates for office, all in order to enable you to be free to do the other things that you may wish to do, such as practise your religion, or your own sexual preferences, or to read what you like, etcetera, that is, to preserve your autonomy. In order to guarantee these enabling rights, the parties in the position of equal power will agree to set up rights-protecting institutions such as parliaments, or the police force, but the persons given special powers in these institutions are given only delegated powers. These powers are not intended to give them advantages over other people in securing the freedom to do what they want by denying freedoms to those over whom they have power. Their role is to ensure equal freedom of all.

Rawls' First Principle of Justice has provided the focus for the previous discussion but Rawls does not always arrive at the same conclusions on the issues discussed as impartialism does, for example, he seems to think that there are circumstances where it is acceptable for some people to have greater political freedom than others, provided this is a temporary step towards the universal possession of such freedoms. I will take up this, and related, issues in the next chapter.

6   The Distribution of Liberty

6.1   Introduction

Rawls (1972, p.302) states that the only grounds for restricting liberty is the sake of liberty itself. There are two cases of such a restriction. Firstly, if liberty in one area is to be reduced this can only be because doing so strengthens the overall system of liberty shared by everyone. This reinforces the interpretation given previously that everyone shares a single system of liberty, not that each person has his or her own, equal system. Secondly, if liberty is not to be distributed equally, then this must be agreeable to those citizens with the lesser liberty (p.250).

Questions about how social and economic inequalities are to be distributed are the subject of his second principle of justice. The issues it deals with are to be addressed only if the requirements of the first principle have been met (p.244). This means that no social or economic inequality is permitted, even if it is to the greatest benefit of the least advantaged if the result is that each person does not have an equal right to the most extensive system of basic liberties. The force of this priority, then. will depend on what is understood by having an equal right to the most extensive system of equal basic liberties. Some of this has been discussed previously. What is to be noted now is that it appears that the priority doesn't necessarily hold for non-basic liberties. To understand what the Priority Rule requires, then, we need to look at what Rawls means by 'basic liberties'.

6.2   The Priority of Liberty

Rawls' list of basic liberties is as follows:- (1) Equal participation in the political procedure in that everyone has an equal right to free speech, freedom of assembly, to vote and to stand for public office (p.61, pp.221-224); (2) The rule of law, which includes the principle that laws should not require people to do the impossible, the requirement that similar cases be treated similarly, the principle that there is not an offence unless there is a law dealing with the matter, the demand that laws be known and expressly promulgated and precepts involving the notion of natural justice, for example, that judges be fair and impartial, and that people may not be judges in their own case (pp.235-243); (3) Equal liberty of conscience, which includes freedom of religious belief, freedom of thought, freedom of conscience, freedom of life-style when this doesn't harm others, freedom of person, freedom to hold personal property, freedom from arbitrary arrest and seizure (p.61, p.450). In addition to these, there is the freedom of the person and the right to hold personal property freedom from arbitrary arrest and seizure of goods (p.61).

It is these liberties, then, whose total cannot be reduced or which cannot be rendered unequal in order to achieve social or economic inequalities no matter how great a benefit they may bring to the worst off. Rawls, however, does not believe that the first principle of justice always has priority over the second. It only has priority once a certain threshold is reached in terms of the satisfaction of urgent basic wants. This means that, when the desire to satisfy urgent basic wants is compelling enough, then it is no longer the case that each person has an equal right to the most extensive total system of equal basic liberties in the sense of either:- (1) each person has an equal right to the same total system of equal basic liberties but it is no longer the most extensive one possible at the time, or (2) the system of liberty is such that not everyone has an equal right to equal basic liberties (pp.542-543).

It might be that Rawls believes it rational of the parties behind the veil of ignorance to waive the priority of liberty if the threshold hasn't been reached for only one of these options. This does not, however, seem to be the case. He says, for example, that it is not rational for the persons in the original position to accept a less than equal freedom to satisfy their basic wants if these wants are not compelling, which does suggest that it is rational to accept a less than equal freedom when the wants are urgent. This shows that he is committed to (2) above. His general position also seems to commit him to (1).

There are, then, a number of issues that need to be considered in Rawls' account of the priority of liberty before we can determine whether impartialism agrees with it or not.

6.3   The 'Civilisation' Threshold

As we have seen, Rawls believes that there is a threshold below which the principle does not apply because it is rational of the parties behind the veil to prefer inequalities of the basic liberties in order to satisfy urgent basic wants.   Rawls (p.543) says that this is rational when:- (1) there are obstacles to the exercise of the equal liberties; (2) urgent wants need to be satisfied; (3) it is not important under these conditions to secure the free internal life of the various communities of interests; (4) people do not aspire to some control over the laws and rules that regulate their association.

Before we assess these claims, we need to consider exactly what it is that the parties behind the veil agree to when they agree to give up the priority of liberty, beginning with case (2) looked at earlier, namely, where people have unequal rights to the basic liberties.

6.4   Less than Equal Liberties

In what ways can the basic liberties be unequal? Only by one person, or group of people, having more of them than another. I will limit myself to the equal participation and rule of law cases for the moment. According to Rawls, the principle of equal participation is that each person has an equal right to take part in, and to affect, the result of the constitutional process that determines the laws by which he or she is to be governed. I will look at this first.

Suppose that Ben, say, is tempted to give up some, or all, of this right for some economic gain. This means that someone else, Ann say, has promised him that, if she is given a greater right to take part in, and determine the outcome of, the law-making process, then she will give him more money, or whatever, than he would have received if his participation was equal to hers.

Ben will want to be as able as Ann to determine the outcome of any law-making process because he will want to ensure that he is not coerced by others. If he doesn't have this equal say, then the outcome of any law-making process in the real world is likely to favour Ann. He will not agree to Ann's greater say if this means that she gains the power to break her promises to him, or to make him do as she wants without recourse to remedy. The principle of equal participation has to do with the balance of power in society. He will not agree to her having the balance of power over him such that she can ignore his interests, even if in the first instance, or always, this benefits him. The risk is too great. There can be no guarantee that this power won't be abused or even that the promise will be honoured, that is, no guarantee that he will not be coerced for her benefit without any comparable compensation.

If Ben agrees to certain sacrifices in order to gain economic benefits, he will only be able to do so if he can opt out of the arrangement if the promises are broken. He can only do this if, in combination with others if necessary, he retains sufficient power to do so. If, however, he has surrendered his right of equal participation, then he has lost his power to cancel the deal. He cannot participate in the decision-making process in order to reverse decisions contrary to his values. He will, then, not agree to surrender his right to equal participation (although it is more a right of equal determination) just for an economic benefit, for the reasons just given.

Rawls would agree that this is so after the civilisation threshold has been reached but does not believe that it automatically holds prior to the threshold. He is probably correct that some people will not concern themselves greatly with spiritual and cultural interests, with the free internal life of the various communities of interests, or even that people will not aspire to control the laws and rules that regulate their association, while their most urgent and basic wants, presumably food, drink and shelter, remain unsatisfied.

All that this shows, however, is that certain ideals of life won't rate very high if the continued existence of life itself is at stake, including ideals that are intimately associated with equal liberty. Nonetheless, while 'modes of social union consistent with equal liberty, and the ends and excellences to which people are drawn', may not rank high in conditions of scarcity, it does not follow that the equal basic liberties themselves will not remain paramount. Why should Ben surrender his equal determination of laws to Ann just because Ann promises to improve the supply of food, drink or shelter as a consequence? There are many subsistence cultures which do not hand over political power to their economic entrepreneurs in this way. Ben would have to be sure that Ann would keep her promise, and that she would not then use her extra power to make his lot even worse than it was before. The only way this latter can be ensured is if he doesn't surrender his equal rights in determining decisions.

Ben can adopt either of two models here. He can insist on equal direct determination in decision-making or he can adopt some form of equal indirect determination. In either case, he will insist that his direct determination be equal to anyone else's, or that his indirect determination be equal. His first preference will always be that his determination be direct, as this is the most effective way for him to ensure that his values are represented to others as he perceives them. Any indirect process will distort his preferences.

Nonetheless, he may be prepared to accept that direct representation has more disadvantages than indirect representation as a method for making most decisions. He may still want to insist on direct determination for the most important decisions, whatever he thinks these are. It is not appropriate to go into details here, but constitutional questions are an obvious candidate. There may be other cases, too, where an issue is so important it warrants a referendum.

Ben, then, will insist on equal determination whether it be direct or indirect because this is the only way for him to ensure that he has some control over the decisions that affect his values. This will mean that he will insist on freedom of speech and freedom of assembly because these, too, are essential if he is to be able to marshal support so that decisions in the real world are determined as he wishes them to be, given that his structural power to determine decisions is no greater than anyone else's.

This leads to questions about how to resolve disputes between large bodies of people in situations where basic rights are not involved. Rawls suggests this be done by a constitutionally controlled majoritarianism for societies above the civilisation threshold. The kinds of arguments that I have adduced so far indicate that a similar system would apply below the civilisation threshold. Cases of national survival such as war might be suggested as exceptions, although it is precisely such cases that are likely to result in a permanent loss of civil liberties if citizens are not vigilant.

Be that as it may, the crucial point is that Ben would not agree to surrendering equal determination for economic gain or even security because this means giving oneself over to the power of others in a way that is not retrievable within the system, but is only retrievable by the forcible overthrow of the system. Giving oneself over to the power of others in this way is irrational because it means that one cannot even ensure that the benefits for which such a transfer was made will be received, so that one may be even worse off after the transfer than before. As there is no way that Ben can guarantee this, he will not agree to it.

6.5   Indirect Determination of Decisions

Ben can, however, agree to something like it, and perhaps this is what Rawls has in mind. Suppose he decides that, under certain circumstances, he has more to gain under indirect participation in decision-making at the national level than he has in direct participation, provided there are certain constitutional safeguards. In particular, suppose he believes that he has more to gain economically, that is, he hands the power to make decisions about the allocation of resources to some group such as a parliament or some individual such as a President.

In doing this, he surrenders a freedom. He is no longer equally free to determine such decisions as anyone else because he has set up a group of people, of which he may not be a member, to make decisions in this area unrestrained by any direct input from him. He will still insist upon indirect input, that is, he will insist that there be some peaceful, lawful mechanism whereby he can stop, or contribute to stopping, the activities of his rulers if he sees them as acting contrary to his values, for example, they are not producing the extra wealth they promised him. In most systems, this mechanism of indirect determination of economic decisions is the election, but there may be other methods (for example, the Gallup Poll).

We have a system, then, where Ann, say, has a freedom lacked by Ben. Now, Ben will be prepared in a position of equal power to agree to such an arrangement provided these powers or freedoms are not irretrievable ones, and provided that they are delegated powers in the sense discussed earlier. The system is a two-stage system, that is, Ben will only agree to Ann having direct powers, whereas he has indirect ones, if her indirect powers are equal to his, for example, as in an election. If this is not so then his retrievability of these powers is weakened, helping Ann entrench herself with these additional powers in ways which he cannot affect even when she no longer makes decisions that take his values as of equal consideration as her own. Moreover, he will not give Ann these extra powers under systems whose effect is to benefit her at his expense.

So, even below the civilisation threshold, Ben will not agree to surrendering his equal right to determine decisions just because Ann or whoever offers him greater wealth, if his surrendering this right is either permanent or for such a long period of time that he can be irredeemably harmed by her actions while powerless to do anything about it.

At the most, he will surrender his direct freedom to determine decisions to Ann provided he retains the same indirect freedom to determine freedoms as she has, and provided he retains the same direct freedom (and indirect freedom) as anyone to retrieve these delegated powers, or to replace her with someone more responsive to his interests. As a rational agent, he will not surrender to her the power that enables him to prevent her reneging on her promise or making his situation even worse than it was prior to the transfer of power, even for the promise, or the receipt, of wealth.

In surrendering power to Ann, he does so only on the condition that she treat her own interests as a private citizen as equal to, not superior to, his own. He will insist that there be machinery built into the operation of the parliament or the presidency that prevents her misusing her additional power. As one reason why he agreed to the establishment of the parliament or the presidency in the first place was to better his financial position, he must also agree to Ann's having the power to compel him to do certain things, for example, to surrender part of his moneys as taxes, or whatever.

What he will not give her is the power to benefit herself at his expense, or the power to deny him the right to vote her out of office. There appears to be as much reason for him to insist on this below the civilisation threshold as above it. In fact, given that the consequences of misallocation of power below the civilisation threshold are the more serious because survival itself is more at risk then there is probably more reason for ensuring the maintenance of the equal right to determination.

It might be argued that this conclusion is empirically implausible. In feudal times, peasants put themselves unreservedly under the power of a lord to gain protection against marauding hordes etcetera. This is true, but the rationality of an action when people are actually in a situation of unequal power does not necessarily carry across to a position of equal power. It may be the case in real life, when one already lacks power, that it is rational to submit unconditionally to one ruler rather than another as the lesser of two evils. This in no way shows that it is rational to agree to let these rulers have this unconditional power in the first place, which is the issue that is before our impartialists.

While democracy would be what the parties would choose in the position of equal power, they recognise that, throughout most of history, such a choice has not been a viable option for most people. In most eras, the grounds for choosing between rulers has been such factors as their blood ties to some previous ruler, or some such pre-democratic claim to legitimacy. The parties in the position of equal power are able to reason about such alternatives. It may well be the case, for example, that they would agree that people in those historical circumstances should have chosen one candidate rather than another on such grounds as the greater stability and peacefulness of society if rules of succession are abided by. Whether this is so will depend, to a considerable degree, on the behaviour of whoever is the successor ordained by custom. He or she may behave so unjustly that, in the absence of a feasible prospect of democracy, rebellion is warranted. Determining the conditions that make such efforts at usurpation morally acceptable are within the province of the parties in the position of equal power, that is, they might agree, for example, that Henry VII was justified in seeking to unseat Richard III and that those who joined him this effort made the morally most defensible choice.

Another piece of evidence for the implausibility of rejecting the civilisation threshold might be that, throughout history, women have surrendered an almost absolute power over their lives to their husbands. To say that the actions of half of humanity are irrational is to put one's definition of rationality into question. Once again, what it is rational to do given that you are already in a situation of unequal power is distinct from the question of whether it is rational to agree to that power distribution in the first place, or to the power distribution which caused it to come about. It may be that, in any age when pregnancy, breast-feeding, etcetera prevent women from being trained as soldiers and thereby makes them vulnerable to the attacks of the above marauding hordes, that it is rational for them to put themselves under the protection of a single man even when this gives him the power to treat them badly should he so choose. They can only hope that he will not so choose. In a position of equal power, however, they would insist on some arrangement that gave them a right to equal treatment in a situation of unequal power.

What has been shown so far, then, is that Ben would not agree to having a lesser liberty than Ann in the matter of determination of political power, even if this lesser liberty offered or delivered a large economic benefit, and even if this occurred below the civilisation threshold.

Certainly, he is more vulnerable to her misuse of power below the threshold than he is above it.

I will now turn to a consideration of two other basic liberties, namely, the rule of law and the equal liberty of conscience. I will also look at the case where Ben, say, has to choose between a less extensive equal liberty or a less than equal liberty.

6.6   The Rule of Law

Essentially, the same considerations apply here as applied with equal determination. While Ben may be prepared to hand over power to judges because there are many advantages in doing so, he will not agree to less than equal liberty with respect to the rule of law just to get an economic gain. If Ann, say, is the judge and has powers that ordinary citizens such as Ben do not have, it is solely so that she can enforce an equal liberty for all, including Ben. He will not agree to give power to Ann to judge his case if she is merely going to use her position to benefit herself, or to benefit judges as a class, at Ben's expense. Nor will Ben agree that she should judge his case if she is the other party to the case, even if high financial rewards are offered, because this as an accepted practice can lead to her stripping him of the benefit he gained this time by a decision of a later case.

The point about each of the rules of law is that they are procedures designed to ensure that the parties who make, and administer the law, do not use the power given to them to benefit themselves consistently at the cost of those not so placed. To this extent, the rule of law is a rights-preserving institution in that those who administer the law still only have an equal freedom with everyone else in the areas that it exists to enforce. Fruit fly inspectors, for example, can enter anyone's yard to see if their trees have fruit fly. This is to prevent anyone having fruit fly. It does not mean that fruit fly inspectors are to be free to have fruit fly ridden trees but no-one else is.

Now, the rule of law is particularly important in those situations where survival is at stake, that is, where those who are the stronger are likely to advantage their own survival at the expense of others. Ben is just as unlikely to agree to suspend his right to the rule of law on a permanent basis below as above the civilisation threshold. This is so even if, were Ann to have total power, she could meet his urgent survival needs but, if she did not have total power, then he would starve. The most that Ben would concede to Ann here is that he give her a temporary but redeemable power, with appropriate mechanisms in place to ensure that the power is redeemable.

6.7   Equal Liberty of Conscience

This is not the same as freedom of speech or freedom of assembly. These are necessary parts of Ben's being able to maintain an equal right of participation and determination with Ann. Equal liberty of conscience is not a liberty needed to preserve other liberties but one of the other liberties to be preserved. Rawls seems to operate a distinction between types of desires that is relevant here. Firstly, there are desires like the desire for food, the desire for drink, etcetera, that is, what might be called 'basic' desires. These can be satisfied by someone supplying the necessary materials. Secondly, there are desires for freedoms, which can be called 'liberty desires'. These freedoms are not necessary to meet the basic desires, nor are they necessary to meet any desires but rather they are just another kind of desire. They cover such things as the freedom of speech, and the freedom of assembly.

Actually, Rawls misnames these. On his analysis they are not desires for freedoms at all, but desires for the things themselves, for example, the desire to speak, the desire to assemble. It is almost as if he would call the desire to eat 'the desire to be free to eat'. For Rawls, the civilised life is one where you can speak to people, exchange ideas, write poems, read novels, go to plays, where you can assemble with others to listen to music, or play sports, etcetera. They are, in a way, ends in themselves. They are manifestations of the Aristotelian principle, of the complexities of human interaction that provide us with satisfaction. As such, they only become desires that figure largely in our lives when urgent and basic desires are met. It is not so much the case that we will only want to have freedom of speech or freedom of assembly above the civilisation threshold as it is the case that we will only want to engage in certain kinds of speaking or certain kinds of assembling above the civilisation threshold.

But this is just as true of the freedom to eat or drink, and so on, in certain ways. It will only be wanted when the desire to eat and drink in these ways arises, and this will not occur until a certain level of civilisation. However, even at levels below the civilisation threshold, each of us will want to eat in order to survive, and will want the freedom to eat in order to survive. We will not want people preventing our eating when it is essential for our survival.

Now, it may well be that we can only prevent this if we are free to speak about how to stop it. This means that we will want to be able to have freedom of speech, not for any fancy civilised reason, but as a tool to enable us to survive. It is an enabling freedom. [1]

Likewise, with the freedom to assemble. It may be that only if we are free to assemble that we can prevent interference to our freedom to eat or drink or have shelter. Freedom of conscience, and freedom of religious belief in particular, are unlikely to be freedoms that help us secure our freedom to eat, drink or build shelters, unlike all the other freedoms listed earlier (determination, rule of law, freedom of speech and assembly, the right to a trial, etcetera).

Freedom of religious belief (or practice, more so) is one of those cases of wanting to be free to do something for its own sake. We will want freedom of speech and assembly in order to protect our freedom to practise our religion, but we will not want the freedom to practise our religion in order to protect our freedom to speak or to assemble. Practising one's religion doesn't help bring about greater freedom of speech or assembly unless prayer is more efficacious than it appears to be, or unless our practices invoke magical powers that have a causal effect upon those who would suppress our speaking or assembling.

The upshot of this is that freedom of conscience is not a basic freedom in the sense of an enabling freedom that makes it possible for us to perform activities that are essential to our protecting our interests on an equal basis with others. Freedom of speech is a basic freedom because it enables us to speak in a public forum, and speaking is essential to our protecting our interests against those who would alter the balance of power so as to advantage their interests at the cost of ours.

One of our interests may be practising our religion. Freedom of speech helps protect this. Another of our interests may be speaking itself (of various kinds), or assembling itself (again, of various kinds), or participating in making the laws and rules that regulate our association for its own sake, that is, what Rawls (following Benjamin Constant) calls the 'liberties of the ancients'. Being free to do these, however, even for their own sake, means that we can use these very freedoms to protect other freedoms. Not all activities that we do for their own sake, if we are free to do them, have the same usefulness. Liberty of conscience is one such. It is not, therefore, a basic freedom in the sense specified.

It is, therefore, possible that Ben would give Ann power to deny him freedom of conscience for economic gains. He would not give her this power, however, just because she wanted to prevent him from having freedom of conscience more than he wanted not to be prevented from having it himself, that is, he would not agree to it just because her desire to deny it to him was 1000 units strong whereas his desire to keep it was only 500 (or even 999) units strong. This is ruled out within impartialism. Ann, therefore, has to find some acceptable reason why she should want him prevented from having freedom of conscience, given that she would rather have it herself than prevent him from having it, but, that if he is to be prevented from having it, then so is she. It may be that, further developed, this gives liberty of conscience the kind of priority over the second principle that Rawls hopes for it.

It should also be noted that the case that concerns Rawls is really a coercion case. The case is that Ann has the means to supply Ben the essentials of life but he doesn't have the means to supply these for himself. Ann, however, will only supply them to him on the condition that he agrees to give her permanent total power over him, that is, that he renounce his basic freedoms. This is acceptable within impartialism, however, only if Ann would be prepared to surrender her freedoms to Ben if he, rather than she, had the only access to the means of survival. The cases between the two of them must be symmetrically acceptable when reversed. Ben, however, as a noncoercionist, wants not to be coerced by Ann more than he wants to coerce her, and Ann wants not to be coerced by him more than she wants to coerce him. This means that neither would accept the other having total power. For either to do so would be to show themselves to be coercionists

6.8   A Less Extensive Liberty

We have seen, then, that the parties in a position of equal power will not agree to there being a lesser than equal liberty even if, were Ann to have total power, she could meet Ben's urgent survival needs but, if she didn't have total power, then he would starve, or some such. At least, Ben would only agree to such an arrangement if he only wanted to live for the sake of living, rather than that he wanted to live to achieve anything of his own life plans. Even this case is weakened, however, by the fact that there seems to be no plausible situation where he could eat only if Ann had permanent total power. The most that could plausibly happen is that Ben could only get food if Ann had *temporary* total power. Further, it would have to be the case that he is in this situation for reasons other than that she contrived to put him there, that is, that she had misused a superior power to render him helpless.

If suitable circumstances arose, then, Ben might agree to surrender his basic liberties but only for as long as was necessary to get beyond the bare survival stage. Moreover, he would insist on retaining the right to assess Ann's performance so that he could replace her, or adopt alternative strategies, if she wasn't supplying him with the means of bare survival or if she appears to be less than conscientious in bringing about a better than bare survival situation for him.

Ben, then, is in the paradoxical situation that he might, if his survival depended on it, surrender as many of his basic freedoms as necessary to ensure survival, provided he retained enough of these basic freedoms to ensure that his surrender of the others paid dividends and to regain them when the grounds for surrendering them have passed. (It should be kept in mind here that Ben and Ann could be representing whole classes of people respectively, such as aristocrats and commoners, feudal lords and peasants, proletariat and bourgeoisie.)

The other strategy that Rawls suggests might be adopted below the civilisation threshold is to have a less extensive total system of equal basic liberties. This assumes that, at the time, a more extensive total system of basic liberties was possible but only at the cost of economic hardships. The distinction made earlier between the political liberties and the rule of law as enabling freedoms and the liberty of conscience still applies here, where liberty of conscience is not the same as freedom of speech or freedom of assembly but rather the liberty of religious practice. Freedom of speech will include freedom to speak about religious matters as these relate to the control of power in the society.

It is not clear how a less extensive equal basic liberty would increase wealth. Perhaps the idea is that political liberty and the rule of law is a costly business, that is, people need to be taxed to support it. Below the civilisation threshold people are more concerned with having their money in order to survive than they are to ensure a fair system of justice and a participatory political system. While there may be some truth in this, it cannot be the case that they will agree to no political participation because this means an unequal liberty, that is, giving power to some group without retrievability. Likewise, for no rule of law.

The scenario that is possible is that they are prepared to bypass the benefits of certain grander systems of participation etcetera in order to secure survival. They may be prepared to live in clans rather than tribes, or tribes rather than states, if this reduces their financial burden. This, however, will only be so as long as the relationship between clans is such that their wars with each other do not put life and property at so much risk that it is worth becoming a tribe or a state with greater overheads in administration that require greater taxes.

Nonetheless, at the clan level, each of the parties in a position of equal power will insist on equal basic liberties for all members of the clan. Likewise, once the clans become tribes and the tribes states. As the costs of remaining at a less sophisticated level of organisation increase, so the motivation to amalgamate and have less face-to-face, more bureaucratic systems of participation and justice increases. These will only be possible at an economic cost, namely, taxes.

The nature of participation will vary. The smaller the group, the more direct participation there is likely to be. Unfortunately, the smaller the group the more vulnerable to attack it is, the more the lives of its members are at risk if its environment is accessible to the ravaging hordes. As groups become bigger, as cooperative effort increases wealth, the concepts that people have as to what their lives are about, that is, what they will value, will change. What was not possible in the small society may become possible in the bigger one. In a large society people will be free to do things that they could not do in the smaller. In cities, where there is no longer the close scrutiny of family and neighbours of one's activities, there is a freedom to be private that does not exist in the smaller society. This may well come to be valued by many.

There is also, as Durkheim and others have pointed out, the dangers of anomie and alienation. There is also likely to be a freedom of lifestyle, that is, an individuality or lack of conformity that is missing in the smaller society. It is possible to interpret these as greater liberties, but they are not greater basic liberties, in the sense of enabling freedoms. Rather, they are freedoms that may be obtained and maintained by the exercise of the enabling freedoms. It may well be that, once a certain economic level is reached, people will prefer more privacy, more diversity, more opportunity for cultural activities like the arts, and so on, than they will prefer to possess material goods. This, however, is something they will hand over to a social and economic policy determining group such as a parliament to sort out by procedures that arbitrate between the interests of conflicting groups in the society.

Below the civilisation threshold they may not want their possession of material goods put into competition with liberties such as privacy, individuality etcetera. Physical security, physical comfort may matter more. Even here, however, either the members of the group as a whole or some equivalent of a parliament will be the determinant body. It is just that the preferences of those it represents so overwhelmingly favour the material over the cultural, or whatever, that it will not dare deprive its electorate of one for the other. The less surplus wealth, above and beyond that needed for material comfort, the less likely people are to be prepared to be taxed to fund other people's demands for support in cultural, etcetera, activities.

None of this, however, affects everyone's interests in ensuring an equal say in the decisions that are made, at least indirectly. In fact, if people want to keep their material goods rather than fund cultural activities, they will need their basic liberties to give them the power to control the activities of their representatives. To the extent, then, that being below the civilisation threshold affects people surrendering liberties for economic gains it is not the basic liberties that they will be prepared to surrender nor the equality of these liberties.

To what extent will the basic equal liberties be surrendered for economic gain without losing their equal nature? The problem here is the choice between losing your wealth and weakening the guarantees you have that you will be free to use your wealth. It is a question of sacrificing some of your wealth in order to guarantee the free exercise of the rest of it. The less wealth one has, the less of it one can afford to lose and the less of it one has to spend freely. Nonetheless, one can lose one's life, or one's freedom of movement (being jailed etcetera) and one will be prepared to spend as much as is necessary to give reasonable security against these eventualities. The poorer the society, the less sophisticated will be its method of securing justice, that is, it will not be able to afford an apparatus of lawyers, courts, appeals, and so on.

Even so, its members will still want the innocent cleared and the guilty punished and will be prepared to spend a reasonable amount of their wealth to ensure this. It is doubtful how much this can be reduced to a formula. Likewise, they will want their government to make decisions responsive to the will of the majority but they may not be able to afford all the modern apparatus associated with this. The best that they can do here is to ensure that enough is spent on the parliament and the justice system to ensure that it is able to respond to demands that more be spent in those areas where the majority of people are unhappy with its performance. How much this is will have to be a matter of judgement, but it applies even when there are few civilised liberties as when there are many.

6.9   Barry's Treatment of Rawls' Derivation of the Priority of Liberty

Barry claims that Rawls' official doctrine is acceptable only if wealth is given a virtually non-existent value in comparison with liberty. Only if this is so would a society be prepared to do as Rawls seems to require, namely, to go from general affluence to general poverty just to secure a negligible gain in liberty (1973, p.60).

I have argued that, understood as I have described it, the priority of the first over the second principle is not outlandishly extreme. This has involved showing that the basic liberties only include the freedom of participation and the rule of law but not freedom of conscience in any sense additional to freedom of speech and assembly. (Conscientious objection to a war, for example, may be a non-basic liberty, as may freedom of sexual preference, and a lot of the standard civil liberties.) This removes some of the problems that Barry finds with Rawls' account. It still remains possible that it is 'outlandishly extreme' to sacrifice any amount of wealth for either an increase in the total system of equal basic liberties or for an increase in the equality of the total system of basic liberties. Barry is probably right here. It is, once again, going to be a matter of judgement.

Consider a case where a drop from general affluence to general poverty means one innocent person will not be found guilty who otherwise would have been. Presumably, the more we spend on our system of justice, the less miscarriages of justice are likely to occur, for example, the quicker cases can be heard, the more thoroughly evidence can be collected, and so on. There will need to be a balance reached here that the parties in a position of equal power are prepared to accept given the wealth of the community, given that any one of them may be the innocent person and that each of them may be one of those who pays taxes.

Similar points obtain for participation. In a modern democracy we could hold referenda on all issues. The parties in a position of equal power would have to calculate whether the added participation is worth the cost, both financial and in terms of time out of one's life. Once again, they would have to settle on a balance. Nonetheless, the balance is to be struck in such a way as preserves the effectiveness of the basic freedom of each of them for, without these freedoms, their wealth is of dubious value, being at risk from those who control the decision-making and judicial processes. If anything, they would err in the direction of more money going on guaranteeing basic freedoms, that is, the enabling freedoms, than is strictly necessary.

The rest of Barry's discussion concerns itself with taking seriously Rawls' 'civilisation threshold' for the priority of liberty. The arguments I have adduced so far have been designed to show that this threshold is not to be taken seriously as far as the basic or enabling liberties are concerned. Barry's points still hold with respect to the non-basic liberties.

What is crucial, I think, to a correct understanding of the relation between wealth and liberty is the distinction between enabling freedoms and 'freedoms' in general. Rawls has freedom as an ideal. He wants people not to sacrifice for increased wealth any of their political liberty or the rule of law, the tolerance of diversity, the freedom to engage in the arts, the freedom to be an individual, to not conform, the freedom to be private etcetera. He has an ideal of the 'civilised person' that he doesn't want people behind the veil of ignorance sacrificing for greater wealth, so he wants to build constraints in to the veil that prevent this. He has, however, failed to distinguish those elements of freedom that may be an ideal, and those elements that are not, that is, the enabling freedoms.

The ideal freedoms, however, are not really under threat even under the impartialist model because the noncoercionist requirement will guarantee that the parties in the position of equal power will not agree to swap them for wealth. Consider the freedom of privacy. The parties are not considering cases where Ben, say, wants to coerce Ann into lack of privacy more than he wants not to be coerced into it himself. Rather, he wants not to be coerced out of privacy more than he wants to coerce Ann out of hers. He will, therefore, have a prima facie preference for the freedom to be private. Certainly, he will want some greater good to accrue to his sacrifice of privacy.

Can this greater good only be a greater freedom? We have seen that this notion is not a clear one. The more kinds of desires that a person can come to have the greater need for freedom (in a sense) follows because the greater the number of areas of his or her life there are that can be obstructed by others. So an increase in material wealth, which creates greater capacity to satisfy desires, also creates greater opportunity for obstruction. As long as people are not obstructing these freedoms just for obstruction's sake (that is, they are not coercionist) then the relation between Rawls' ideal freedoms and wealth is negotiable through the parliament, provided it really can be shown that there is economic gain from the denial of these freedoms. Liberty of sexual preference is a case in point. It may be the case that homosexuality being illegal is of economic benefit to sufficient people to justify it. (The benefit might not be strictly 'economic'. For example, the military effectiveness of an army may be affected by its allowing homosexuals in its ranks.)

What is crucial, however, is that the parties in the position of equal power agree that the economic or whatever gain justifies restrictions on a particular sexual preference. Suppose Ann was a heterosexual and Ben was a homosexual. They would have to agree that the sexual preference of either of them could be banned under certain circumstances if failure to ban it, for example, put their lives at risk, or a wide range of their other freedoms and interests. If, for example, soldiers fight better when they are not sexually distracted at the front, therefore all front line troops have to be heterosexuals without the opposite sex present, then it would be an impartially acceptable policy to ban homosexuals because not doing so puts even homosexual at the risk of a loss they would prefer not to have. Either no-one can have sex, or they all can. On this example, the soldiers at the front could be all heterosexual men or all heterosexual women, or else there are no restrictions on men and women, heterosexual or homosexual, at the front.

The same arguments would apply with a 'veil of ignorance' model, so Rawls has even less cause for worry about his ideal freedoms because the parties behind the veil will only accept that Ben, say, be coerced into losing an ideal freedom for Ann's economic or other gain if she is prepared to lose that freedom for his gain. This means that they have to be prepared to ban heterosexuality for Ann's economic gain in certain circumstances as well as her homosexuality for Ben's gain. People, however, want the economic gain precisely to indulge their own versions of the luxury freedoms. The parties in the position of equal power have to accept that the gain is worthwhile regardless of how many people there are in either sexual group.

Note

1   An indication that such a point is not just a philosopher's conceit can be
         found in the comments of one of the jurors for the United States trial of
         Oprah Winfrey versus Texas cattleman Paul Engler.   The Adelaide
         Advertiser (February 28, 1998, p.48) reports Ms Pat Gowdy as saying
         'Our rights have suffered enough in this country. Our freedom of speech
         may be the only one we have left to regain what we have lost.'
         Comments like this, it seems to me, undermine 'false consciousness'
         theories like those we looked at in Chapter 2 which assume that the public
         is easily manipulated by governments, advertising, the media, etcetera.
         Notions like 'false consciousness', 'reification', 'mystification',
         'patriarchy', 'construction of consciousness', 'discourse', 'repressive
         tolerance' often seem to be postulated as theoretical constructs when the
         public (or women, or some racial group or the working class or whoever)
         chooses what the theorist believes must be against their own interest. In
         this respect, these theorists are like those religious thinkers who offer the
         devil as an explanation for why the world rejects their religion. In order
         to establish the existence of the entity that the theorist proposes he or she
         must be able to be identify it by criteria independent of the difference in
         values between him or herself and the public. As far as I am aware, none
         has done so. This kind of unfalsifiability is frequently a problem in what
         might be called 'critical social science'. For an example of related
         problems in structuralist and functional analyses of society, see Liston
         (1990).

7 The Distribution of Opportunities

7.1   Introduction

In the previous two chapters we have seen that impartialism reaches similar conclusions to Rawls about the distribution of liberty, namely, that everyone has an equal right to the enabling liberties, although we had to modify Rawls' list of liberties slightly. We saw, however, that the parties in the position of equal power would not always agree to the system of equal enabling liberties being the most extensive one possible given the economic circumstances. They would have to calculate on a cost-benefit basis the degree to which their wealth or its enjoyment was put at risk by the extent of the equal enabling liberties they possessed. The more money spent on protecting the equal enabling liberties, the less likely they were to be denied the enjoyment of their wealth but also the less wealth they would have to enjoy. At some point, there would have to be a diminishing return on increased expenditure on the enforcement of the enabling liberties. At this point, it would be rational for them to refuse to extend the total system of equal enabling liberties even though it was possible to.

Rawls' Second Principle of Justice deals with social and economic inequalities, rather than with inequalities of liberty. I will only concern myself with the first part of the principle, which Rawls calls 'The Difference Principle' which requires society to arrange social and economic inequalities so that they can reasonably expected to be to everyone's advantage (p.60). Rawls later glosses this principle so that it reads that these inequalities are to be of 'the greatest benefit to the least advantaged' (p.83).

The parties behind Rawls' veil of ignorance do not know who they will be in the real world. They have to decide on the distribution of wealth for a world of uncertainty. Rawls argues that the rational principle for whichever principle guarantees them the best minimum. My task in this chapter is to see whether Rawls' arguments for maximin also hold for impartialism.

7.2   Average Utility or Maximin?

Ann and Ben in the position of equal power are to determine how to solve conflicts of desire over the arrangement of social and economic inequalities in the real world, that is, in a world where an equality of power is not guaranteed. Barry argues that Rawls has made a 'monumental confusion' in his case for preferring maximin over the principle of average utility. The confusion is that Rawls casts the calculations of the parties behind the veil in terms of the choice of which society to enter rather than the choice of which institutions within a particular society to choose.

Barry (1973, p.92) concedes that it might well be rational to choose the society with the highest minimum when choosing between societies, provided you knew the minima for each society but didn't know the proportions of people in each representative position. However, the parties behind the veil have to decide which criteria are to be used to judge the institutions of whichever society it is that they eventually find themselves in. The parties do not know the proportion of the population in the different representative positions or what the levels of representative positions (including the lowest) in their society are. In such a case, Barry thinks, the information bearing on maximin and maximising average utility are symmetrical. Maximising average utility will produce the highest possible obtainable average individual expectation and maximising the minimum will secure the highest possible minimum individual expectation, so the issue becomes whether rationality recommends pursuing the highest average expectation or the highest minimum expectation. As the parties behind the veil do not know their attitude to risk, then, Barry concludes, all information 'which could provide a basis for making a rational choice of a criterion' has been removed (1973, p.96). Is this so?

The parties behind Rawls' veil of ignorance are to resolve conflicts of desire in the real world between Ann and Ben, say, over arrangements of social and economic inequalities. Ann and Ben are in the same society. The parties behind the veil do not know which of Ann or Ben they are and are deciding which of two types of institution they wish to have in the society. Let's call these institutions V and W. Let's suppose that V and W have the same utility but V has the lower minimum. Let us further suppose that, within the institution V, we can divide the representative positions into two, namely, the position occupied by Ann and any other position which we say is occupied by Ben. Ann's position has a higher utility than Ben's.

Suppose, now, that Ann's utility in V is at Ben's expense, that is, that there could be an institution W where Ben would have a higher utility but Ann a lower one, while the average utility remains the same. The question is whether the parties behind the veil will prefer V to W. They can be allowed knowledge of the utility levels and minima of these institutions without biasing their decision because the veil prevents them knowing which of Ann or Ben they are. We can also allow them to know which representative role Ann and Ben occupy as long as we turn the situation into a two-party conflict where neither of the parties behind the veil can calculate their chances of being either Ann or Ben.

As rational agents, the parties behind the veil will go for whichever of V or W maximises their chances of getting what they want. Barry's problem remains, however. Without knowing their own attitude to risk there does not seem to be enough information for the parties behind the veil to make a rational choice between V and W. This is because, as far as the parties know, Ann and Ben could both be high risk takers who would prefer a system where they could either have great economic inferiority or great superiority to a system where they would have economic equality at a level much less than the economically successful in the other system. If Ann and Ben are low risk takers, then they will adopt a maximin strategy and most of Rawls' conclusions about social and economic management of inequality go through. If they are high risk takers, however, then other arrangements for social and economic inequalities will be more rational than maximin. Whether the most rational one will be the principle of average utility is outside the scope of this discussion.

Rawls does not impose the difference principle on the parties behind the veil but, rather, tries to derive it from the veil conditions. As we have seen, Barry believes that he fails. I will now see whether impartialism is better able to derive the difference principle from its axioms.

7.3 Power Relativities

As we have seen, the parties in the position of equal power would agree to Ann and Ben having equal enabling rights. This is because the parties there must be noncoercionists. As maximisers of desire-satisfaction, Ann and Ben will want each to be free from coercion by the other to pursue the satisfaction of whatever desires they wish by whatever means they wish, provided that these desires and the means to them are ones that they would agree in a position of equal power that they should be allowed to pursue. In order to ensure that Ann does not use coercion to get Ben to maximise her desire-satisfaction at the expense of his own, Ben will agree to certain rights-protecting institutions. These institutions will themselves have coercive powers which are intended to prevent Ann from coercing Ben or else to coerce Ann into restoring to Ben what is rightfully his if she has wrongly denied him his rights by her greater coercive powers.

It is essential if Ann and Ben are to have equal enabling rights in practice as well as in theory that the rights-protecting institutions not be open to manipulation by either party. If Ann, for example, is able to bribe the judiciary so that it uses the coercive power of the law to preserve her wrongful possession of what is rightfully Ben's, then the rights-protecting institutions become rights-denying institutions. As Ann and Ben want not to be coerced more than they want to coerce, they will agree that Ann not be so much more powerful than Ben that she can pervert the course of justice. This will mean that Ann is not to be so much more powerful than Ben that she can permanently control the legislature and executive of the society because these bodies ultimately control what occurs in the courts and in the police force.

Not only can such bodies as the legislature and executive manipulate the law enforcement agencies in favour of entrenched groups but they can consolidate the power and wealth of some groups by discriminating against others in legislation. Ann and Ben in a position of equal power will agree that neither of them is to have this kind of power over the other. The wealthier that Ann, say, becomes relative to Ben, however, the greater her power to bias the rights-protecting institutions in her favour.

This means that Ann and Ben will agree that the relative difference in wealth between them not be such as to enable Ann to bias the rights-protecting institutions in her own favour to any significant extent. This bias does not need to be an illegal bias such as the case mentioned earlier of bribing judges. Both Ann and Ben would be concerned about a legal system in which court cases were regularly decided in favour of one side rather than another because the winning side could afford an expensive lawyer and the losing side could not afford a lawyer at all.

Wealth, however, is not the only method by which a group could bias the rights-protecting system in its own favour. Another could be by all the positions of power in the rights-protecting system being occupied by members of this group. This would only be a problem if this group either had a common interest in favouring its members against nonmembers, as it might if they were all part of the same family, or the same religion, or the same race, or whatever. It is this kind of possibility that Rawls' Principle of the Fair Equality of Opportunity is supposed to frustrate. Ann and Ben in a position of equal power would agree with Rawls that neither of them should be able to bias the rights-protecting system against the other by having a monopoly on the positions of power within the system.

The rights-protecting system, then, can be subverted by methods other than inequalities of wealth. The reasoning about how to prevent such subversion by inequalities of wealth also applies to subversion by other sources of power. Ann and Ben, then, will agree that Ann, say, not be so much wealthier than Ben that she can use the rights-protecting system to coerce him to do what satisfies her desires.

One way of minimising her capacity to do this is for the two of them to be equally wealthy. Ann and Ben in a position of equal power would not, however, require that their interests-protecting freedoms be preserved by this particular strategy. They might be prepared to let Ben earn more money than Ann but only if this did not significantly increase Ben's power over Ann vis a vis the rights-protecting system.

This gives us an alternative to the difference principle, which I will call the 'relativities' principle, and which is spelt out below.

The Relativities Principle:- *Social and economic inequalities are to be arranged so that any improvement in the conditions of the better-off be accompanied by an improvement in the value to the worst-off of the rights-protecting system.*

This principle could be met in at least two ways. Firstly, by actually increasing Ann's wealth whenever Ben gets an increase in wealth so that he has no significantly greater power over the rights-protecting system than Ann. Secondly, by modifying the rights-protecting system so that Ben has no significantly greater power over it than Ann even though Ben is so much wealthier than Ann that had these modifications not been made to the system he would have had significantly more power over it than she would. Possible ways of implementing this kind of strategy are by subsidising the poor when they employ lawyers so that they get reasonable representation, subsidising political parties so that the parties of the poor compete for votes on an comparable footing with those of the rich, forbidding media monopolies, subsidising access and public radio and television, educating the poor in the processes by which they can protect their rights, and so on. Ann and Ben, then, will at least agree that economic and social inequalities satisfy the relativities principle.

Ben, however, can coerce Ann by means other than having greater power than her over the rights-protecting system. If he has greater wealth than her, he may be able to control her means of livelihood so that she is dependent on him for her own, or her family's, survival. This means that he can coerce her into not seeking redress through the rights-protecting system for his infringements of her rights by threatening to cut off her means of livelihood. Or he could trade on her vulnerability to extract concessions from her that she otherwise would not give, such as the sexual favours that the grocer extracts from his female clients in Zola's 'Germinal'.

Likewise, Ben could threaten to cut off Ann's means of livelihood unless she uses her enabling rights, such as the right to vote, to hand over to him greater power over the rights-protecting system. As Ann and Ben want not to be coerced more than they want to coerce they will be more concerned to protect themselves from this kind of coercion than they will be to maintain their superior wealth. There are two ways that Ann, say, could be protected from such coercion by Ben.

Firstly, it could be required that, if the society is wealthy enough, then it ensures that no-one is dependent in this way on anyone else, that is, it provides either a minimum wage or unemployment benefits or some such that is sufficiently high to ensure that Ben has little coercive power over Ann to get her either to surrender her right to use the rights-protecting system or to get her to use the rights-protecting system to confer greater power on Ben. An alternative model might be that everyone was guaranteed a minimum of land on which to produce the necessities of life as well as at least a reasonable surplus, or some such.

Secondly, if the society is not wealthy enough to do this, it would be agreed that Ann and Ben be more or less equal in their financial insecurity, that is, that the difference in wealth between each of them is not such as to lead to Ann's becoming dependent on Ben. The parties in the position of equal power, then, would adopt what I will call the 'independence' principle, namely:-

The Independence Principle:- *Social and economic inequalities are to be arranged so that people are not so dependent economically on anyone that they will surrender to such a person (or persons) their equality with respect to the rights-protecting system, or their recourse to that system, in order to preserve their income.*

The most, then, that can be derived from the impartialist axioms are the 'relativities' and 'independence' principles. Impartialism, therefore, is not subject to those criticisms that are directed solely at the maximin aspect of Rawls' theory, for example, Barry's criticisms of maximin as the rational strategy under the conditions that Rawls specifies (Barry, 1967) or the detailed criticism that Wolff offers of the various versions of maximin that Rawls proposes. (Although see Corrado 1980 for a defence of maximin.)

It should be noted that I do not mean that any of the above proposals such as the relativities principle or the independence principle are to be imposed on a citizenry in the real world by overruling the democratic process. The parties in a position of equal power place a lexical priority on process rather than on the outcome of process. While each of us as individuals may believe that a particular social arrangement is the fair one, and we believe we have the arguments that convince us, at least, that these are the arrangements that would be chosen by the parties in the position of equal power, we still have to engage in the process of convincing a majority of the polity that we are right. Even this majority is subject to whatever constitutional constraints on the powers of government have been agreed to by majorities voting on the basic political structure.

7.4   Maximising Income

For Rawls, the parties behind the veil of ignorance must prefer a situation where Ann, say, has $200 and Ben has $300 to one where they have $199 each, given that the spending power of each dollar is the same. The relativities principle does not require this. Ann and Ben in a position of equal power, however, would be prepared to let some conflict-resolving process such as majoritarianism determine in the real world between the two options, namely, whether they will stay on $199 each in order to ensure that neither has more power than the other to use the rights-protecting system to their own advantage or whether they will allow an inequality of wealth, and therefore of power, because this inequality of wealth generates greater scope for desire-satisfaction for all.

Ann and Ben in a position of equal power might decide that the enabling rights are best protected by economic equality, even if this is at a low economic level. Admittedly, Ann and Ben may only be able to obtain the higher freedoms such as privacy, etcetera, if they go for economic inequality but, in a position of equal power, there is no guarantee that Ann and Ben would see themselves as required to prefer the higher freedoms to the lower ones. Provided that they have political equality in a tribal society, they will not require the introduction of economic inequalities if this is necessary to move them to a society that provides a wider scope for individuality, or a greater variety of consumer or 'cultured' satisfaction.

Nonetheless, it may be the case that the move to greater scope for individuality is difficult to avoid once societies can no longer close themselves off from other societies. Ann and Ben, then, in a position of equal power, would have to devise principles governing the relationships between societies that resolved conflicts of desires between societies by non-coercive means. This may mean an educative relationship within each society that undermines the conformity of the culture and leads to pressure from politically equal citizens for the goods, or freedoms, available to citizens of other societies. While this may be what is required once there is a conflict of desires between societies, impartialism does not require it in a self-contained society provided all its citizens are political equals in that their equal enabling rights are equally preserved by the rights-protecting system.

7.5   Liberty and the Equal Worth of Liberty

Rawls (p.204) makes a distinction between 'liberty' and 'the worth of liberty'. According to him, the worth of liberty is a function of one's capacity to further one's ends, either at the individual or group level, within the complete system of liberties of equal citizenship. The greater the wealth and authority the greater the capacity to achieve one's aims. One has a lesser worth of liberty, for example, when one has a greater inability to take advantage of one's rights and opportunities as a result of poverty and ignorance, and a lack of means generally.

Impartialism, however, sees the worth of liberty and liberty itself as inextricably linked when it comes to the enabling rights and the rights-protecting system. The rights-protecting system must ensure that each person's enabling rights are of equal worth. Ann and Ben in a position of equal power will not agree to any social or economic arrangements that give Ben, say, greater power over the rights-protecting system than Ann. Where he has unequal rights or powers within the rights-protecting system, as with the rights of police officers or parliamentarians, these need to be stringently controlled so that abuses of them are quickly detected and severely dealt with.

While the rights-protecting system must ensure that everyone has equal worth of enabling rights, impartialism does not require that there be a system that ensures that everyone have equal worth of freedom if this means that Ann, say, is able to get as great a proportion of her desires satisfied in the real world as Ben. As we have seen, in a position of equal power, Ben and Ann will agree that Ben, say, can earn more than she does provided:- (1) that he does so by non-coercive means or, at least, by only those coercive means that they, in a position of equal power, have agreed to allow in the real world, and (2) that his extra wealth is within the range permitted by the relativities and independence principles.

If Ben's extra wealth meets these conditions then he has greater worth of freedom than Ann but he is no freer. This must be so if the relativities and independence principles have been met. He is no freer than her because he is no more able to coerce Ann into doing what satisfies his desires than she is able to do this to him. Nonetheless, he is able to satisfy more desires than she is.

7.6   Primary Goods

Behind the veil, Ann and Ben do not know anything about who they are in particular in the real world, therefore they do not know which desires they have. The range of possible conflicts of desire between them is enormous. For any desire that Ann has, for example, Ben could either want her not to satisfy it or else he could have some desire of his own that is incompatible with it. It would simplify their task behind the veil of finding principles to resolve conflicts of desires if this range could be reduced.

Rawls suggests that the range be reduced in two ways. Firstly, that Ann and Ben behind the veil only propose principles that resolve conflicts of desire over primary goods. Secondly, that they resolve conflicts of desire in accord with the principle that the desire that exercises a person's capacities more, or exercises more complex capacities, is to be preferred. This automatically resolves many conflicts of desires, leaving the parties behind the veil only those conflicts of desire to resolve where either side exercises capacities equally or exercises equally complex capacities. As we have seen, Rawls (p.426) calls this principle the 'Aristotelian' principle.

Both these ways of reducing the range of conflicts of desires that the parties behind the veil are to consider do not result from using the veil of ignorance, however. They are not general conclusions about the kinds of principles that resolve conflicts of desires that have been reached as a result of applying the veil to their reasoning. Rather, they are limitations externally exposed on their reasoning. As a consequence, there will be two kinds of conflict of desire which they do not resolve, namely, (1) the conflict between those who want conflicts of desire resolved in terms of primary goods and those who don't and (2) the conflict between those who want conflicts of desire resolved by using the Aristotelian Principle, and those who don't. Rawls sets up his theory so it favours one side over the other in each of those conflicts but, as his preference is not itself derived from the veil, it may be a partialist preference.

I will now look at the primary goods, then at the Aristotelian Principle, to see whether they are consistent with impartialism and, if they are not, what consequences this has for the kinds of principles the parties in a position of equal power would choose to resolve conflicts of desires.

Rawls thinks of the primary goods as things that every rational person can be assumed to want (p.62). The most important of these are, in his view, rights and liberties, powers and opportunities, income and wealth and self respect. These are the 'social' primary goods. He also lists a number of 'natural' primary goods, namely, health, vigour, intelligence and imagination. These are 'natural' because, they are not directly under the control of the basic structure of society although they are influenced by it.

The question for impartialist theory, then, is whether or not conflicts of desires are to be resolved only by principles that deal with these primary goods, or whether there is something other than primary goods in terms of which principles should be formulated.

Barry (1973, p.22) suggests that Rawls has introduced the primary goods into his theory because, otherwise, the parties behind the veil would have to formulate these principles in terms of want-satisfactions. Rawls, he says, is in an awkward dilemma because he dislikes what is implied by the want-regarding view, wishing to assert, for example, that Ben's desire (say) to practise his religion freely should have priority over Ann's desire (say) to stop him, even in cases where Ann's desire is stronger than Ben's or Ann's community outnumbers Ben's. I will call this the first horn of Rawls' dilemma.

The second horn of Rawls' dilemma, according to Barry, is that he simultaneously wants to derive principles of justice from an original position whose occupants are denied specific information about themselves. This seems to lead inevitably towards formulating principles in want-regarding terms. The connection, he thinks, is unavoidable.

Impartialism, however, is able to avoid the first horn of the dilemma without introducing the primary goods. It can remain a purely want-regarding theory. This is because, as we have seen earlier, the principles the parties in a position of equal power are to adopt have to be symmetrified ones, that is, the principle that Ann's religion is to be suppressed because Ben's desire to suppress it is stronger than her desire to practice it can only be agreed to in a position of equal power if Ben is prepared to allow his religion to be suppressed if Ann's desire to suppress it is stronger than his desire to practise it (or some desire of equivalent strength).

What matters, then, is not that Ben's desire to suppress Ann's religion is stronger than her desire to practise it but, rather, that his desire to coerce her is stronger than his desire not to be coerced by her. Even if he meets this requirement, however, his desire to suppress her religion is ruled out by the noncoercionist requirement that the parties in the position of equal power reason as if they wanted not to be coerced more than they want to coerce. Impartialism, then, achieves the result that Rawls wants without bringing in primary goods.

The second horn of Rawls' dilemma is not a problem for the kind of theory that I have advanced so far, as I have formulated its principles in want-regarding terms.

7.7 The Aristotelian Principle

According to Rawls, people enjoy the exercising their innate or trained abilities, other things being equal. Moreover, their pleasure in this increases the more these capacities are realised, or the greater their complexity. This is because the more proficient people become at something, they more than enjoy it. Given a choice between two activities they do equally well, they prefer the one calling on a larger repertoire of more intricate and subtle discriminations, (p.426). For example, someone who can play both chess and checkers (draughts) generally prefers chess.

Barry (1973, p.27) sees this as Rawls' most important attempt to limit the range of desires that his theory has to consider. Barry (1973, p.28) then proceeds to argue that either the Aristotelian principle is an empirical generalisation or else a partially constitutive definition of 'rationality'. If it is the latter, then, in his view, Rawls has advanced a substantive concept of human excellence under the cover of a neutral-appearing concept of rationality, even though this may not have been Rawls' intention. I will not repeat Barry's arguments here but will merely note that impartialism requires no more of the term 'rationality' than Barry gives it, namely, that what makes people's plans of life rational is that they result in there getting more rather less of whatever things it is that they happen to want.

Whether the Aristotelian principle is true of human beings or not doesn't really matter from the viewpoint of impartialism. What does matter is that the parties behind the veil not be required to reason as if it is true. If it is true, then the parties behind the veil will take this into account in their reasoning about how people in the real world should act. If, however, it is not true, then they should not reason as if it is. If the Aristotelian principle is imposed on them rather than being an actual condition of the state of affairs about which they are reasoning, then the parties would be reasoning as if they know they favoured the more complex over the less complex, etcetera.

While this produces the result Rawls is after, it doesn't show that those who reject the Aristotelian principle are partialists. In fact, Rawls' own result could be the partialist one. To show that it is not, he would need investigate whether the parties behind the veil would agree on his result if they didn't know whether they were Ann who accepted the Aristotelian principle or Ben who didn't. This means they need to arbitrate between Ann and Ben from behind the veil, and do so without begging the truth of the Aristotelian principle.

Haksar claims that, without the Aristotelian principle, Rawls would not be able to show why the parties behind the veil would value autonomy or why they would give liberty priority over income. While this may be true of Rawls' theory, it is not true of impartialism. We saw in Chapter 6 that the parties in the position of equal power will give the enabling rights priority over income. Their reason for doing so, however, is not because it is part of their ideal that, as Hart says , each person should be the kind of public-spirited citizen who prizes political activity and service to others as among the chief goods of life, unable to contemplate as tolerable an exchange of the opportunities for such activity for more material goods or contentment (1975, p.252). Rather, they merely want these freedoms as guarantees that they will be able to satisfy whatever wants they happen to have, including their desire to live in accordance with a public spirited ideal if they have it. Nonetheless, it remains the case that they do give the equal basic freedoms priority over such other goods as wealth, so Rawls' major claim remains intact.

7.8   Wants as the Units of Social Evaluation

Barry (1973, p.21) comments that, as far as he is aware, no case against treating wants as the units of social evaluation has never been set forth systematically. He suggests three reasons why so many people are opposed to a want-regarding view. These are:- (1) that they feel there is something fundamentally wrong in treating a whole range of different wants as being alike for the purposes of calculation - wants such as the desire for personal gratification, the desire to give others pleasure, the desire to add to the world's store of truth and beauty, the desire for spiritual improvement and enlightenment; (2) that they find it impossible to believe that any set of principles which only discriminates between wants in terms of relative intensity could give results that could be conscientiously endorsed: and (3) that the results of applying the most promising set of want-regarding principles one could think of to actual or hypothetical situations might turn out to be morally unacceptable.

I will look at each of these in turn to see whether they constitute reasons for rejecting impartialism.

7.9   Immoral Desires

The first objection that Barry mentions is really the view that there are some desires that shouldn't even be taken into account in calculating what should be done. Rawls (p.261) certainly holds this view. He thinks that a theory of justice need give no weight to desires for things that are inherently unjust, or that can only be satisfied violating just arrangements.

Rawls' concern here is with a theory like utilitarianism which admits into its calculations as to which act is the right one any desire whatever, including desires to be cruel, vicious, dishonest and so on. Utilitarianism has a procedure for determining which acts are right or wrong. It performs calculations in terms of the consequence of the various desires from the viewpoint of maximising happiness, or whatever particular interpretation is given to utility. It does not exclude any desires from this procedure. It can be contrasted with a theory which has a procedure for deciding which acts are right or wrong but only applies this procedure to a certain domain of acts. The procedure itself does not identify this domain. The domain is determined antecedently to any application of the procedures in accordance with criteria quite independent of the procedure. Rawls sees his own hypothetical contractarianism as a theory of this kind.

Impartialism, however, is more like utilitarianism than Rawls' theory in this respect. It does not say in advance that there is any desire whose conflict with other desires it will not consider. The impartialist axioms are to be applied to any conflict of desires whatsoever, not just to ones selected by some independent criterion. Nonetheless, the effect of the impartialist axioms is to eliminate egoistic and coercionist desires from any calculation as to what is to be done. In this way, impartialism differs from utilitarianism.

Unlike Rawls' theory, however, it does not isolate these desires by a criterion independent of its own procedure. Rawls' theory poses two problems of justification. Firstly, there is the problem of justification of its procedure for deciding right and wrong. Secondly, there is the problem of justification for its limiting the scope of these procedures to some desires rather than others. Impartialism has only the first of these problems. Impartialism, then, has the virtue of utilitarianism in that it deals directly with desires rather than needing some other, possibly suspect, alternative such as primary goods. It has also the virtue of Rawls' hypothetical contractarianism in that it is a consequence of impartialism that certain desires are morally reprehensible in themselves.

7.10   Relative Intensity

Impartialism, like utilitarianism, only discriminates between wants in terms of relative intensity or, possibly, Bentham's related criteria such as duration, propinquity, fecundity, etcetera. As we have seen, it does not reject certain principles because they fail to meet the formal constraints of the concept of right and it differs radically from utilitarianism in how it deals with the relative intensity of desires.

It is concerned with the relative intensity of the desires to coerce and not to be coerced but it doesn't measure Ann's desire not to be coerced against Ben's desire to coerce. It then requires that principles which rely on Ann's desire to coerce being greater than her desire not to be coerced be eliminated from the calculations. Whether or not the principles it eventually arrives at could not give rise to implications that could conscientiously be endorsed is best tested by seeing what implications for action its principles actually do have. This test would also meet Barry's third point.

Stronger objections than the ones Barry lists to wants as the basis for calculating which acts to do are needed before they constitute grounds for rejecting impartialism merely because it does use wants rather than primary goods as its basis for calculation. I haven't so much rebutted these objections to wants as the basis of calculation of the right as shown that impartialism bypasses them. They are objections that are met by producing a theory that does the kinds of things the objections suggest can't be done.

It is also the case that impartialism bypasses the problems utilitarianism faces with the 'interpersonal commensurability of utilities'. It judges principles in terms of the intensity of Ann's desire not to be coerced against the intensity of the desire to coerce of the same person. If the latter is greater than the former, then there is no problem of comparing Ann's preference to coerce with Ben's preference not to be coerced because impartialism has excluded Ann's preference from any consideration in the determination of principles for resolving conflicts of desires.

None of the above is to deny that there is much of value in the notion of primary goods. As we have seen, the parties in the position of equal power will treat certain primary goods as of supreme importance - namely those rights and liberties that I have called the basic or enabling liberties. The other primary goods that Rawls mentions, such things as opportunities and powers, income, wealth and a sense of self-worth cannot be shown to the kinds of things that any rational person (say, Ann) would want because possessors of these goods are always advantaged in the satisfaction of their desires regardless of what these desires may be. It is always possible to devise scenarios in which Ann, say, is better off with less of one of these primary good than with more, as it is with the natural primary goods such as health. Wealth, for example, can get you killed in a proletarian revolution, or if you are the victim of kidnappers. Health can get you conscripted into the army whereas being a cripple may save your life. Thomas Mann, for example, by the end of his novel *Dr Faustus*, has made it comprehensible that his main character, Adrian Leverkuhn, could so want to be a composer of genius that he would deliberately infect himself with syphilis because he thought genius of the relevant kind could only be obtained through madness.

Rawls (p.72) suggests that natural primary goods such as intelligence, vigour, health and imagination are less directly under the control of the basic structure of society than the social primary goods. While this is true, there is much that a community can do to improve the intelligence, vigour, health and imagination of its citizens. Not only can these be improved by government policies on public housing and public health, they can also be improved by policies on education and assistance to families. When it comes to social planning of this kind, especially with respect to children,, it seems to me that the parties in the position of equal power would give the non-liberty primary goods, whether social or natural, an important place in their deliberations. This is because, in anticipating what will the qualities that a child needs to develop to get the most out of his or her life, we cannot assume that they will have one set of goals rather than another. We must seek to develop those aspects of character and personality that will most assist them to achieve their goals whatever those goals may be or, if this is not entirely possible for the reasons just given, to achieve those goals that a suitably thorough empirical study of the human situation suggests they are most likely to pursue. This last point, however, needs to be treated with caution. In providing children with an education that meets this last point, we should not render them incapable of choosing goals other than those most common to humanity as a whole, that is, they should remain autonomous agents, ones who possess person-freedom as well as interests-freedom.

Gerald Dworkin, however, suggests that it may well be the case that there are goals that should be ruled out of court. Rawls, he argues, only reaches the liberal conclusions he does, particularly about matters of religion, because he assumes that there is no religious truth to be found. If it were the case that some religious claims were true and others false then it may well turn out to be the case that some religious doctrines, and the goals they legitimate, are heretical and should be suppressed. This raises questions about the epistemological underpinnings of contractarian theories. In the next chapter, I will use Dworkin's criticisms of Rawls to sketch out some elements of an impartialist theory of knowledge.

8 Impartialist Epistemology and Religious Truth

8.1   Introduction

Gerald Dworkin (p.139) claims that many of the substantive conclusions that Rawls reaches depend on implicit and controversial assumptions that are incorporated into his theory in a non-obvious way. In particular, he argues that Rawls' theory entails religious tolerance only because it assumes justified true belief in religious matters is not possible.

In this chapter I will argue that impartialism does not make this assumption, even if Rawls does. In addition, I will look at how the impartialist axioms can be applied to epistemological questions to produce resolutions of conflicts of desires over what to believe, for example, if Ann wants Ben's belief about some matter to be suppressed, what kinds of reasons would be unacceptable.

8.2   Dworkin's Criticisms

While Rawls' contractors know nothing which enables them to identify their real life counterparts, they do have knowledge of the general laws of science and human behaviour. Under such circumstances, Rawls believes, they will contract to prefer religious tolerance to intolerance. Dworkin (p.138) claims that this preference can only be deduced from the original position if it is assumed that the parties know or believe that justified true belief in religious matters is impossible. To show that this is so, he postulates that the parties behind the veil of ignorance all believe that redheads know the truth in religious matters. If this is so, then, Dworkin thinks, the parties behind the veil of ignorance may well contract to prefer religious intolerance over tolerance. In doing so they would not be showing bias because they would be giving preference to the true or highly

168

probable. They would not consider their integrity to be damaged by the suppression of false views if the truth on a matter could be ascertained.

8.3 The Relevance of Dworkin's Criticisms to Impartialist Theory

8.3.1 Dworkin's Non-Sequitur

Dworkin (p.138) postulates that the parties behind the Rawlsian veil of ignorance know that redheads have religious truth. If this is so, then, he believes, it would be rational to make redheads into authorities with the right to suppress false views. He gives us the first premise of an argument, namely,

(a) It is not biased to give preference to the true.

From this premise he derives the conclusion:-

(b) Redheads have the right to suppress false views.

This conclusion only seems to follow if Dworkin treats 'giving preference to the true' as identical to 'suppressing false views'. If this identity is made, then the argument would go through given the minor premise (2) below. The full argument, then, becomes:-

(1) It is not biased to give preference to the true (suppress false views).

(2) Redheads have the right to suppress whatever it is not biased to suppress.

Therefore:-

(3) Redheads have the right to suppress false views (give preference to the true).

It is by no means obvious, however, that giving preference to the true and suppressing the false are identical. A utilitarian, for example, who only values truth as a means to happiness may feel that someone who insists without argument that happiness-producing falsity must be suppressed while unhappiness-producing truth need not be thereby shows distinct signs of bias. Using impartialist arguments we can see further difficulties with this supposed identity.

8.3.2 A Provisional Impartialist Argument

In Dworkin's opinion, people behind the veil of ignorance who know that redheads have the truth, would contract to suppress all views that disagreed with redhead views. We can express the principle by which they would act as:-

(4) Suppress all false (non-redhead) views.

From an impartialist point of view, however, Dworkin's rider that the people behind the veil of ignorance know that redheads have the truth is a problem. The impartialist position is unconditional. All principles are open to dispute. Only if this is so are we in a position to say that the principles eventually contracted for are really person-neutral, respecting the integrity of each moral agent, considering all their interests equally. Nonetheless, we can discover whether or not people are impartialists by seeing how they would argue given common assumptions. If all parties are presumed to know something to be true, they will reach certain contracts about which symmetrical principles they will obey. A person who refuses to obey these, even though he or she accepts the common assumption, will not be impartialist. Those who do obey them will also obey whatever new contracts would eventuate were the common assumption shown to be unfounded. We can therefore operate on the basis of a provisional impartialism, remembering that the conclusions we reach only hold as long as our conditional assumption isn't challenged.

Given Dworkin's condition, then, the grounds on which we oppose the suppression of false views can't be that the freedom to express all views, including false ones, maximises the likelihood of the truth emerging. The truth already has emerged as far as all the parties are concerned. What other kinds of grounds might we have for opposing the suppression of false views?

8.3.3 The 'Error' Principle

Suppose there is a conflict of desires between Ann and Ben such that Ann wanted to suppress Ben's views just because she thinks them false. She is therefore operating on the principle 'Suppress all views that Ann believes false'. Impartialism, however, will only accept this principle if it can be meaningfully symmetrified. Meaningfully symmetrified, it becomes, 'Ann is to be free to suppress whichever of Ben's view that she thinks false if Ben is free to suppress whichever of her views he thinks false'. Ann and Ben would only accept this symmetrified principle, however, if they were coercionists. If Ann wanted not to be coerced by Ben more than she wanted to coerce him, then she would rather that those of Ben's views she considered false were not suppressed than run the risk that those of her views that Ben considered false were suppressed.

The impartialist axioms, then, lead us to the conclusion that it is not a reason to suppress someone else's views that you think them false. This I will call the 'error' principle.

The Error Principle:- *It is not a reason in itself to suppress someone's opinion that you think it false.*

8.3.4 The 'De Gustibus' Principle

Suppose Ann merely wants to suppress Ben's views because she doesn't like them. She is operating on the principle 'Suppress any views Ann doesn't like'. Meaningfully symmetrified, this becomes, 'If Ann is to be free to suppress views that she doesn't like, then so is Ben'. Ann and Ben would only accept this symmetrified principle if they were coercionists. As a noncoercionist Ann would rather be free to express views that Ben doesn't like than to be free to suppress Ben's views that she doesn't like at the risk of having her own views suppressed instead.

The impartialist axioms, then, lead us to the conclusion that it is not a reason to suppress someone else's views just because you don't like them. In fact, this can be extended to the conclusion that it is not a reason in itself to suppress anything anyone else wants to do that you don't like it. This is an application of what I called the 'degustibus principle' in Chapter 5.

8.4   The 'Self-Protection' Argument

If rational agents risked their desires not being satisfied as a result of false views not being suppressed, then they would all contract to suppress false views. Is it true, however, that not suppressing false views poses this threat? Often, in the real situation, we risk frustrating our desires by acting on a false view we believe to be true. Dworkin, however, has ruled out this way of frustrating desires because everyone knows the truth. Any rational agents, then, who know the truth yet act in accord with what is false either have acted irrationally or else are satisfying their desires by choosing to do what they know is based on a false claim.

People, however, who are satisfying their desires by acting on a claim they know to be false will not contract to be bound to suppress false views, so an argument is needed to show why it is not acceptable under impartialist conditions to satisfy one's desires by acting on what one knows are false claims. This is the utilitarian consideration raised earlier. I will not provide such an argument here but merely point out that one is needed if the false is to be suppressed on the 'self-protection' ground, given Dworkin's condition.

Rational agents only act irrationally by acting in accord with the false if thereby they frustrate their desires. By acting irrationally they act in contradiction to what is definitionally required for them to be a rational agent, that is, a maximiser of desire-satisfaction. In the example being discussed here our rational agent (say, Ben) is presumably contemplating a future case where he ceases to be rational. He knows the truth, he knows that acting in accord with it will maximise his desire-satisfaction, yet he suffers irrational urges to act in accord with the false. It is by no means clear that suppressing the false will remove this problem unless the availability of false views is the cause of his irrational urges. This would be a rare case.

It is only in this situation that a rational agent might contract to suppress the false for self-protection. Even in this kind of situation, however, a rational agent would impose stringent conditions on the circumstances under which he would allow the false to be suppressed. Firstly, he would require that those who suppressed the false for his benefit always had his agreement that their idea of the true coincided with his own. After all, the case we are discussing is one where everyone knows the truth but some people are irrationally acting contrary to it. The whole case changes if there is disagreement about what is true or false.

Given that everyone agrees on the true, and continues to agree throughout on what is the truth, then rational agents will agree in advance that, should they be caused to act irrationally by exposure to the false, then either they will have the false suppressed or else they will have treatment that eliminates their irrational urge to act on the false.

It is clear, however, that this agreement depends entirely on there being no disagreement on the true. In the real situation this is a highly implausible assumption. Moreover, from the impartialist point of view, the absence of actual disagreement is irrelevant. Someone always could disagree. An unprovisional impartialist argument would need to accommodate this possibility. The fact that a person would abide by the principles contracted for under Dworkin's condition shows that they are impartialists but does not show that the principles they have contracted for are properly person-neutral.

8.5   Aquinas' Argument

Rawls believes that his two principles of justice are incompatible with Aquinas' argument for the death penalty for heretics. Aquinas claims that, as corrupting the soul is far graver than counterfeiting money, yet counterfeiters are punished by death, then likewise, heretics, who corrupt the soul, should be punished by death. Rawls rejects this argument because it cannot be established by commonly recognised modes of argument. Dworkin (p.136), however, thinks that Rawls dismisses too quickly the possibility that it is true that heretics corrupt the soul and that, if they do so, then this deserves the death penalty. Dworkin wishes the arguments we have discussed earlier to show that Rawls cannot so easily dismiss Aquinas' view.

The problem, however, is that, once we accept Dworkin's condition that everyone knows the truth, there are no heretics. There may be heresies, in that people may postulate false views for discussion purposes, but no heretics in the sense of people who believe the heresies to be true. The corrupting influence, therefore, has to be the heresy. The heresy, however, corrupts by making someone cease to believe what is true, which immediately alters Dworkin's conditions. Once someone doubts the redhead view, a contract needs to be established on how doubts are to be removed.

While Dworkin's conditions continue to obtain, there seems to be no reason for banning the heresy, other than a fear that the mere existence of the heresy will lead to a situation where Dworkin's conditions don't obtain. As rational agents, however, people will not come to believe the heresy unless they have good reasons for thinking they will thereby maximise their desire-satisfaction. Consequently, rational agents have nothing to fear by the availability of the heresy. While they know that redheads have the truth, they will not frustrate their desires by acting contrary to the truth, therefore heresy doesn't need to be suppressed.

The only exception here is the one mentioned in the previous section. This, however, can be met if the person (say Ann) who knows she will act irrationally, agrees to have her own access to the heresy suppressed rather than suppressing everyone's. As rational agents, other people will want minimum restriction on their freedom. Restricting their access to heresies just to prevent Ann's irrationality would only be acceptable if it protected the maximising of their values. On the other hand, if Ann comes to think that redheads' views are false, she will not have the supposed heresies suppressed at all.

8.6   The 'Disapproval of Goals' Problem

It may be that you know a view to be true, for example, let's assume that promiscuity leads to eternal damnation. Even knowing this, you may like being promiscuous so much that you are prepared to suffer damnation. In a case like this you are not corrupted by false views.

Rather, you know the truth about how to get eternal salvation, but your values are such that you value eternal salvation less than present pleasures. Here you have not frustrated your desires by a false belief, so being exposed to false views to the effect that promiscuity is compatible with salvation does not lead you to behave as you do. Other people may dislike your preference but, as rational agents, none of you will contract to prevent such a preference solely on the grounds of dislike. This is the degustibus principle we discussed earlier. It will have to be shown that even you are committed to a higher order principle which rules out this preference.

8.7   Impartialist Epistemology

So far we have operated as if Dworkin's condition applied. We have assumed that everyone knows that redheads had religious truth. Even with this assumption we have seen that it is very difficult to find a case where 'Suppress all false (non-redhead) views' is acceptable under impartialist conditions. While it may not be biased to prefer the truth, in the sense of your preferring to believe what is true, it can be biased to suppress the false. Forcing people to believe only the true is prima facie a case of bias in favour of valuing truth over all values that might conflict with it, such as happiness or equality. It is only justified if valuing truth over all other values is what rational agents would contract to do when equal on all advantaging characteristics. Although I will not argue for it here, I believe rational agents would contract to encourage people to develop a disposition to prefer the true to the false but they would not actually suppress the false. Be this as it may, Dworkin has not shown that Rawls' deduction of religious tolerance depends on scepticism about religious truth. My argument has shown that, even if everyone agreed on religious truth, there would be no need for the universal suppression of the false.

Of course, if it is the case that all false views are corrupting, this would no longer hold, and it is possibly this kind of case that Dworkin most has in mind. As I indicated earlier, this kind of claim has its problems, in that Dworkin's conditions only continue to hold while the claim remains false, that is, once someone is corrupted by a false belief it is no longer the case that everyone knows that redheads have religious truth.

If Dworkin's case is not invalidated by this apparent paradox, then he has shown that Rawls' deduction of religious tolerance is a provisional one. It is sound only if religious knowledge is not attainable. To render it unprovisional, Rawls needs to show that his contractors would contract to regard religious knowledge as unattainable. Rather than use Rawls' system, I will show that impartialist theory produces an epistemology which is sceptical about religious belief.

8.8   Intuition versus Knowledge

Rational agents will, as I indicated before, want as few restrictions as possible on their freedom to satisfy their desires, so they will need to be convinced that their desire-satisfaction is maximised by their adopting true beliefs rather than false ones. This, however, is not difficult to do in the area of beliefs about what is causally efficacious in maximising their desire-satisfaction. A person (say, Ben) is more likely to maximise his desire-satisfaction if he acts in accord with true rather than false beliefs about the means of satisfying those desires. Consequently, any rational agent whatsoever will want to have true beliefs about the means of satisfying his desires, even if he is indifferent about the truth of any other beliefs he might hold. Any rational agent, then, will want to maximise the likelihood that he lives in a society which educates him in such a way as to maximise his chance of recognising this truth when he sees it, as well as maximising his disposition to find it. When people propose criteria of truth, then, he will want to arrive at the best criteria, at least as far as the true means to maximising his desire-satisfaction are concerned. These criteria will have to be relevant to the purpose of having true beliefs, that is, they will have to indicate the likelihood that a belief about the nature of the world matches, or corresponds to, how the world actually is. Unless the criteria satisfactorily do this, a rational agent as such need have no special interest in them.

Ben might propose that the truth of a belief be determined by his having an 'intuition'. The word 'intuition' here covers such publicly unverifiable items as faith, revelation, visions, dreams, mystical experiences. A rational agent will only accept this criterion if he thought there was good reason to believe that how he felt reality to be corresponded with how reality actually was. (The only reality we are concerned with here is the reality of means to satisfying desires.) This will be true even if the agent advocates the criterion himself. He will want his own intuitions to give him accurate guidance to the true means for satisfying his desires. If the agent is not the advocate of the criteria he will want some way of determining when its advocate's intuition is a reliable guide. Just because the advocate feels that reality is of a particular kind is no guarantee that it is. Both parties, then, as rational agents, will want to be able to check the advocate's feelings against the world itself in some way.

There appears to be only one plausible candidate for such a checking procedure, and this is observation of the world. Observation, however, will not he enough because the causes at work in the world may not be directly observable. Claims about such causes will need also to be checked against the world in some way, presumably by predicting observable consequences of there being such unobserved entities. This will mean proposing theories. Theories, however, will only be able to be the basis of action if we act as if their past predictive successes are a reliable guide to future predictive successes. [1]

By doing so, we are not making the unjustified assumption that the future will be like the past. Rather, we are adopting the only strategy available to us if we are to plan our lives so as to maximise our desire-satisfaction. If the universe is totally random in that its past behaviour bears no relation to future behaviour, then there can be no person-independent basis for preferring one causal hypothesis to another. These criteria combined suggest that a rational agent will prefer that theory which correctly predicts how the widest range of things will behave, as determined by repeatable observation. His main interest in modifying a theory will be to increase its predictive success rate. In so far, then, as Ben is interested in the true causes of public phenomena, he is bound to use empirical truth-criteria of the kind just described. Of course, there is still considerable controversy about empirical truth-criteria, as the continuing debate about the views of Hume, Winch and Feyerbend shows.

From the impartialist point of view, however, this is not a problem. If those who deny the empirical criteria just described at the level of philosophical debate in fact use them in their choice of means to ends, then their challenge to these criteria as a basis for action is purely speculative. A provisional impartialist argument will suffice against them, because they hold to these criteria for all practical purposes. It is not good enough, for example, for a creationist to make a last ditch assault on the truth of evolutionary theory by appealing to unresolved disputes in the philosophy of science if his or her own everyday actions are most adequately interpreted as based on the very same criteria by which evolution is to be preferred to creation. All he or she can do is investigate the empirical evidence to see whether new evidence changes the picture.

What then of the person (say, Ann) who doesn't just philosophically challenge the status of these truth-criteria but who refuses to live her life in accord with them, like Pyrrho, the Greek sceptic who refused to draw inductive conclusions from falling down a cliff, or being hit by a cart or bitten by a dog? Even Pyrrho, presumably, was inductivist enough not to starve himself to death as a result of scepticism about the efficacy of eating. There may, however, be someone sufficiently serious about their scepticism to do so. Such a person could not meaningfully participate in an argument about whether some arrangement is causally more effective in favouring one person's values rather than another's. The parties in such an argument must at least have those beliefs in common that are necessary to get such an argument going at all. They must believe communication is possible, that commitments can be honoured, and so on.

This doesn't show that the sceptic's view is false but merely that those who engage in the kind of argument that is the subject of this debate have thereby committed themselves to personally regarding scepticism of this kind as false. This is all that is needed to proceed with an evaluation of the arguments that they then produce about what ought to be done in the realm of values. How, then, does all this relate to religious tolerance?

Suppose that Ann proposes that it is a good enough reason to suppress Ben's belief that she has an intuition that it is false. This means she advocates the principle 'Suppress whichever of Ben's beliefs that Ann has an intuition is false'. This is similar to the case where Ben's belief was to be suppressed because Ann believed it to be false but she is claiming her intuition as a source of knowledge of greater authority than a mere belief. Symmetrified, this becomes, 'Ann is to be free to suppress any of Ben's beliefs that she intuits is false and Ben is to be free to suppress any of her beliefs that he intuits to be false'. The outcome is the same as the Error Principle. Impartialists will not accept intuition that someone's belief is false as a reason to suppress it.

Unless religious beliefs can be tested by criteria that do not turn out merely to be some person's private opinion, unless they are testable by public repeatable criteria, then rational agents under impartialist conditions will not agree to require adherence to them. After all, these criteria do manage to produce orthodoxy in science. The claim that the attractive power of bodies diminishes according to the inverse square of their distance from each other is as certain a claim as any, and is taught as true in schools and universities. It is not taught as merely the opinion of some groups of scientists.

There is no reason, in principle, then, why public repeatable criteria could not produce the same kind of certainty in religious matters, so there is no need for impartialism to assume in advance of such an investigation that religious beliefs will turn out to be unprovable. If it does turn out to be unprovable on the basis of public criteria, then, for the reasons already given, the parties in the position of equal power will oppose religious intolerance. Even if it does turn out to be provable, it has still to be shown why heresy in religion should not be as equally tolerated as heresy in science. After all, those who continue to believe that the earth is flat or that evolution is false are not hunted done and executed, even if they are not taken seriously. What makes it important to religious believers to suppress heretics is often their disagreement with heretics over moral matters rather than over matters of empirical or metaphysical fact. Disagreements over moral matters are, at least, conflicts of desires, so their resolution is the province of the parties in a position of equal power.

The religious and scientific epistemological issues we have just discussed suggest the question of what, if anything, impartialism has to say about epistemology in general. One important application of theories about what we can know is in the justification of what ought to be taught to the young people of a society. In the next chapter I will take up the issue of what knowledge, if any, impartialists would expect to be acquired by the children of a liberal democratic society and whether or not they would insist that it be taught as part of a compulsory education. As a framework within which to place the discussion, I will use the taxonomy of knowledge proposed by Paul H. Hirst in his paper 'Liberal Education and the Nature of Knowledge.'

Note

1   A useful overview of the contemporary state of the debate in philosophy of science over induction can be found in Couvalis. I will not enter in the debate in this book but do make some remarks on the justification of scientific practice in Chapter 9.

9 Impartialist Education

9.1   Introduction

Hirst argued that knowledge could be exhaustively divided into seven distinct forms, each with its own unique concepts, distinctive logical structure, testability against experience and unique methods of testing. The seven forms he proposed were mathematics, the physical sciences, the human sciences, history, religion, literature and the fine arts as one form, and philosophy and moral (including political) knowledge as another. However, rather than using Hirst's proposal as a classification of forms of knowledge I will use it to separate out logical distinct kinds of belief. If it is taken as a categorisation of kinds of 'knowledge' then we have to be convinced that the entities çentral to the category actually exist and that there are effective procedures for determining which claims within that category are true or false but this is highly contentious. After all, if there is no God, or no after-life, or no such power in the universe as karma, that is, if there are no supernatural entities at all, then all religious claims are false and so religion cannot be a form of knowledge. Likewise, what exactly is 'known' in the study of literature and the fine arts, or in philosophy and morality, and what reliable test procedures do these disciplines have for separating the true from the false? (For detailed discussion of these issues see Barrow, 1976; Pring, 1976; Watt, 1974.)

Nonetheless, these seven disciplines can be regarded as an exhaustive list of 'putative' forms of knowledge in that they cover all the kinds of claim in which a person might pretend to a knowledge-based authority or expertise. Every belief falls under one of them. They are, in effect, 'modes of believing'. The natural sciences, for example, cover all beliefs about things, including humans, viewed as physical systems. The social sciences cover all beliefs about things, especially humans, in so far as they are intentional systems whose behaviour is explicable in terms of such notions as desire, consciousness and rationality. History covers all beliefs about the human past. Religion deals with beliefs about the

180

supernatural. Mathematics deals with beliefs about number and pattern. Philosophy and morality deal with beliefs about how we ought to act and what we ought to accept as true. I will take up the province of literature and the fine arts later but either the beliefs they deal with fall under one of the other six modes or else they provide us with a seventh distinct domain.

If one, then, wished to manipulate the beliefs of other people for some political or other goal, all the beliefs one might try to manipulate would be in one of these areas. In particular, one will want to ensure that people are prevented from investigating the epistemological status of the beliefs by which one is manipulating them. This is because the success of one's exploiting others depends on their holding as true either a belief that could be shown to be false if they knew how to test it or, alternatively, a belief that can be shown to be neither true nor false because there is no genuine test for its content. If people are able to investigate the epistemological status of the claims that underpin one's exploitative activities, and they are inclined to act on the results of such an investigation, then one's power to exploit them reduces or disappears. If one could hide from people the epistemological status of each of these seven modes of believing then one would be well-placed to manipulate their beliefs so that they accepted one's political, religious or whatever ideal.

Why, however, would the parties in the position of equal power wish to eliminate manipulatory practices from any state-supported education of the young? After all, it will involve placing limitations on the freedom of teachers and parents to have their taxes used to teach what they believe is important. It will deny certain religious and cultural groups government support in moulding young minds with ideas central to the values of these groups. As we have seen, the parties in the position of equal power have an initial tendency to agree to whichever is the option that maximises freedom. What grounds are there for overriding this prima facie principle in the case of public education?

The answer to this lies in the fact that the parties in the position of equal power are also noncoercionists. They want to not to be coerced more than they want to be free to coerce others. The freedom that matters most to them is the freedom from submission to the arbitrary will of others. What needs to be shown, if limitations are to be placed on what can be taught as part of state-funded compulsory education is that the loss of freedom involved in a restricted curriculum prevents an even greater loss of freedom in more important areas of life, especially in terms of basic or enabling rights. Now, we run the risk of such a loss of important freedoms if children grow up suspicious of, and hostile to, anyone who is not a member of their particular religious or cultural group because their parents have kept them locked away in isolated communities that preach fear and distrust of non-members. This risk can be overcome if children are required to attend school, provided the schools themselves teach the right subjects in the right way. I suggested above that the seven disciplines that Hirst identified cover all the different kinds of belief that people may wish to manipulate. While it is not necessary that these disciplines be the particular subjects that are taught in schools, the school curriculum, however organised, should raise the kinds of questions central to these disciplines that I discuss below.

Before I look at the curriculum, however, I would like to briefly address the question of whether what I have to say about the curriculum should apply to all schools or only to state-funded ones. The problem, really, is whether the parties in the position of equal power would exempt private schools from the requirements placed on government schools. Ann, as a person in a position of equal power, would not consent to her taxes in the real world being used to fund schools where children were taught to hate or despise or seek to humiliate or divest of their basic and enabling rights or their civil liberties members of the groups to which Ann herself belongs. The symmetry principle requires her to apply this principle to those schools that do the same to groups to which she does not belong. In fact, the same considerations suggest that she would want such practices banned in all schools, whether government-funded or not. However, in so far as the doctrines of different religious or cultural groups could be taught without inciting racial hatred, gender bias, disregard for the civil liberties of others, then these could be taught in non-government schools, provided these schools covered the essential components of the curriculum described below. It is possible that the parties in the position of equal power might even allow non-government schools to impart a parochial education, provided there were good reasons to believe that the children would exposed to a sufficiently pluralist environment outside of school to overcome the bigotries and prejudices that might otherwise result.

An auxillary issue is whether or not the parties in a position of equal power would allow non-government schools at all. As with other matters, the parties will want the onus of proof to be on those who wish to ban an option. It would have to be plausibly argued that permitting non-government schools would put people in general in greater danger of coercion than banning them. As banning something already involves coercion, this would need to be compensated for in the gain in security that outlawing private schools would achieve. It is, however, by no means obvious that the existence of private schools, in itself, increases the long-term risk of increased coercion from a graduate body that is intolerant and aggressive. Even if there is such a risk, strategies less severe than a ban are preferable, such as public criteria that private schools (and government ones, for that matter) need to meet - criteria that are effectively policed by some kind of inspection system itself open to public scrutiny.

9.2   The Non-Manipulative Curriculum

9.2.1   *The Science Curriculum*

Scientific claims, as we have seen, have to do with the behaviour of bodies regarded as physical systems. As a rule, they involve law-like generalisations and hypotheses to the effect that some theoretical entity explains the generalisation. How would the parties in a position of equal power arbitrate between a conflict of desires over which of a number of competing scientific claims should be taught in schools and universities? This depends on what the purpose of teaching such claims might be. There are two broad purposes to be considered here. One is that the claims be taught as part of a general programme to get students exposed to the truest available picture of the world. Alternative purposes would be those that have some other, non-truth oriented aim, for example, teaching whichever claim most suits some political or religious ideology.

Ann, say, as a rational agent, will not want Ben to manipulate her so that she believes false claims if these claims serve his interests or causes at the expense of hers. In fact, in so far as she wants to adopt whichever course of action in any instance is the best means to her goal of the moment or to her overall life goals, she will want to base her choice of course of action on the relevant claims that are most likely to be true. As a consequence, she will want to be equipped with the best techniques for identifying those claims most likely to be true, either by herself doing the research that establishes likely truth or by knowing what it is that makes for expertise on the subject and how to identify which groups have the relevant reliable authority. As this is what she wants for herself, the symmetry requirement means that any principle which gives it to her must give it universally, so these factors will be the ones relevant to the content of a truth-oriented science curriculum. A science curriculum oriented towards the dissemination of any particular ideology would be ruled out by the fact that those parties with a different ideology would not agree to it. The least coercive option for them all is the truth-oriented curriculum. Moreover, it is the one that most respects each of them as an autonomous rational agent.

Current scientific practice provides a model of techniques aimed at maximising the discovery of truth. Hypotheses and theories are open to public scrutiny because of their essentially empirical or observational nature.

Testable predictions are postulated as consequences of the claims. These are tested by a range of public and repeatable procedures such as experimentation, epidemiological surveys and so on. These are published in journals vetted by established experts in the area in order to ensure that only work that is cognisant of basic procedures and the latest research receives the attention of the scientific community. Textbooks are compiled from such research and chosen by university staff who themselves have passed through examinations and other forms of checking to establish their competence in the field, and so on. The nature of all of these arrangements seem to be warranted either by the pursuit of truth or by the need to narrow the material examined in the pursuit of truth to the most promising candidates. Of course, there is always the possibility that such structures may be corrupted by external factors in particular cases but it is difficult to see what systems different from these might be put in their place if the pursuit of truth is their purpose, although there may well be ways in which this system might be refined and improved.

The implication of the above for schooling is that science should be taught both as a set of processes and as a body of knowledge. It needs to be taught as a set of processes so that children come to understand the source of the authority of scientists. They need to engage in making hypotheses and eliminating those that fail to pass appropriately designed tests. However, this kind of 'discovery' or 'enquiry' approach cannot teach them the body of scientific knowledge that is crucial to the kind of scientific literacy that minimises superstitious judgements about matters of political significance. The children also need to be introduced to the most comprehensive picture that science has to offer of the kind of universe we leave in and the major causes at work within it. This picture needs to be the one that has the support of the vast majority of research scientists in the field, otherwise teachers are misrepresenting to children the status of what they are told.

As a contrary approach, consider the one that Plato offers in *The Republic*. His general approach there is such that he would try to restrict scientific understanding to people who had shown their loyalty to his political ideal by having passed through an exhaustive selection process designed to identify those most likely to perpetuate the system of values he has set in place. Even if those who are going to be rulers eventually come to realise that what they thought were scientific truths were in fact lies, they would only have been allowed to become rulers because they were the kinds of people who would accept the need for the Noble Lie to preserve their ideal in power. Plato, then, sees the method for obtaining his political ideal to be an 'indoctrinatory' one which plays on the ability of rational people to form beliefs on the basis of evidence by manipulating the evidence, by controlling all aspects of the information flow so that the people appear to themselves to be arriving at independent rational beliefs that bind them to obedience to the rulers.

Rousseau, in the *Emile*, offers another contrast. He criticises Plato's approach on the grounds that the wrong information is too likely to get out among the masses. If it does, and they are still able to think for themselves, they might reject what their leaders have told them and so come to reject the ideal that Rousseau favours. What Rousseau wants to do instead is to change people's desires so that their overwhelming desire is to obey the laws of the rulers because they have come to see these laws as inescapable in much the same way as laws of nature. This will lead them to limit their desires in the same way as we limit our desires to what is possible within the laws of nature, for example, by not trying to fly without mechanical aids. If they do this, then it will not matter that they discover that the science they had been taught was false because they would want to maintain the political system more than they wanted to believe the truth. What is crucial, however, is that they are not allowed to reason about what makes scientific claims true or false before their conditioning has had effect. [1]

9.2.2   *The Human Sciences Curriculum*

Hirst included the human sciences in his list. This includes such things as psychology, economics, sociology, possibly anthropology. These are sciences in that they try to find law-like generalisations about human behaviour or to give theoretical explanations of that behaviour. Such claims are tested by hypothesising what agents will do under particular circumstances, given a particular account of rationality. They are tested by observation to eliminate alternative hypotheses. Such claims can be used to foster political ideals advantaging one section of the community at the expense of others, as in the claims about the IQs of Negroes, women and the working class. The parties in the position of equal power would be truth-oriented about such claims for the same reasons as given for science and history. It should be noted, with respect to the human sciences, that where a theory of society embodies a particular contentious set of values as one of the parameters by which it explains society, then that theory should not be treated as the truth of the matter. Examples that come to mind are such theories as Marxism, Critical Theory, feminist theory, post-structuralist theory. Suppose, for example, such a theory explains the operation of science in our society in terms of science serving the interests of capitalism. There are many thinkers who believe that such a theory should be taught as part of the science curriculum. However, students must first be taught some criteria for evaluating such theories, as well as having had a solid grounding in science itself. They need to think about what kind of evidence would enable us to arbitrate between this theory, say, and theories that see science as driven by internal, knowledge-based factors. To treat a particular theory of society as a given in one's examination of social institutions is to mislead students about the actual state of play amongst researchers in the field. It is seeking to bias them in favour of one's own set of values.

9.2.3   The Mathematics Curriculum

The scope for manipulation in mathematics is less obvious than in the sciences but, even there, the approach adopted by the parties in a position of equal power would be a truth-oriented one, for the reasons given earlier, although the criteria for truth will not be the empirical ones to be found in science. Nonetheless, children should be taught mathematics in such a way as they understand the evidence for mathematical claims so that they are in a position to appreciate what it is that makes someone an expert on mathematical questions. Again, the mathematics taught to them in schools should be anchored in the consensus of the mathematical community as to its truth.

9.2.4   The History Curriculum

In the case of history we are dealing with claims about what happened in the past or explanations of what happened. They are tested, in part, by empirical observation in much the same way as with science in that hypotheses, usually in the form of narratives, are formed on the basis of the residues that the past has left behind such as documents and artefacts. These hypotheses are, again in part, testable in terms of whether or not further documents and artefacts discovered in the future are the ones we would expect to find if the narrative were true. If one wishes to get people to adopt a particular political or religious or whatever ideal, then teaching false beliefs about the past may be effective, as may ensuring that they do not have the opportunity to consider the epistemological status of historical claims. Illiberal regimes often try to legitimate their power with mythical accounts of the past, as with apartheid South Africa or communist Russia. Winston Smith, in Orwell's *1984*, helps Big Brother exploit the citizens by his re-writes of history in the Ministry of Truth. This is precisely the kind of Noble Lie that Plato would have supported when he recommended that Homer's stories of disgraceful acts of the heroes of the past be censored. Rousseau, too, wished to control the beliefs that children obtained from history by eliminating it from the curriculum altogether. He advises this because he thinks that history provides children with contrasting models of human behaviour, encouraging them to think about right and wrong in terms other those acceptable to the rulers, leading them to challenge the teacher to justify why one model is better than another instead of just experiencing the model made available by the rulers to be as natural and inescapable as the law of gravity.

Impartialists however, would deal quite differently with cases that amount to conflicts of desire over what to teach about the past. As we saw in the case of science, a person such as Ann in the position of equal power will want to be free in the real world of manipulation by Ben of her beliefs about the past to serve his ends at the expense of hers. She will want him to engage in the exercise of belief-changing by using techniques whose purpose is to select beliefs on the basis of their truth. In schools, this will mean getting children to make hypotheses about the past and to suggest what residues they might be able to find that would support or disprove a particular narrative. This would have to be limited to claims they had the resources to check for themselves. With respect to more remote historical narratives, they would have to rely on the researches of scholars but, at least, their own efforts at research would have led them to understand what warranted regarding one person rather than another as an authority on a particular aspect of the past. Again, teachers would have a responsibility to present to the children as the most authoritative account of some event the one that most scholars in the field supported. To do otherwise would be to give one's own opinions an unjustified status, as would getting the children to think that the children themselves were well placed to form a contrary opinion

9.2.5   *The Religion Curriculum*

Religious claims, in so far as they are not subsumable under historical or scientific claims, are claims about the supernatural. While empirical methods may be able to establish that the events important to any particular religion may have happened, they do not seem able to arbitrate between competing religious theories as to which supernatural entity or power best explains a phenomenon. While an individual may be an expert in the doctrines of a religion, he or she cannot be an expert or authority in whether or not those doctrines are true. A person such as Ann will not want her beliefs about supernatural matters manipulated by Ben for his benefit at her expense. She will want him, instead, to offer arguments to her in terms of the truth of such claims, arguments that appeal to evidence available to both of them, not merely that appeals to experiences private to himself. The result of this, as far as what can be compulsorily taught to children, is that religion cannot be treated like science or history. It cannot be taught as if there are people in the community who really are experts or authorities in the truth of religious doctrine, that is, it cannot be taught 'confessionally'. Instead, schools would need to teach *about* religions in a way they do not teach about science. They have to teach it 'nonconfessionally'. Such teaching would try to help the children see how people as rational as themselves might to come to hold such doctrines and to engage in the practices associated with the religion. This would be part of trying to reduce the hostility towards different groups in the community that is one of the important functions of schooling - differences in religion being one of the major sources of such hostility. However, this does not mean ignoring those aspects of a religion that are contentious from a human rights point of view.

9.2.6 The Literature and Fine Arts Curriculum

Literature and the arts are possible vehicles for the manipulation of people in that they often express a particular conception of some aspect of the world, and convey a particular emotional response or attitude to it. This means that the exploiters can use them to expose children (and adults) to a conception of some aspect of the world and ensure that this expression conveys the particular emotional response the exploiters want. This is the reason why Plato is so concerned with drama, music and dance. If the rulers want to develop in people a sense of obedience, self-control, restraint, then the music and dance of a society have to be monitored to ensure that this is its effect. People cannot be allowed to feel that they have a right to respond to the world in their own way.

Our question, though, is what would the parties in the position of equal power say was the appropriate way to get people to acquire beliefs or attitudes from literature and the arts? Certainly, Ann, as we have seen, will not want Ben to manipulate her by these means for his advantage at her expense. This is not to say that she will rule out his trying to change her beliefs and attitudes with respect to literature and the arts, any more than she would with the disciplines we have already examined. It may well be the case, for example, that exposure to literature and the arts, like exposure to history, broadens our sympathies, introduces us to ways of viewing the world, ways of experiencing, that we would otherwise never encounter. The arts may provide us with knowledge about the kinds of feelings different people have in different situations or the strength and force of those experiences, as when music heightens the emotional impact of a scene in a film or a play. The arts can put us inside the heads and hearts of other people. This kind of knowledge can demystify the strange for us, making us less likely to react to others with hostility and suspicion. It may also make us aware, as our provincialism and naivety might not have done, of the variety of unacceptable attitudes and motives that can be present in the human breast.

Were Ben to use the arts to produce these effects in Ann, however, she would not want him to lead her to believe that the opinions of some people about these matters should be given greater weight than those of others unless she herself could test and evaluate such claims in terms of publicly available evidence. In schools, then, teachers would need to be careful not give children the impression that the weight of authority lay behind some particular judgment as to the rightness of a particular kind of emotional response to a particular kind of situation unless there were widely accepted criteria of expertise in these matters. This is not to say that there will not be experts *about* literature, in a scholarly sense. Rather, it is to advise caution in identifying people as experts *in* literature, in the sense of being experts in whether the response that a writer seeks to produce in us towards a particular object is the correct one, for example, whether the attitude of admiration that the author seems to have for the hero of the novel is the one we should have or whether the poet's response to a flower is merely sentimental. Nonetheless, there may still be experts in *how* to produce certain effects. This is what makes an artist skilful at his or her art.

9.2.7   The Philosophy and Moral Knowledge Curriculum

The final form of belief that I have derived from Hirst's forms of knowledge is that of philosophy and moral knowledge. With respect to morality, the parties in the position of equal power can do none other than require that children be taught to resolve conflicts of desires between each other in terms of what would acceptable to the parties in a position of equal power. This will involve encouraging them to judge their relationships with others in terms of such things as fairness, the golden rule of do unto others as you would be done by, putting themselves in other people's shoes. As the moral problems they face become more complex, so their application of the impartialist axioms or their less technical equivalents would become more sophisticated. Children would need to be taught *in* morality rather than about it, at least with respect to the basic or enabling liberties. This would not exclude their criticising and contesting such values but it would require their operating within such values while they did so. However, at the level of personal values, that is, of preferred life-styles and so on, they would be taught *about* values. No particular set of them would be imposed on them in the classroom.

As a follow-up to this point I will use the next section to briefly discuss what some writers have seen as the educational implications of the kind of 'Critical Theory' advocated by Jurgen Habermas.

9.3   Habermas and Critical Theory

I will begin with a comment from Habermas (p.40) to the effect that, in a situation of ideological enlightenment, those who do the enlightening are superior to those who are to be enlightened. This superiority, he says, while a vindicating one and theoretically unavoidable, is, nonetheless, fictive and in need of self-correction. The process of enlightenment is such that there can only be participants. There would appear to be two ways in which the Critical Theorist (Ben, say) might claim to be superior.

Firstly, he could claim to be superior because he knows the true concept of the good, say, equal wealth and power. It is part of this concept of the good that no individual is superior in moral worth, that is, even though the Critical Theorist knows the true concept of the good, his interests are not to count more than anyone else's. Nonetheless, his concept of the good is to count more than anyone else's. It is not part of Critical Theory that this component of the theory is negotiable. If it were, it would collapse into liberalism because it would have to allow the possibility that everyone agreed on all the facts other than the concept of the good yet could rationally differ on the concept of the good. This means that, contrary to Habermas' assertion, Critical Theory does not treat the superiority of its advocates as fictive and open to self-correction.

Secondly, Ben could claim to be superior in a way that is fictive and self-correcting in the sense that there is no guarantee that the Critical Theorist has the best possible apologia for why people resist what the theory claims is the true account of their good. New converts may well be able to see false consciousness at work where their teachers have not postulated it before.

Either way, the Critical Theorist remains wedded to a particular concept of the good which is only rejected by those who are unenlightened. Moreover, the criterion of enlightenment is acceptance of the Critical Theorist's concept of the good. The temptation for the Critical Theorist, then, is to manipulate the speech situation to bring about agreement with his concept of the good while telling the other participants that they are really equals and that no-one's opinion has a privileged status. Moreover, he may really believe that he is putting this into practice. Nonetheless, he begins from the assumption that the other participants are oppressed and that their refusal to acknowledge this oppression is just further proof of their conditioned state. Under such circumstances he is likely to regard it as more important that they come to believe what he thinks is the truth than that he not manipulate them. He will not see his manipulation as unjust because, for him, they are getting what they deserve or being made more likely to get it, namely, equal wealth and power or whatever he counts as their true good. Even so, if his fellow participants were aware of what he was doing, they would probably regard themselves as being used and refuse to consent to further participation. They would see his behaviour as condescending and unfair because he is using methods on them to get them to agree with his concept of the good that he would not like them to have used on him to get him to agree with their concept of the good. I will now look at an example of how this can happen, using the work of Paulo Freire.

9.4   Paulo Freire and Manipulation

The choice of Paulo Freire may surprise many who see his work as a paradigm of the non-coercive. Supporters stress the non-indoctrinatory nature of his methodology, which involved raising the consciousness of peasants while teaching them to read. The procedure, however, assumes that the peasants are oppressed whether they realise it or not and is designed to bring them to this realisation. One lesson, according to Thomas Sanders (p.8), involves showing the peasants a number of pictures, then asking questions about each of them. In one picture a couple performs the cueca, which is a Chilean folk dance. The coordinator asks the group whether it is possible for the composer of a cueca to be a great composer. The intent behind such a question, says Sanders, is to get the peasants to see that one can be as much an artist in composing a cueca as one can be writing symphonies.

As this makes clear, the coordinator already has an answer to the question, one that other people in the group could think is wrong. After all, while few people would doubt that a man who composes popular music is an artist, they might well doubt that he is as much of an artist as a famous composer like Beethoven. However, the coordinator's role, according to Sanders (p.9), is to get the rest of the group to appreciate the deeper meaning of what they previously took as an obvious, accepted reality but which the Critical Theorist believes is a mistaken picture of how things really are. The coordinator's role, says Sanders, is not to give his own opinions. Like group psychotherapy, the Freire method stimulates the participants to move themselves from inauthentic interpretations of life to creative initiative by making a realistic assessment of themselves and their environment. What, however, would happen to the peasant, teacher, parent or child who argued persuasively from the position that the Critical Theorist regards as inauthentic, who holds a different view about the good? Presumably expulsion from the group. This is far closer to indoctrinatory practice than the kind of evidential education a liberal would favour.

Critical Theorists may feel that this account of their position is somewhat unfair in that their theory makes much of equal power, of autonomy and giving people self-determination. However, they do seem to be caught on the horns of a dilemma. They could truly treat the people they are trying to convert as equals, which means they genuinely have to regard their own concept of the good as up for grabs, as something not proven, and be able to propose a resolution procedure that does not presuppose the truth of their concept of the good. If they do this, they have to accept that rational people with as full an access to the empirical facts as themselves might well accept that some inequalities of wealth and power of which the Critical Theorist disapproves are, in fact, fair. Accepting the possibility of such a plurality of values, however, seems to make Critical Theorists no different from liberals, except that they believe that people are ignorant of certain facts about their condition whereas liberals are more inclined to think that people might know these facts quite well. Nonetheless, because they explain people's acceptance of inequalities of wealth and power in terms of ignorance of the facts, there is still point to treating people as autonomous and self-determining agents who will change their minds when convinced of the facts. Such a position does not justify the standard criticisms made by Critical Theorists of parliamentary democracy.

Alternatively, they are caught on the other horn of the dilemma. They are not liberals because they hold unshakeably to the view that anyone who disagrees with them about the wrongness of particular inequalities of wealth and power must suffer from false consciousness, even were it to be the case that there were no empirical facts that the Critical Theorists were more aware of than other people. In this case, then their theory does seem to allow them to ignore people's autonomy and self-determination.

To conclude this chapter on impartialism and education I will briefly consider what, if anything, impartialism has to say about school governance.

9.5   Impartialism and School Governance

Before we look at the impartialist view on school governance, I will clarify
the sense in which I will use the word 'democracy'. As a rule, the word
'democracy' refers to decision-making processes where those affected by
the decision have an equal vote either in the actual decision itself ('direct
democracy') or in the selection of representatives who then make the
decision ('representative democracy') and the decision that prevails is the
one chosen by the majority of voters in a direct democracy or by the
majority of representatives in a representative democracy. In this sense of
democracy, it is possible for the voters to make decisions that infringe the
civil liberties of minority groups. When we combine 'democracy' in this
sense with the view that there are controls in place to prevent the
infringement of civil liberties then we have what I will call 'liberal
democracy'. Usually this involves having some constitutional restrictions
placed on the powers of parliaments. To be a liberal democracy, however,
any society with such limitations on the power of parliament must have put
them in place as a result of a democratic vote, that is, a majority vote of
citizens or citizen representatives. In the United States of America, for
example, changes to the constitution require a majority of the parliaments
of the states to vote in favour of the proposal. In Australia, all that is
needed is a majority of the people across the nation as a whole and a
majority of the people in a majority of the states. Australia's constitution
is not changed by any vote of any of the parliaments. Britain, by contrast,
does not limit the power of its parliament by a constitution of the
Australian or American kind but does claim to have such limits as a result
of tradition and custom.

So far, what I have been talking about is what I will call the
'macro-democratic' structure of our society, that is, the over-riding source
of legal power. Our macro-democratic structure involves the constitution,
the federal government and the various state governments. These
determine the laws which provide the framework within which any other
decisions get legally made in our society. As we have seen, impartialists
are committed to the final authority in a society residing in a macro-
democratic process. It does not insist that it be direct democracy rather
than representative democracy, or federal democracy as in Australia and
the United States of America as opposed to a single parliament as in
Britain. However, it does insist that each person has the same value for his

or her vote as any other person. To do otherwise is not to treat people as of equal worth as choosers.

Now, an important question in political theory is whether all, or some, of the decisions in a macro-democratic society that are made below the macro level should also be democratic, that is, should our society also be micro-democratic? In particular, from an educational point of view, should schools be micro-democratic and, if so, who should constitute the electorate? Should it just be parents, just teachers, just children, or parents and children, or parents and teachers and children? Should the principal be elected? If so, by whom? Should the decision as to whether there will be a principal be decided micro-democratically? Should teachers be elected, and so on.

The impartialist position on this is straightforward enough at the most general level. Whether or not there should be micro-democracy in schools is a matter to be determined macro-democratically. If people want it, then they should make it clear to political parties that their support for such a proposal will be crucial to their re-election. Impartialists certainly would be opposed to any strategy that involved overthrowing macro-democracy in order to establish micro-democracy in schools or anywhere else. It may seem paradoxical that anyone would suggest that the macro-democratic nature of our ultimate political authority be removed in order to achieve micro-democratic changes but there are non-liberal positions that do seem committed to such a plan. Of course, it may well be the case that our current macro-democratic laws already make micro-democratic reform possible in those schools where parents or teachers or whoever want it. Impartialists would have no objection to such groups proceeding, provided they stay within the macro-democratic law.

The interesting educational question on micro-democracy for impartialists, however, is whether impartialism of its very nature requires them to push for micro-democracy in schools. Is it the case that children will grow up better able to fulfil liberal ideals if they have been educated in micro-democratic schools? This is an important question. Nonetheless, even if the answer turns out to be 'Yes', impartialists must operate within what is permitted by the macro-democratic structure. If the parliament has decided that the control of school administration lies with the Minister of Education and he or she has decided that the ultimate authority in each school is the principal, then this is a macro-democratic decision that liberals must respect until they can persuade the parliament or the Minister of Education differently.

Similar points hold about curriculum content, teaching methodology, discipline policy - even standardised testing, to take a currently controversial example. Of course, teachers, like any other group of employees, also have liberal democratic rights to strike, etcetera, if they believe their employers are seriously in error in some way but, again, this is a matter that must be settled within the macro-democratic framework. Resort to illegal activities is not justified from the impartialist point of view unless one is convinced that the law is a vicious infringement of civil liberties and the only hope of change is to bring this injustice to the attention of the public through civil disobedience, as in the freedom walkers in the American south in the 1960s, or Gandhi against British rule in India in the 1940s. As a rule, however, the kinds of disagreements found between governments and citizens in liberal democratic societies do not involve infringements of civil liberties but conflicts over the good of the nation or of a group. As such, they are appropriately settled through liberal democratic processes, that is, by influencing parliaments.

We have seen the kind of education that impartialists would mandate for a liberal democracy. In the next chapter I will look at what relationships liberal democratic states should have with illiberal and undemocratic nations, using Rawls' answer to this question as a basis for discussion.

Note

1　For a more detailed account of the interpretation of Rousseau given here, see L.G. Croker. On this interpretation, Rousseau's emphasis on childhood freedom is not the progressive educational idea that it is often thought to be by many educational theorists but is part of an overall totalitarian strategy to guarantee obedience to the State which, in Berlin's sense, represents the higher self of each citizen.

10 Liberal Tolerance and the Laws of Nations

10.1 Introduction

In his paper, 'The Law of Peoples' (1993b), Rawls claims that the toleration by liberals of well-ordered non-liberal regimes at the international level is parallel to the liberal toleration of other conceptions of the good in the domestic case. (Let's call this the 'domestic analogy' argument.) From this, he concludes that the appropriate relationship for liberal societies to have to these regimes is one of 'principled toleration'. Liberal societies would not be warranted, from the viewpoint of political liberalism, he believes, in attacking such societies militarily or in bringing economic or other sanctions against them to get them to liberalise their institutions (p.81). In this respect, Rawls thinks, these regimes differ from tyrannical or dictatorial regimes of whom a principled toleration is not possible. Rather, the best that liberal societies can do is negotiate a modus vivendi with such powers.

     In this chapter I wish to show that, using Rawls' own principles, the international case is not relevantly parallel to the domestic case and that, as a consequence, liberal societies cannot relate to well-ordered hierarchical non-liberal societies in terms of principled toleration. There is, in effect, no difference in principle between these societies on the one hand and tyrannies and dictatorships on the other. While liberal societies will usually find it prudent, or even morally necessary, to remain at peace with all three kinds of non-liberal societies, they are entitled, in principle, under the appropriate circumstances, to attack these societies militarily and/or to bring economic and other sanctions against them to get them to revise their institutions. As we have seen, the parties in the position of equal power are constrained in such a way that we would usually expect the conclusions they reach to match those that would be reached behind Rawls' veil of ignorance. It is important, therefore, from an impartialist

197

point of view, to see whether or not Rawls' conclusions about the laws of nation and liberal tolerance do follow from his own premises.

I will begin with a review of the relevant sections of Rawls' argument.

10.2   Representation and Rationality

Rawls believes that well-ordered hierarchical societies can be represented in the original position. If this is so, then they can be included in a law of peoples that is compatible with liberal ideas of justice. In order for any party whatsoever, whether an individual or a corporate body, to be represented in the original position, that party must be able to be categorised as free, equal, reasonable and rational in the particular sense that Rawls gives to each of these notions. This is because the original position itself models a fair decision procedure for such parties. I will now consider whether or not hierarchical societies are the kinds of party that can be rational in the requisite sense.

Rationality, for Rawls (p.50), is a notion that applies to a person or a collective entity in so far as either is a single, unified agent that exercises powers of judgement and deliberation in seeking ends and interests peculiarly its own. Rationality applies to the way these interests are chosen and affirmed, how they are prioritised, and how the means to their satisfaction are selected. This involves adopting the most effective means to ends and picking the more probable alternative given that other things are equal. Rational agents, however, are not limited to means-ends reasoning because they can evaluate final ends in terms of their significance for their overall plan of life, and by how mutually coherent and complementary these ends are.

What, exactly, makes a party (whether individual or corporate) a 'single unified agent'? In the case of individuals, according to Rawls (p.53), the kind of rationality that the representative of a citizen is supposed to pursue on that citizen's behalf is to maximise his or her essential interests as a person. Individuals, then, must be the kinds of things that have an essential interest that can be pursued as if each one of them is a single, unified agent. Likewise, what makes it possible to for a party behind the veil of ignorance to represent a liberal society as a single unified agent is his or her ability to deliberate among available principles for the law of peoples by reference to the fundamental interests of democratic societies in accordance with, or as presupposed by, the liberal principles of domestic justice (p.54).

In Rawls' view, a well-ordered hierarchical society can be represented in the original position only if it, too, has fundamental interests as a single, unified agent. It achieves this unity through what he calls a 'common good' conception of justice. This conception of justice enables it to meet certain necessary conditions for being seen as legitimate by its own people (p.43). This conception of justice will only give it the required legitimacy if the society is concerned to take into account in an impartial way what it reasonably believes to be the fundamental interests of all members of society (p.61). There must also be a consultation process through which the concerns of sub-ordinate groups in the society are seriously considered by the dominant group or its agents. In essence, then, Rawls is trying to find an account of how an hierarchical society can be said to speak with one voice in the way that the legitimacy of democratic procedures makes possible for a liberal society, even though there may be disputes and disagreement between parties at the domestic level.

While the development of a parallel between liberal and hierarchical societies in terms of a unifying conception of justice would, if successful, give each type of society the necessary features to be represented in the original position, there are good reasons to believe that this parallel is more difficult to establish than Rawls indicates. This can be seen if we compare the cases of those who reject the conception of justice central to each kind of society, that is, the case of the anti-liberal dissenter in a liberal society and the case of the anti-hierarchical dissenter in a hierarchical society. I will now examine the differences in the two cases.

10.3   Anti-Liberal and Anti-Hierarchical Dissenters

It may, at first, appear to be a problem for the representability of a' liberal society in the original position that there are people in that society who reject its conception of justice. If the conception of justice is what makes the society well-ordered, that is, each person accepts and knows that everyone else accepts the same principles of justice (Rawls, 1972, p.5), then the presence of even one dissenter to the conception of justice renders the society ill-ordered. Given that the well-orderedness criterion appears to be the same as the rationality criterion for corporate individuals, presumably including nations, then a liberal society with even one dissenter would appear to be non-rational in the required sense and, therefore, not something that can be represented in the original position.

As it happens, there is a special relationship between liberal societies and the original position such that the presence in the liberal society of an anti-liberal dissenter does not render the liberal society ineligible for representation in the original position. This is the fact that the original position has been constructed precisely to model a fair argument procedure for free, equal, reasonable and rational persons (whether individual or corporate). A liberal society is one that has a conception of justice correspondent with the kind of conception of justice that would be accepted by persons in the original position.

This means that the anti-liberal dissenter who rejects the conception of justice found in a liberal society must also be rejecting the original position and the kind of decision procedure it models. In effect, then, the anti-liberal dissenter is rejecting one of the four central tenets embodied in the original position, namely, that people are, or should be regarded as, free and equal, reasonable and rational agents. If this is so, then the existence of such a dissenter is no threat to the representability of a liberal society in the original position. It is only intended to represent persons (whether individual or corporate) who accept the four tenets listed above.

Hierarchical societies are in quite a different position. Their conception of domestic justice is not one that would be agreed to by the parties in the original position, so anti-hierarchical dissenters to their conception of justice cannot be excluded from representability in the original position on the same grounds as the anti-liberal dissenter. In fact, the anti-hierarchical dissenter's actual grounds for dissent may be a commitment to exactly the conception of justice that the original position embodies.

By rejecting the hierarchical society's conception of justice, the dissenter (say, Ann) does not show that she believes that those parties who disagree with her conception of the good are irrational, unequal, lack free will and are unreasonable. (What Rawls means by these terms is explained in the next paragraph.)

She, then, is in quite a different position to the dissenter from liberalism. As a dissenter from liberal society, she posed no threat to the legitimacy of the liberal society. In no way did she undermine the unity of the liberal society in the sense necessary to enable it to have a life-plan, a conception of its own essential interests, a harmony in its concept of the good. This is because the dissenter from liberalism failed to meet the conditions necessary to have her point of view, or herself, represented in the original position. The dissenter from within a hierarchical society (say, Ben), however, need not be like this. He may well be entitled to be represented in the original position. In order to deny him this right (or any group of which he is the representative), the hierarchical government would have to deny that the dissenter met at least one of the conditions necessary to be represented in the original position (which the liberal government can do, because the anti-liberal can be shown not to meet at least one of these conditions - namely, the reasonableness criterion). Suppose, however, our anti-hierarchical dissenter accepts the reasonableness requirement (which is more than the hierarchical government does vis a vis its own citizens, even though it does vis a vis other states). Then the hierarchical government must exclude the anti-hierarchical dissenter from representation on what are, in effect, empirical grounds not metaphysical or philosophical ones. What they are saying is that one of the following is true of all anti-hierarchical dissenters. They all:- (1) lack the moral power to form, revise and rationally pursue a conception of the good, to be a self-authenticating source of rational claims and capable of taking responsibility for one's own ends (p.72); (2) lack the capacity for a sense of justice and for a conception of the good (the two 'moral' powers) and the powers of reason and lack these to the requisite minimal degree to be a fully cooperating member of society (p.19); (3) lack the capacity to do what is best for their essential interests. (And this needs a criterion other than that they disagree with the government what their essential interests are - it is, after all, a *capacity* that is lacked.)

Now why should subordinate groups in a hierarchical society accept the legitimacy of a government whose conception of the good, that is, whose common good conception of justice, rests on its denying one or more of the above empirical facts about the group. The hierarchical government cannot get represented in the original position unless it can show that it possesses the kind of unity to be found in the individual when it comes to having a life-plan or consistency of direction of decision-making. Liberalism can reject its anti-liberal dissenters in such a case because they would be rejected as representable in the original position on the grounds that they don't meet the relevant requirements . Subordinate groups in a hierarchical society, however, cannot be rejected on this ground. They can only be rejected on the supposed empirical grounds of failing to meet (1) to (3) above, and there is no reason to believe that this is true of the vast majority of the members of subordinate groups. Certainly, they do not fail to meet (1) to (3) above solely because they do not accept the conception of the good of the hierarchical government or even because they fail to accept the common good conception of justice proposed by the government. They, then, would not regard the government as representing them and this cannot be ignored in the way that it can for the anti-liberal dissenter.

The hierarchical government, therefore, fails one of the crucial requirements for being represented in either Rawls' original position or in a position of equal power, namely, it fails to meet the 'rationality' or 'essential interest' requirement. Unless all members of the society who are entitled to be represented in the original position or the position of equal power regard the government as legitimate in the sense that they would choose to select a government in this way, then the government does not speak with a single voice. It cannot be said to represent them.

There is, then, this significant divergence between the cases of liberal societies on the one hand and hierarchical societies on the other. The only way in which this problem for a hierarchical society can be overcome is if it has not a single dissenter to its common good conception of justice. Only if this criterion is met will a hierarchical society be 'well-ordered' in Rawls' sense. As it happens, there are probably no actual hierarchical societies that meet this criterion. Real hierarchical societies are all ill-ordered, so to speak. They, therefore, are not the kinds of society with whom liberal societies can enter into a principled agreement on a law of peoples. As a consequence, liberal societies would be entitled to go to war, impose economic sanctions against such societies, although they may choose not to do so for good moral and prudential reasons.

Nonetheless, it may be the case that a well-ordered hierarchical society does come into existence one day. Would liberal societies be bound not to go to war against it, and not to impose economic sanctions, etcetera? I will now turn to the case of the well-ordered hierarchical society.

10.4 The Well-Ordered Hierarchical Society

All the members of a well-ordered hierarchical society accept the common good conception of justice enforced by the dominant culture. What kind of thing can this common good conception of justice be? Rawls says that it is a 'comprehensive doctrine' as held by the dominant culture (p.43). It cannot arbitrarily privilege the interests of some members of society while the interests of the others count for nothing. What the government reasonably considers to be the fundamental interests of all members of society must be impartially taken into account (p.61). This common good conception of justice does not require that the government regard all people as free and equal citizens, as in a liberal democracy, but it does require that persons are regarded as responsible members of society who can appreciate their moral duties and obligations and perform their part in societal life (p.62). It does not give individuals the right of free speech but they do have the right, as members of associations and corporate bodies, to express political dissent. It is the duty of the government to take their dissent seriously and to reply to it in a conscientious manner (p.62). Judges and officials cannot refuse to listen to objections on the grounds that anyone who objects is thereby incompetent and incapable of understanding government policy (p.62).

The common good conception of justice also secures citizens certain minimum rights, namely, the rights to subsistence and security, to liberty and property, as well as to formal equality as expressed by the rules of natural justice. Even so, the state religion in a hierarchical society may be the ultimate authority on certain questions within society and rightly determine government policy on various crucial issues (p.63). Nonetheless, the comprehensive religious and political doctrines of the dominant culture must not be unreasonable. They must provide some degree of liberty of conscience and freedom of thought, even if these freedoms are not in general equal for all members of society in the way they are in liberal societies (p.63). Also, this inequality of religious freedom means that a hierarchical society must allow its dissenters the right of emigration (p.63).

So, we have a dominant culture which has a conception of the good that is 'reasonable' in the sense that it tolerates or does not repress other conceptions of the good, or, at least, does not do so entirely. It does not, presumably, seek to impose its own conception of the good on to the subordinate cultures in the nation. In effect, this 'reasonableness' requirement is the equivalent at the domestic level of a 'nonexpansionist' requirement that Rawls places on the international behaviour of nations that can be represented in the original position, namely, that they are not expansionist in the sense that they do not seek to convert other nations to their religion by coercive means (p.61). Similarly, the dominant culture in a hierarchical society should not be engaged in actively converting other cultures (adherents of alternative conceptions of the good) by coercive means.

Even so, the dominant culture is 'reasonable' in a somewhat limited way. While it allows subordinate cultures to live in accordance with their conceptions of the good, it does so with the proviso that they must conform to those components of its own conception of the good that specify what is good for everyone. For example, if it is part of a Moslem conception of the good that it is for the good of everyone, whether they be Moslems or not and whether they agree with this restriction on their freedom or not, then the Moslem government can impose a rule such as 'khatwah', that is, that it is a crime to be in 'close physical proximity to another man's wife'. In other words, the government can, according to a common good conception of justice, legislate that it is in the common good that adultery be illegal, even though it may not be regarded this seriously by the subordinate cultures in the society.

What, however, would lead a subordinate culture to accept that this kind of limitation of the lives of its members was legitimate, as opposed to putting up with it because they were politically too weak to have any option? It could only be one of two things (a) that they accepted that the dominant culture really was correct that this was in the common good of all or (b) that they held, as an essential part of their conception of the good, that subordinate cultures should accommodate themselves to the dominant culture's conception of the good unless this flagrantly transgressed some essential of their own conception.

The first option, however, is not an available one because this restriction on their freedom is, per hypothesi, one they do not include in their conception of the good and so cannot believe to be in the common good of all because they do not believe it to be in their good. It is hardly consistent to have a particular conception of the good (say, Good 1) which includes an account of what is good for people, while accepting that some other conception of the good (say, Good 2) which rejects Good 1 or aspects of it, nonetheless covers the full good of all people. It is almost as if the subordinate culture were saying that the dominant culture knew better what was in its good than it did itself. If this is so, then the subordinate culture, one would assume, would convert to the conception of good of the dominant culture.

The second option is a possibility. Jehovah's Witnesses, for example, seem to be a group that accommodates itself to the laws of any country in which its adherents find themselves, provided they are free to proselytise. This is because their struggle is not to improve things in this world but to ensure that as many people as possible will obtain the beliefs that will enable them to live forever in God's kingdom after Armageddon. Even so, they do not actually believe that the dominant culture is achieving the common good by making everyone conform to its conception of the common good, even when they believe that the dominant culture honestly believes that it is for everyone's good, rather than merely putting it forward as a mask for their real expansionist intentions or whatever.

Suppose, however, that there was a subordinate group that actually thought that the dominant group was achieving the common good by restricting the freedom of all citizens, including members of subordinate groups, in accordance with the dominant group's own conception of the good. Let's call such a group a 'lackey' group. This group would not need to have its civil liberties curtailed in the way Rawls describes. It could have freedom of speech and freedom of assembly and the right to form political parties and vote, and all the other liberal freedoms. Given its acceptance of the leadership role of the dominant group, it will use these freedoms in a way that is no threat to the dominant culture and its conception of the good.

There would no need, then, for a hierarchical society to suppress the liberal freedoms. That it does so surely must be interpreted as its perceiving that there is a need for such suppression, which can only be the case if the subordinate groups are not of the 'lackey' kind described above. If they are not, then the nation is not of the kind that can be represented in the original position, or in a position of equal power, because it contains anti-hierarchical dissenters. Of course, the suppression of the standard liberal civil liberties may also motivated by the existence of dissident voices within the dominant group itself.

Rawls, then, has failed to show that his own principles require liberal societies to practise 'principled toleration' towards well-ordered non-liberal regimes. The international case, contrary to Rawls, is not relevantly similar to the domestic case. Well-ordered non-liberal societies are not the kinds of societies that can legitimately be represented either within Rawls' original position or in a position of equal power. As a consequence, Rawls has provided us with no acceptable argument as to why liberal societies should respect the right of a well-ordered non-liberal

206 Power, Impartiality and Justice

society to deny to its citizens any of what I have called the enabling (basic) rights that standardly apply in a liberal society. I argued earlier that freedom of religion and freedom of conscience were not basic or enabling rights and, therefore, might be traded by people in special circumstances for other benefits. However, my assumption in making such a claim was that the members of any society who made such a choice at least had the basic or enabling rights, that is, that the choice really was theirs and not that of some other group that imposed the decision upon them. Certainly, one of the prime functions of the basic or enabling rights is precisely to protect the right of individuals not to have a particular religious group favoured in the policies of the government and the laws of the land.

As an aside, it is interesting to note that non-liberal societies wish to be treated in the international forum as their citizens wish to be treated in the domestic forum. Non-liberal societies often appeal to a notion of national sovereignty, that what occurs within their own borders is, in effect, a private matter for the nation itself to deal with. It should not be subject to interference in these matters from other nations. The notional of national sovereignty, however, bears the same relation to the community of nations as the notion of individual sovereignty over his or her life does to the community within the nation. If the community of nations has no right to interfere in the private affairs of its members, then why does the community within the nation, or the government of that nation, have the right to interfere in the private affairs of one of its members? In so far as the government claims that there are circumstances that override the right of individuals within its community to privacy, then there will be circumstances in which the community of nations can override the right to privacy of an individual nation. A government that does not respect the civil liberties of its citizens can hardly expect the community of nations to take seriously its claim to parallel civil liberties as a nation.

In the next chapter I wish to look at what, if anything, impartialism has to say about the rights of nonpersons, for example, animals and human foetuses. To provide a structure for this discussion I will look at the criticisms that Vinit Haksar levels at Rawls' theory with respect to these matters.

11 Impartialism and Nonpersons

11.1   Introduction

Vinit Haksar believes that the normative conclusions that Rawls derives
from his veil of ignorance are vitiated by the metaphysics that it
presupposes. In this chapter I will look at Haksar's arguments to see
whether they work against Rawls but, more particularly, whether they
would also apply to the parties in the position of equal power.

In his criticism of Rawls, Haksar seeks to turn one of Rawls' own
notions against him. This is the notion of a 'reflective equilibrium'.
Rawls (1972, p.48) proposes this notion as a solution to the problem of
how we are to decide which of the judgments that a person makes about
the justice of a set of arrangements are the most justified ones. He
suggests that these are unlikely to be the ones that the person makes prior
to examining any conception of justice. Instead, it is likely to be the one
that the person comes to after he or she has weighed up various proposed
conceptions in terms of the particular judgements they lead to about which
arrangements are the most just ones, then either changed the original
judgment in light of the fact that it does not fit into the best conception of
justice he or she has encountered or else adopted a conception of justice
because it fits the original judgement, as well as other judgements that he
or she wishes to preserve.

Haksar argues that his own moral theory, which he calls
'perfectionist egalitarianism', produces a greater reflective equilibrium
than any of the alternatives between our moral and political principles (his
equivalent of Rawls' 'conceptions of justice'), on the one hand, and our
moral intuitions (his equivalent of Rawls' judgments of the justice of an
arrangement) on the other hand, provided we also try to establish a
harmony between these and our metaphysical principles. In particular, he
believes that perfectionist egalitarianism produces a more comprehensive

reflective equilibrium than contractarian egalitarianism of the kind proposed by Rawls. It is my intention to show that impartialism is preferable to Haksar's perfectionist egalitarianism because it reduces the reliance on intuition unavoidable in his approach.

Haksar's theory is egalitarian, he says (pp.65-66), because it holds the following two principles:- (1) there are certain rights held equally by all human beings, especially the right to equal respect and consideration, and (2) these rights are owed to the individual for his or her own sake, not because his or her possession of these rights has desirable consequences of some kind.

He regards his theory as perfectionist because it holds the following three principles :- (1) some forms of human life are intrinsically inferior to other forms of human life (2) human beings, with the possible exception of some such as congenital idiots, have more intrinsic worth than animals (3) human ways of life, at any rate those that are not anti-social such as Nazism, have more intrinsic worth than animal forms of life.

Haksar claims his perfectionist egalitarianism to be superior to Rawlsian contractarian egalitarianism because the particular moral judgements that Rawls favours cannot be derived from Rawls' own theory unless perfectionist and metaphysical considerations are added to it.

Haksar argues that the following claims cannot be derived from contractarianism without appeal to independent metaphysical or perfectionist considerations (1) that congenital idiots are members of the egalitarian club (2) that human foetuses are members of the egalitarian club (3) that children are members of the egalitarian club (4) that animals are not members of the egalitarian club and (5) that the senile and permanently comatose are members of the egalitarian club.

His claim raises two issues that I wish to consider (1) Is it true that these positions can't be derived for contractarianism without appeal to independent metaphysical or perfectionist considerations? (2) If it is true, does this demonstrate that perfectionism is a better moral theory than contractarianism? It may be that an adequate moral theory does not need to be able to accept all of these positions or be able to derive them from its basic premises. It may be that it can accommodate them, where necessary, by some other means consistent with its contractarianism. I will be concerned to see whether impartialism rather than Rawls' version of contractarianism can answer these questions. Before I look at Haksar's arguments, I will take up the issue of how to distinguish persons from non-persons.

11.2   Persons and Nonpersons

Singer (p.75) follows John Locke in treating rationality and self-consciousness as the defining characteristics of personhood.   The consequence of such an account is that most animals, foetuses, children, congenital idiots and senile adult humans are not persons. This means that they cannot be parties to the arguments in a position of equal power about what principles should govern conflicts of desires.   This, in turn, raises questions about whether only the desires of persons should be taken into account by such parties in their reasoning.

While nonpersons cannot be parties to the argument in a position of equal power, it still remains the case that the parties in a position of equal power can have a conflict of desires over whether or not the desires of nonpersons should be given equal consideration with the desires of persons.   This question itself makes a prior assumption that also needs scrutiny, namely, that it is desires that matter, that are the coinage of the debate, and not some other factor. It may be, for example, that one of the parties to the debate is concerned to maximise the amount of intrinsic value in the world, where this is believed to exist independently of desires, that is, even if the universe contained no desiring creatures one state of it could be of greater intrinsic value than another.

So, the first issue that needs to be dealt with is whether it is desires rather than some other matter that should be the coinage of the debate. This, of course, is itself a question to be debated by the parties in the position of equal power. What can certainly be said of them is that they are desiring creatures. Neither party to any debate can repudiate the value of the desires of desiring creatures. If one party wishes to deny the value of the desires of desiring creatures, it thereby creates a paradox about the value of their desire that the desires of desiring creatures not be valued. What they would be seeking in the position of equal power is to persuade others that the desire that the desires of desiring creatures not be valued be valued sufficiently by the parties in the position of equal power that they will all agree not to value such desires. But one of the desires to be valued is the desire not to value such desires, so, in valuing it, they are not valuing it, and in not valuing it, they are valuing it. It appears, then, that the parties in the position of equal power are committed to the value of at least some desires of at least some persons.

In order to avoid the same kind of paradox, if there is a party that desires that the people in a position of equal power value the intrinsic worth of ecosystems, say, or of non-sentient life or whatever, then such a party seems committed to at least the value of this desire. The same applies to those who desire that the desires of animals or non-person humans be taken into account. They must at least value this desire.

It appears, then, as if desires will be the coinage that underpins the debates in the position of equal power. However, must the parties there only take into account the desires of persons or must they also give some weighting to the desires of nonpersons. I will now look at this question.

11.3   Nonperson Desires

Given that desires are the coinage of the debate, what grounds might be offered for giving priority to one kind of desire over another? As we have seen, one kind of ground that cannot be offered by Ann, say, is that the desire's being her desire makes it special, warrants its trumping any desire that is not hers. At least, she cannot offer such a principle without supplementing it in some way, for example, by tying it to an ability she claims to have to be always reliable on matters of moral judgement, or some such. In holding the unsupplemented version of such a view, she is committed to always using any superior power she has in the real world to resolve a conflict of desires in her own favour regardless of what might have been agreed to in a position of equal power, that is, she is a partialist and so cannot be party to arguments in the position of equal power.

Who owns the desire, then, in the absence of some compelling case about a particular owner, cannot be a grounds for preferring one desire to another. The grounds for preference, it seems, have to be internal to the desire. A plausible case can be made that there are important internal differences between the desires of persons and the desires of non-persons. Persons have desires about the satisfaction of their desires whereas non-persons do not. Singer (p.81) makes this distinction in terms of how desires can be frustrated. There are two ways, he says, in which desires can be frustrated.

The first way is that one could say that a desire is frustrated when its owner experiences the frustration of having the desire thwarted. An example is where someone (say, Ben) wants to go to the movies, arrives at the ticket box but finds all the tickets sold or that he forgot his money. He feels frustrated. He is aware or conscious of not getting what he wants, not just in the sense that he knows that he is not getting what he wants but also in the sense that his emotional state changes. He experiences anger or irritation.

The second way is that one could say that a desire is frustrated when its owner (Ben) doesn't live to have the desire satisfied or, perhaps, when he loses all consciousness of whether or not his desires have been satisfied, as when he is in a coma. In this case, he doesn't experience any frustration because he is either dead or unconscious but, nonetheless, he may well have had desires about what he wanted to happen tomorrow, or next year, or when he retired, which he will now never be able to satisfy.

Both animals and humans have desires but there is a crucial difference between the desires of most animals and those of most humans. Whereas most humans have desires about what they would like to happen to them in the future, most kinds of animals do not, or, if they do, they have them in a very crude form.

This difference is clearly illustrated with the desire for life. A being only has a desire for life if it is able to comprehend what it is to be alive and what it is to be dead. Singer (p.81) argues that most animals do not have the requisite concepts of 'life' or 'death'. Cases in which they behave as if they do are only apparent. Their apparent struggle to preserve their life is really just an expression of their preference to avoid a painful or threatening state of affairs.

Conscious beings, then, can be divided into two classes (i) those who have a concept of what it is for them to be the same being over a period of time, who have a concept of death and who have desires about their own long-term futures, and (ii) those who lack these. The former are 'persons' and the latter are 'non-persons'. If Ben kills a person, then he kills a being whose desire to live is, thereby, frustrated. If he kills a nonperson, his taking of its life does not frustrate any desire it has to live because it is not conceptually capable of such a desire. If he hurts a person or an animal, then, in both cases, they will wish to avoid the pain he causes so his initiating and persisting with his action frustrates the same kind of desire for each of them.

Conflicts of desires about which nonperson type desires are to be acted on or not in the real world, about which are to be valued or discouraged there, are one of the kinds of conflicts that the parties in a position of equal power will have to settle. Generally, such conflicts would be about the non-person type desires of persons in the real world, that is, desires for food, drink, sleep, sex, simple pleasures such as sun-bathing and having one's back scratched, straight forward cases of avoiding pains, fear, and so on.

As we have seen, however, the parties in the position of equal power will not accept principles on these matters that differentiate between cases on the basis of whose desire it is - at least, not without some story being told as to the special features of that person. Instead, the principles will be based on features internal to the desires such as their intensity and duration - in fact, the kinds of criteria that Bentham spelt out in connection with his felicific calculus (1789).

It would seem, then, that the parties in the position of equal power cannot privilege a non-person type desire in a person over an equivalent desire in a non-person without showing themselves to be the kind of person who would privilege their own nonperson desire over a similar desire in another person, that is, without showing themselves to be the kind of person who would use superior power in the real world to favour a particular instance of a non-person desire, just because they were its owner, over an equivalent non-person desire in another person or in a non-person.

It should be noted, however, that what the parties in the position of equal power will find wrong about the frustration of a nonperson's desires is not that this shows a tendency or inclination to frustrate the nonperson type desires of persons. Rather, they will agree to treat the frustration of certain nonperson-type desires (as well of certain person-type desires) as wrong in itself. One does a wrong to the owner of the desire in hurting him or her or it. The relevant wrongness does not lie in what is done to those persons who feel outraged that non-persons are hurt, although this, in itself, may constitute a different wrong. Although impartialism is similar in many respect to Kant's ethical outlook, with the decisions of the parties in a position of equal power playing the role within impartialism of the Categorical Imperative, it parts company with him on the treatment of animals, rejecting his claim (1779) to the effect that we have no direct duties to animals. They are there merely as a means to an end, which is humanity. The moral interest in our treatment of animals, Kant thinks, is that people who are cruel to animals will become hard in their dealings with humans.

While nonperson animals, then, are members of the egalitarian club when it comes to the satisfaction or frustration of non-person type desires, impartialism does not have them as members of the egalitarian club either in terms of a right to life or in terms of their value as desiring creatures. They lack the value that attaches to desiring creatures with person type desires. Impartialism, therefore, differentiates between persons and nonpersons without having to import perfectionist assumptions.

This, however, still leaves Haksar's other challenges. Not all humans are persons. Foetuses aren't persons, nor are very young infants, nor congenital idiots, nor the senile nor those in permanent comas. I will now turn to the arguments that Haksar uses to show that congenital idiots are members of the egalitarian club.

11.4 Congenital Idiots and Perfectionism

The congenital idiot (say, a man) is an interesting case because he lacks even the potential to be a person. There might be an argument based on potentiality that entitles us to include nonpersons in the egalitarian club on the grounds that they will become persons in the normal course of events. Haksar argues this for foetuses and infants. But this is not available for congenital idiots who, by definition, have no such potential.

Haksar thinks congenital idiots should be treated as associate members of the egalitarian club whereas animals shouldn't. He does this, even though he agrees that there are no relevant differences between congenital idiots and animals. His argument for this begins with the case of defectives who began with the full potential but whose potential was destroyed. Such people are to be treated as members of the egalitarian club because, he believes, once a member always a member. He calls this the 'doctrine of the transitivity of ends in themselves.' As congenital idiots are often indistinguishable from non-congenital idiots, and as non-congenital idiots are to be counted as members of the egalitarian club in Haksar's view, he claims that there is a 'pragmatic' argument for treating congenital idiots as members of the club. If the congenital idiot is given inferior status, then there is the danger that, not only noncongenital idiots but also ordinary humans, will be treated as inferior by mistake or by malicious design (p.75).

This argument depends on the lack of clear demarcation between congenital and noncongenital idiots and, to a lesser extent, on a similar possibility of 'confusion of similars' between defectives in general and normal humans. It also rests on there being clear demarcation between humans and animals which means that there is less likelihood of abuse arising from the practice of giving animals inferior status than there is if it is given to congenital idiots.

Haksar's pragmatic argument isn't really a perfectionist one. It does not establish that congenital idiots are members of the egalitarian club. Nonetheless, it attempts to show that a perfectionist is not merely being arbitrary in treating congenital idiots with greater consideration than animals. A contractarian, however, can adopt the same strategy.

11.5   Impartialism and Congenital Idiots

Congenital idiots, like animals, are not persons with conceptions of themselves continuing into the future and with desires about that future. As a consequence, neither will have their desires frustrated by being painlessly killed. Unless some morally relevant difference can be found between them, then, it seems that it is equally permissible to painlessly kill congenital idiot humans as it is to do so to animals. When, then, might the parties in a position of equal power agree to give preferential treatment to congenital idiots? They would do so under the following circumstances:- (1) the usual 'indirect' classical utilitarian kinds of circumstances, that is, where other people would be made unhappy by congenital idiots being treated the same as animals, and (2) the 'pragmatic' argument that Haksar has given, stripped of its reference to confusion between congenital and noncongenital cases.

The parties would accept the argument from 'confusion of similars'. Given that persons desire not to die, except under exceptional circumstances, this desire can be frustrated by their being confused with congenital idiots who lack such a desire. Circumstances may well arise in which a person is mistaken for a congenital idiot if killing congenital idiots painlessly is permitted. The best insurance that this will not happen is to treat the congenital idiot's right to life as equivalent to that of a person's.

11.6   Abortion and Potentiality

Haksar argues that foetuses should be members of the egalitarian club. This is because egalitarianism requires what he calls the 'dynamic' as opposed to the 'static' view of intrinsic worth.

The static view is that an individual (say, a man) is only entitled to be treated as a member of the egalitarian club if he possesses at the time the abilities that warrant membership of the club, for example, self-consciousness, rationality, etcetera. It is not enough that he has the potential for these abilities. Haksar attributes this view to Feinberg (1974). The dynamic view, which Haksar endorses, treats an individual as a member of the egalitarian club if he has or had the relevant potential. Whereas the static view would exclude foetuses, infants, the senile, the comatose, the psychopath, the catatonic schizophrenic and the dead from the egalitarian club, the dynamic view includes them.

My interest in these classifications is that Haksar claims that contract theory must also opt for either the static or the dynamic view of intrinsic worth, yet it cannot choose between these options unless it relies on noncontractualist considerations. It must, in Haksar's terminology, import 'perfectionist' assumptions.

I have already shown that the parties in a position of equal power would contract that the same criteria are not to be used in deciding how to treat persons as are used in deciding how to treat non-persons. Nonpersons include foetuses, infants, the senile, the comatose, the catatonic schizoid, and the dead - in fact, all of Haksar's list except the psychopath. Whereas persons are automatically members of the egalitarian club, nonpersons are not, as we saw with the case of the congenital idiot. If nonpersons are to be treated as if they were members of the egalitarian club, then argument is needed as to why this should be so. A contractarian, then, is committed to the 'static' view of intrinsic worth unless there is a contractarian argument to show that present and/or past potentiality to be a person entitles an individual to membership of the egalitarian club.

Haksar clearly regards it as a defect in a moral theory that foetuses, infants, the senile, the comatose, the catatonic schizoid and the dead are not granted certain rights granted to persons. He believes that all of these groups, except the dead, have a right to life. Those who were once persons are entitled to have contracts or promises honoured if these were made about situations that might obtain if these individuals ceased to be persons. Haksar, therefore, seeks a reflective equilibrium between theory and particular moral judgements such that his theory generates at least these particular moral judgements. Contractarianism may not generate exactly these particular moral judgements. The mere fact that it does not do so is not necessarily a defect. Haksar needs independent arguments to show why a perfectionist reflective equilibrium is to be preferred to a contractarian one.

Haksar attributes the rights he does to the kinds of non-persons listed earlier because he treats 'potentiality' to be a person as a rights-conferring characteristic. It may well be the case that there are good contractarian arguments for treating potentiality this way, although these contractarian arguments may not confer the relevant rights on all of the groups that Haksar wants.

In a position of equal power, the parties would contract that similar rights to life should be given to the comatose, the senile, the catatonic schizoid as are given to normal persons. They would certainly not treat the comatose, etcetera, as liable to whatever categories of painless killing are permitted with respect to animals. This is because the parties would themselves want not to be killed while in a coma or while a catatonic schizoid as long as they possessed the potential to become a person again.

Potential, therefore, is clearly relevant in determining the moral rightness of an action if the beings under consideration are likely to suffer at the prospect of being killed while they retain a potential for recovery. This is not the case, however, with foetuses and infants, who will not suffer at the thought of their never realising their potential. If foetuses and infants are to be given the same right to life as persons, then arguments other than the 'potential' argument will be needed.

The senile, too, constitute a different case as they have lost their potential to be a person. Their case has become like the congenital idiot case. Nonetheless, people will worry now about how they will be treated when senile. The parties in a position of equal power will contract to alleviate this worry by requiring people to give the senile the same right to life as the non-senile, with the proviso stated earlier. Singer himself gives an example of how this might be done. He suggests that anyone who does not want to be the subject of non-voluntary euthanasia under any circumstances should be able to register their refusal (p.139).

Contract theory of the kind I have been advocating, therefore, requires us to treat those with a potential for personhood as if they were persons, provided they have already been persons. Contract theory, therefore, agrees with Haksar that the comatose, and the catatonic schizoid, should have the same right to life as ordinary persons. Likewise, contract theory concludes that the senile should have this right, unless they voluntarily consented to waive it when they were persons. While this is not the place to spell out in detail a theory of euthanasia, the parties in a position of equal power would contract to build in certain safeguards against misuse of euthanasia, or its careless implementation.

Haksar's own 'pragmatic' justification will apply in those cases of catatonic schizoids who have no potentiality to become persons again. Until there are clear markers separating person from nonperson categories, all catatonics would be treated as persons. This is because the parties know that persons would worry that they might lose their right to life while catatonics, even though the catatonic has the potential to become a person again. This would worry them while they were persons. They would be less concerned about losing their right to life if they had become permanently nonperson catatonics, although even this might worry some of them. This could be overcome by prior consent to, or refusal of, euthanasia. The parties know that, once they are nonperson catatonics, they will not care if they are painlessly killed. As nonpersons they will live in the immediate present and the near past, with very little anticipation, if any, of the future. They will not be afraid of dying but nor will they resent staying alive.

It would appear, then, that the fact that foetuses have the potential to be persons does not provide a conclusive reason why they should be given the same rights as persons. It is not a defect, then, of contractarian theories that they cannot deduce that foetuses have these rights without importing perfectionist assumptions.

It should be noted, by the way, that many of the above points also apply to someone who is asleep (say, Ann). She is not desiring to be alive unless one wishes to say that she really has this desire in a dispositional as opposed to an occurrent form. Nonetheless, the parties in a position of equal power will agree that it was wrong to kill sleeping people just because their desire to live was not consciously present at the time.

What makes most humans different, then, from animals, foetuses, congenital idiots, etcetera, is that they are persons, that they have desires about the satisfaction of their desires. They value their person-freedom, their role as agents in deciding for themselves how to live their lives. They wish to exercise autonomy over their lives. Haksar, however, believes that the parties behind Rawls' veil of ignorance might well choose a society with little or no mental illness in preference to a society with a high degree of autonomy. In the next chapter I will look at his arguments for this claim and see whether or not they also apply to impartialism.

12 Impartialism and Autonomy

12.1 Introduction

Haksar believes that Rawls' parties behind the veil of ignorance must import certain perfectionist assumptions into their arguments if they are to conclude that people in the real world should never deprive each other of their autonomy. Is this true, and do the parties in the position of equal power have the same problem?

Haksar argues for his claim by imagining a Brave New World in which people are effectively conditioned from a very young age to have internally consistent but low-level desires. This system has eradicated all serious mental illness. Mental health, Haksar believes, would be seen by the parties behind the veil as a high ranking primary good that is as much under the control of the basic structure as self-respect is. The parties behind the veil cannot object to such a society on the grounds that it restricts freedoms and, thereby, contravenes Rawls' First Principle of Liberty. Haksar (p.177) argues that there is nothing in contractarianism that rules out making the worst-off better off by bringing them up not to set their sights too high so that their hopes and goals can be easily satisfied, thereby avoiding mental and emotional problems.

Haksar, then, has posed the question of the inviolability of autonomy in terms of what the parties behind the veil would regard as being the worst-off members of a society. It is, he believes, plausible to propose that the parties behind the veil would prefer a society with little or no autonomy and little or no mental illness to one in which each individual had a high degree of autonomy and a high likelihood of mental illness. His argument is, essentially, that the worst-off person in a brave new world will be happier than the worst-off individual in an autonomy-oriented society. This can be granted him. The truth of his conclusion, then, depends on whether happiness is the standard the parties behind the veil will adopt to determine who is the worst-off. It may be that they can be shown to be committed to the view that not being autonomous is worse

218

than not being happy. The way that Haksar has posed his Brave New World challenge to Rawls biases the argument in favour of a 'happiness' solution. This is because he adopts a particular 'hedonistic' conception of what it is to be rational. I will now look at how this 'hedonistic' understanding of rationality leads him to too swift a victory over Rawls.

12.2   Rationality

The parties behind the veil, by definition, do not know which people in the real world they are. As rational agents they will want whichever person they turn out to be to have his or her desires satisfied. This in no way entails that they must, as rational agents, want their desires to be such that they can be easily achieved or that they want their desires to be such that the chances are small of getting mentally distressed because these desires are not satisfied. Just because they may, if their desire is to be a painter as brilliant as Van Gogh, want this to be achieved with no more effort or suffering than necessary, it does not follow that, if there are desires that involve less effort and suffering than this one, then they will prefer them.

'Rationality', as I will use the term, merely requires that, whatever desire we have, we want to achieve it in a way that leaves maximum opportunity for the satisfaction of other desires compatible with the satisfaction of this one. One of the possible obstacles to the maximum satisfaction of other goals is that we take more time satisfying this one than we need, thereby leaving us less time to satisfy less of our other desires. This doesn't mean that all desires need to be satisfied quickly. Some of our desires, of their very nature, may involve a leisurely use of time. Nonetheless, the point remains that, as rational agents, we will not take more time than the nature of our desire requires. This is quite different from the requirement that our desires be such that they can be satisfied with little effort, or at little cost, or with little suffering, or in a quick time.

In Rawls' terms, a rational person (say Ben) has a life-plan. This means that his various desires are structured in an order of priority. It may be, for example, that he wants one particular desire satisfied regardless of whatever happens to the others he would also like to satisfy. A person's life-plan may be such that, although he would like desires D, E and F satisfied, he ranks them such that, if D and F can only be satisfied if E is not, then he would rather E be satisfied and D and F not. To return to a case we have considered before, namely, that of the political dissident (still

Ben) who wants a secure job, enjoys his work, wants to be happily married, have a contented home-life and good friends, while at the same time wanting that there be freedom of speech and other civil liberties in his nation. It may be the case that his nation is ruled by an oppressive regime so that his attempt to satisfy the last of these desires means that he frustrates all the others. Nonetheless, he may want the last more than all the others.

As a rational man, then, he will sacrifice these other desires to the pursuit of civil liberties within his nation. Any judgement to the effect that he should not do this is not a judgement of his rationality but a disagreement either with his choice of desires or with the lexical ordering he has placed on his desires. This is a disagreement in values. An individual's decisions about which desires are to be preferred to which, or what the lexical ordering between desires is to be, are not decisions whose rationality is open to question, except in so far as the lexical ordering is self-defeating. Rationality, as a quality of agents, is not of itself to beg the question in favour of the desires of some agents over those of others. Rather, it merely requires of any particular agent that his actions can be integrated as either consistently achieving a particular lexical ordering of desires or else that he has changed his mind and he is now acting so as to consistently achieve a new lexical ordering of desires.

It is perfectly possible, then, for a rational agent to want both to bring about civil liberties in his nation and avoid mental distress, yet so order his desires that he pursue civil liberties even if this means mental distress. Other rational agents may make the reverse choice. There is nothing in rationality itself that requires the one rather than the other. If someone so defines rationality that it does require one rather than the other, then this merely raises the question of why rationality in this sense should be desired. Rationality, in the sense I have given it, is not itself one of a number of kinds of desires, but merely a specification of what it is to want something more than something else.

If we are psychological hedonists, then we are likely to regard a person as rational only if he seeks to maximise the kinds of feelings concomitant upon the satisfaction of desires. This is because, as Frankena puts it, pleasure is our ultimate desire. It is what each of us aims at. It is what is good in itself (p.85). This means that, over a life-time, the more desires one has that result in these feelings the more 'rational' one has been. I will call these feelings 'happy feelings'.[1]

The dissident I described in Chapter 1 would be judged irrational by these criteria. She should have calculated the happy feelings that would have come from keeping her job, seeing her family, etcetera, weighed these against the happy feelings she will get as a political prisoner in a labour camp, then chosen whichever maximised her happy feelings. As a political prisoner, she will at least have happy feelings associated with her preservation of her self-image as a woman of integrity, and so on, but, qua happy feelings, this will be far outweighed by the happy feelings she would have got as a hypocrite, or as a moral coward.

Rationality defined this way, however, is merely one kind of desire among a number of kinds of desire. There can be conflicts of desire between Group A who want to resolve conflicts of desires 'rationally' in this sense of 'rational' and Group B who don't. The parties behind the veil, as such, need have no commitment either way. This conflict of desires is just one among many. They do not, however, give any special treatment to Group A just because Group A tries to persuasively define 'rationality' to make its criterion for resolving conflicts of desires the only 'rational' one in the desire-neutral sense of 'rationality'. Our political prisoner is quite rational in this desire-neutral sense in that he wants to be a man of integrity more than he wants to maximise the amount of happy feelings he has in his life. To him, the mental distress that is associated with his decision is worthwhile.

Haksar, then, only shows that the parties behind the veil would choose the Brave New World over an autonomy-oriented society if they accept that the criterion of being worse-off is being mentally distressed rather than autonomous. The political prisoner, however, would regard himself as worse-off if he were to be less mentally distressed and less autonomous. Haksar's argument, therefore, begs the point at issue. What he needs to do is to show that the parties behind the veil would believe that a person was worse off when she was mentally distressed but autonomous than when she was neither, even if they did not already value lack of mental distress more than autonomy.

In other words, he cannot attribute to them a concept of rationality that is really a value-judgement in disguise. As rational agents, they are to be construed as out to maximise the satisfaction of their desires. This, however, does not mean that they are only interested in maximising the happy feelings that come from having desires satisfied. Rather, they are concerned with satisfying desires in the sense of bringing about whatever state of affairs is the object of the desire. It may be that the state of affairs that they want to come into existence more than any other is the one in which they maximise their happy feelings. If so, they are psychological hedonists of the kind I have described above.

It may be, however, that the state of affairs they most want to see come into existence is a society with political and civil liberties, or an autonomous society, or the destruction of their enemies regardless of the cost to themselves. Rationality merely requires that they take whatever course of action is most effective in achieving these desires and any other compatible with them. It does not require them to abandon these desires and replace them by others. The same points would seem to apply to the parties if they are considered as being in a position of equal power rather than behind a veil of ignorance, given the symmetry and noncoercion requirements.

12.3 Autonomy

We have seen that rationality itself does not require the parties in a position of equal power to prefer mental health to autonomy. It could still be the case, however, that the impartialist axioms are not strong enough to generate the conclusions that an autonomous society is to be preferred to a Brave New World. Haksar claims that Rawls' principles only become strong enough if they are combined with perfectionist assumptions. It could be the case that impartialism, too, needs perfectionist assumptions. I will now consider whether this is so.

I will say that a person Ann removes another person Ben's autonomy when Ann controls Ben's will in the sense that, whenever there is a conflict of desires between them, Ann can bring Ben to want to do whatever Ann wants him to do.[2] If Ben is not autonomous, then he is not capable of resisting Ann's will. It is not just that she always wins in any conflict between them, but that Ben cannot control what he himself does. He may be aware of this. He may know that what he wants is to do X yet find his will controlled in such a way that he finds himself doing Y which he does not want to do, and does not intend to do. It is as if he watches himself doing Y rather than being the agent who does Y.

Alternatively, Ben may not even be aware that his will is controlled by Ann. He may always think that he wants to do X, when the cause of his wanting to do X is that Ann wants him to. If Ann had the means by which to deprive Ben of his autonomy, this would be a very satisfactory way, from Ann's point of view, of resolving conflicts of desire between herself and Ben. Ann, then, would be prescribing the principle that, when there is a conflict of desires between herself and Ben, then Ben's will be under her control.

Symmetrified, this becomes the principle that Ann be free to coerce Ben by controlling his will and Ben be free to coerce Ann by controlling her will. As neither of them can be in a position of equal power unless they want not to be coerced more than they want to coerce, they will reject this proposal. We have, then, another impartialist principle, namely, the 'autonomy' principle. It is the principle that Ann not be free to coerce B by controlling his will and Ben not be free to coerce Ann by controlling her will. In other words, within impartialism it is wrong for either party to resolve a conflict of desires by depriving others of their autonomy.

The Autonomy Principle:- *No conflict of desires between people is ever to be resolved by one party depriving the other of its autonomy.*

This still leaves it open for Ann to take someone who lacks autonomy but would later develop it naturally, for example, a neonate, and to bring up the neonate so that its will is subservient to hers. She has not deprived the neonate of its autonomy. Nonetheless, she shows a lack of respect for autonomy that most contractarian philosophers would regard as totally reprehensible. Can this reprehensibility be deduced from the impartialist axioms?

In the kind of case I have proposed, Ann is an autonomous rational agent, that is, a person, whereas the neonate is not. It has a potential for autonomy but, as we saw in discussing abortion, potential is not a factor the parties in the position of equal power would take into account as it doesn't affect the actual desires of the participant with the unrealised potential. As a consequence, the discussion so far does not entitle the parties in the position of equal power to conclude that it would be wrong of Ann to deny the neonate the opportunity to realise its potential for autonomy.

This kind of conflict of desires, however, misrepresents the actual argument in everyday life about how Ann should behave. The argument is not between the person Ann and the neonate. By definition, if the neonate is a nonperson then it is incapable of argument. Instead, the argument would be between the person Ann and some other person Ben about how

Ann might treat a nonperson N or even about how Ann should treat Ben should he become a nonperson. In this case, however, the only aspect of nonpersonhood we are concerned with is lack of autonomy.

I will consider first the case of an argument between Ann and Ben about how she should treat him if he were to lose his autonomy temporarily. What we are to have in mind here is that Ann and Ben, who are still both persons, are discussing a scenario in which he is no longer a person. In that scenario, Ben may lack certain kinds of desires such that Ann does not frustrate any of his desires by making him permanently nonautonomous, even though she does this solely to make him a slave to her will. Ann, then, may want to turn Ben into a permanent state of nonautonomy should ever the situation arise where he accidentally becomes temporarily nonautonomous.

In wanting him to be a slave to her will, Ann is prescribing the principle 'Ann is to be free to keep Ben permanently nonautonomous whenever he accidentally loses enough of his autonomy to no longer desire to retain it'. She would only advocate this principle in the position of equal power, however, if she thought that she would be in a position of superior power in the real world, so it fails the symmetry test as it stands. Even then, it is hardly a principle that Ben as a rational agent with desires that may well be in conflict with Ann's, that is, who is not her superfan, could agree to.

Were her principle to be symmetrified, so that it also proposed that Ben be free to keep Ann permanently nonautonomous whenever she accidentally loses enough of her autonomy to no longer desire to retain it, then it would be excluded by the noncoercionist requirement. If Ann is a noncoercionist, as she has to be if unforced agreement is to be possible, then she will not risk being forced because she is nonautonomous just to have a chance to force Ben because he is nonautonomous.

This still leaves the case of the new-born infant. Should a baby with the potential to be an autonomous agent be denied the realisation of this autonomy in order to become the compliant tool of already autonomous agents. Would we ever be justified in operating on children to remove their capacity for autonomy or even of manipulating genetic codes to breed a race of willing slaves? Again, the argument here has to be between the two autonomous agents Ann and Ben about how infants should be treated. This case differs from a temporary loss of autonomy in that infants have never been autonomous. It is not a case of Ann's being concerned to ensure that she be returned to autonomy as soon as possible.

As an already autonomous agent she has no concern to ensure that she becomes autonomous in the first place, and those who are not yet autonomous have no desire of theirs for autonomy frustrated if their potential is never realised.

As we have seen, Ann and Ben would agree that neither them should deprive the other of autonomy. They would agree to whatever non-coercive measures were available that were likely to reduce the chances of one depriving the other of autonomy. One of these would be to create a climate in society in which autonomy in others was valued. If Ann values Ben's autonomy, then she is less likely to regret the fact that no accident has yet befallen Ben to deprive him of his autonomy so that she can take advantage of this to make him a mere instrument of her will.

In fact, it is this tendency to treat other people as a mere instrument of one's own will if one doesn't value their autonomy that would be of greatest concern to them given that they have agreed that neither of them is to coercively deprive the other of autonomy. If Ann is hopeful that Ben will lose his autonomy accidentally then it is difficult to see how Ann can have a sincere desire not to deprive Ben of his autonomy coercively. It would seem that Ann has no real respect for Ben's autonomy but merely is constrained by laws punishing the coercive deprivation of autonomy. Ben's autonomy is best protected from coercive deprivation by Ann if she genuinely wants him to be autonomous. Such a genuine desire would carry over into the desire that Ben regain his autonomy if he accidentally loses it, that is, it carries over into a disposition to want Ben's potential for autonomy restored if the actuality is temporarily lost. A concern for the actualisation of Ben's potential autonomy shows that Ann doesn't regard him as a mere instrument of her will but values his independence. It would be built into the socialisation and educational processes of the community.

It also shows that Ann values the fact that Ben has desires and wishes of his own that come into occasional conflict with hers and which she wants to have resolved by impartialist processes. It shows that she treats him as an agent whose life-plan for her own life is worth equal consideration with her own. She sees him as someone with whom she must enter into argument about how to resolve conflicts of desires. She shows respect for his personhood. All of these qualities of character are qualities they will want to have towards each other as re-inforcements of the agreement that they are not to coercively deprive each other of their autonomy.

If Ann, then, in the real world, sees infants with this potential for autonomy as mere instruments of her will then she shows the kind of lack of respect for autonomy itself that is the cause of concern to both herself and Ben in a position of equal power in the case where she seems to be anxious for Ben to lose his autonomy in an accident. A disposition to value the actualisation of the potential for autonomy in people who have temporarily lost it will be difficult to separate from a disposition to value the actualisation of autonomy per se. The disposition to take advantage of an infant's helplessness to permanently frustrate its potential for autonomy so that it can be an instrument of one's will is difficult to distinguish from the disposition to permanently frustrate anyone's potential for autonomy to make them an instrument of one's will.

It would appear, then, that there is a theory of the virtues that can be derived from the impartialist axioms. I have only sketched here some of the dispositions the parties in a position of equal power would want developed in the real world. What they would regard as crucial, however, is that the people in the real world develop attitudes that foster their commitment to the use of impartialism itself as the method for resolving conflicts of desires. One way of resolving conflicts of desires is by deprivation of autonomy. The parties in a position of equal power, however, agree this should not be done.

It is important, then, that Ann and Ben want people to be autonomous, that they want the principles that govern conflicts of desires to be the ones that autonomous agents would agree to under impartialist conditions. They would discourage the tendency to turn others into mere instruments of one's own will. As a consequence, the potential for autonomy, as well as its actualisation, would be valued because those who did not value it would show a manipulative inclination even towards those in whom it was actualised in that they seem to be playing a waiting game for the moment when this actual autonomy is temporarily lost.

These, then, are the kinds of considerations that can be employed within impartialism to arrive at the conclusions that autonomy is preferable to the kind of Brave New World that Haksar describes. Perfectionist assumptions have not been necessary.

Before concluding this discussion, though, it should be noted that impartialism is not bound to the notion that a rational person (say, Ann) must have a life-plan in the sense of definite goals that have greater priority than others. As a rule this will be the case, but there is nothing self-contradictory in the idea that one live an aimless life, the life of a beachcomber, an unsettled life not structured to achieve anything in particular. One may wish to live for the moment, to take things as they come. There is no logical obligation on us to be ambitious. What would seem to matter, from a happiness point of view, is that we can look back on our lives and feel satisfied with how we lived it. The sensualist, the sloth, the drifter, the opium smoker, may all be able to do this. All that impartialism demands of them is that they do so within the constraints imposed on them by the parties in the position of equal power.

Not only does Haksar think that perfectionist assumptions must be smuggled into the veil of ignorance to ensure that autonomy has a special value there, he also argues that the particular judgements about just institutions that Rawls derives from the veil depend on certain unacknowledged metaphysical assumptions about the nature of personal identity. In the next chapter I will consider whether or not this is so, and whether impartialism has the same problem.

Notes

1   Barrow (1980, pp.62-65) argues that it is logically necessary in order for Ann, say, to be happy that she have a sense that there is a fit between how things are and how one desires them to be. He calls this sense the 'feeling of enmeshment'. It can be achieved either by changing the world to fit whatever desires Ann has or changing her desires to fit the world. If it is rational to maximise this feeling, then it may be more rational to change one's desires than to change the world. Similar problems arise if we talk of 'preferences' rather than 'desires'. We can maximise the extent to which the preferences Ann has over her life are satisfied by changing her preferences to more easily satisfied ones. This fits in with the discussion on utilitarianism in Chapter 1.

2   Stanley Benn (p.116) distinguishes the inner-impelled or 'autarchic' person from the 'heterarchic' person. Heterarchic persons include those who act under hypnosis or who are brain-washed or who cannot even think that they might disobey an authoritarian parent. Haksar's challenge is that Rawls' principles do not rule out heterarchy.

13 Impartialism and Personal Identity

13.1 Haksar's Criticisms

One of the major metaphysical assumptions that an ethical theory can make is an assumption about the nature of personal identity. Haksar (pp.106-107) believes that the particular moral judgements derivable from Rawls' form of contract theory depend on a presupposition of the persistent self. If one adopts, instead, an alternative metaphysics which denies the existence of the persistent self then, Haksar argues, Rawls' anti-utilitarian particular moral judgements no longer follow. Is this also true of impartialism? Before I try to answer this question I will need to spell out in sufficient detail the two contending metaphysical theories of personal identity that Haksar considers.

13.2 Parfit's 'Complex' Theory of Personal Identity

We will need a terminology in which to pose alternative theories of personal identity, without thereby begging the question against any particular theory. Parfit (p.63), for example, suggests that talk of 'selves' or 'subjects of consciousness' is harmless enough as long as we treat them as convenient abbreviations for actions, thoughts and experiences and their various interconnections. Haksar offers no objection to this terminology, so I will use it to pose the disagreement between him and Parfit.

A 'self', as described by Parfit, is a technical term bearing little relation to the ordinary language use of 'self'. It refers to the contents of consciousness of a particular individual over some period of time. It is, in fact, nothing more than a particular time-slice of the consciousness of a particular bodily individual.

Generally speaking, there will only be one self to any one body at any one time. I will refer to the self in the body B1 at the time T1 as the self B1 S1. This self will have visual, tactile, auditory, olfactory, gustatory kinaesthetic, pain, etcetera, sensations from a perspective located within B1. I will, therefore, say that the self B1 S1 is 'located' in B1. It is possible that B1 may contain more than one self at T1, or that there may be selves that are located at a particular spatial point where there is no spatio-temporal body. The terminology of 'selves' does not rule out these possibilities. Whatever is said about the central case of one self in one body at one time can be modified to apply to these cases where (or if) they occur.

The terminology of 'selves' should not beg the question in favour of one metaphysical theory rather than another. This means that whatever makes the time slice of the consciousness of B1 at T1 the 'same' self as the time-slice of B1's consciousness at T2 must not depend on which meta-physical theory of personal identity is true. We must be able to pose any metaphysical theory about personal identity in 'self' terminology without thereby guaranteeing its truth or falsity by definition. This makes the duration of a 'self' a matter of convenience. Sometimes it will suit us to start S1 at the onset of consciousness in B1 for the day and conclude S1 when B1 goes into deep sleep for that day. Other times it will suit us to treat S1 as a year in length, or a mere thought in length.

Another technical term I wish to introduce is 'individual'. I shall say that B1 S20 believes itself to be the same 'bodily' individual as B1 S1, when it believes that its body is the same body as B1 S1's body; B1 SN believes itself to be the same 'suffering' individual as B1 S1 when it believes that B1 S1's pains were also its pains; B1 SN believes itself to be the same 'remembering' individual as B1 S1 when it believes that the experiences that B1 S1 remembers are the same experiences that it remembers. There may, of course, be no such things as individuals. Whether they exist is one of the bones of contention between the competing metaphysical theories of personal identity. We could also have 'intending' individuals, 'feeling' individuals (in the sense of 'feeling' emotions), and so on.

If B1 S1 is the same individual as B1 S2 then I shall say that B1 S1 and B1 S2 are both instances of L1. This can be represented by L1 B1 S1 and L1 B1 S2. If, however, they are not the same individual, this will be reflected by a change in the notation such as L1 B1 S1 to L2 B1 S1. Parfit believes that S1 is the same individual L1 as S2 when two conditions are met.

The first of these conditions is that there is psychological connectedness between S1 and S2. 'Connectedness' is a 'direct' psychological relation, that is, it is the kind of relation that holds between a memory of an experience and the experience it is a memory of, or between the intention to perform some action and the action. Personal identity is a matter of degree. The greater the connectedness between S1's experiences and intentions and S2's memories and actions, then the more inclined we are, Parfit believes, to say that S1 and S2 are part of the same individual L1. The less these connections, the less inclined we are to identify them.

The second condition is that there is psychological continuity between S1 and SN. S1 is psychologically continuous with SN if there is a chain of connections between S1 and SN, for example, SN remembers S3's experiences, S3 remembers S2's, S2 remembers S1's, but SN need not remember S2's or S1's and S3 need not remember S1's, and so on. The more continuities there are between S1's experiences and intentions and SN's memories and actions, the more inclined we are, Parfit thinks, to say that S1 and SN are both instances of L1.

Whether S1 is the same individual as S2 or SN, according to Parfit is a matter of degree. It is a convention we adopt because it suits our purposes in certain kinds of case. Some purposes require a greater number of connections than others. For Parfit, the identity of S1 and S2 is analogous to the identity of England before and after 1066. Was it still the same 'nation'? From the point of view of geography it was but from the point of view of political control it was not.

13.3 Haksar's 'Simple' Theory of Personal Identity

Haksar (p.81, p.83) claims that personal identity is not a matter of degree. It is an all-or-nothing business. The identity of S1 and S2 is not analogous to the identity of a nation. Rather, it is as if there is an underlying 'metaphysical' substance called the 'individual' that endures from S1 to S2, linking them together through changes of memory and intention and, possible, changes of body. Haksar believes that Rawls' contractarianism assumes the truth of the simple view of personal identity. If the complex view is true, then many of Rawls' particular moral judgements would not follow from his veil of ignorance conditions. In particular, he would not be able to avoid utilitarian moral judgements.

My concern is whether Haksar's criticisms of Rawls' contractarianism also apply to impartialist contractarianism. This depends on whether or not the impartialist contractarian must assume the truth of either one or the other of these two metaphysical theories of personal identity (or of any other such theories). I will argue that he or she does not need to do so. To do this I will look at the particular moral judgements that Haksar claims do depend on the simple view and show either that impartialist contractarianism can generate these judgements or else show that impartialist contractarianism can reject these particular moral judgements without depending on any metaphysical view of personal identity in either case.

13.4 Continuity of Body and Potentiality

Haksar (pp.84-86) states that the human infant has the potential to lead a significant life, except for such cases as congenital idiots. He believes that infants with this potential have the right to develop it. Their having this right, he claims, depends on their being the same substance as the adult they eventually become. This right, then, depends on the simple view of personal identity being true. If the complex view is true, he thinks (p.84), then the infant's right to develop its potential can always be sacrificed for utilitarian ends because the infant and the adult need not be viewed as the same individual, as a continuous slice of the same 'substance'. Its potential, therefore, gives it only an instrumental value. There is no reason to think that it is any more intrinsically valuable than other beings at the same actual level of rationality, etcetera, such as ants, bees or sperms.

Such a claim poses a number of questions for impartialist contractarianism. Firstly, does impartialist contractarianism generate the particular moral judgement that human infants with the potential to lead significant lives have the right to develop this potential? Secondly, if impartialist contractarianism accepts or denies this particular moral judgement does it do so because it either accepts or denies one of either the simple or the complex theories of personal identity? We have already discussed the impartialist treatment of potentiality. In this chapter I will take up the question of or not impartialism presupposes the simple view of personal identity.

Let us consider a particular kind of being X, namely, homo sapiens. Each member of X at some time TN is a self, SN, of some particular body BN. Let us consider the case of SN of the body B1. The body B1 has changed over time, as have the bodies of all members of X. At some time T, body B1 was in its infant stage. Now, twenty years later at T20 it is in its adult stage. It is, however, still properly identified as B1 because there has been a spatio-temporal continuity to all its changes. The selves located in B1 in its infant stage were not persons in the technical sense of 'person' introduced earlier, that is, they were not rational self-conscious agents. Nonetheless, given normal conditions of development, the selves in the adult stage of B1 will be persons. The infant B1 then possesses the potential to become a person, but is not yet a person.

What contracts would be reached by people arguing as if behind a veil of ignorance about how such beings should treat each other at their various stages of development? They are to argue as if they don't know whether or not they are B1 or B2 or, if they are B1 say, as if they don't know whether they are the infant B1 S1 or the adult B1 S20. Also, any particular party (say, Ben) behind the veil is to argue as if his desires were the desires of B1 S1 or B1 S20 in the real world. He is not to argue as if what matters is how he, the person behind the veil, wants B1 S1 to be treated should he ever turn out to be B1 S1. Rather, he is to argue as if what matters is how B1 S1 thinks B1 S1 should be treated in the circumstances under consideration. If B1 S1 in the real world is an infant, that is, still a nonperson, then the only desires he will have at this stage of his life are nonperson desires, and these do not include the desire for life, given that he is not yet conceptually capable of such a desire.

The parties behind the veil, however, do know that, if they are B1 S20, then what they are able to do now at T20 to implement their plans will be greatly affected by what has been done to B1 at T1 and at the times in between. They know that S20 will not want his plans frustrated because injuries done to B1 at T1 make it impossible at T20 to do what he wants. They will, therefore, want to prevent people negligently or maliciously causing the infant B1 any injuries at T1, given the assumption that B1 will live to become the self S20. They will contract, therefore, to penalise people who do cause such injuries in order to ensure that such injuries do not occur to them, whether they are B1 or B2 or BN.

They will do this even if they only believe that the selves of B1 from T1 to T19 are selves of the same bodily individual as the self at T20. Whether S1 to S20 is the same individual in any other sense in no way affects the degree to which S20 has been handicapped at T20 by the injuries B1 has received between T1 and T19. People arguing as if behind a veil of ignorance, then, do not need to presuppose any particular theory of personal identity in order to reach a contract about how adult members of the species X should treat infant members of X. This contract, however, does assume that a particular self S20 of some body B of the species X wants handicaps to the implementation of its plans minimised but this is not an assumption about personal identity. It is, rather, a consequence of adult Xs being persons, that is, rational self-conscious agents.

As the parties behind the veil argue from the viewpoint of the being whose interests are affected, they will be indifferent as to whether or not B1 S1 is painlessly killed because B1 S1 is not a person with the concepts of himself as continuing to exist over time with a future and a past. B1 S1 lacks the concepts of life and death, consequently he cannot desire to be alive rather than dead. No desire of his is frustrated by killing him painlessly. As B1 S1, however, the parties behind the veil will seek to avoid threatening and painful situations so they will wish to be protected from these. They will not be concerned to ensure that they develop their potential to lead significant lives because they lack the concepts necessary to possess such a desire.

They will contract, therefore, to prevent cruelty to infant Xs, but it is by no means obvious that they would contract to give an infant X the right to develop its potential to lead a significant life. If they do give it this right it will be for some 'indirect' reason such as the distress caused to adult Xs by the thought that infant Xs lack this right. It will not be because infant Xs have more intrinsic worth than an ant or a bee or a sperm. An infant X is not relevantly different to ants, etcetera, in spite of its potential to lead a significant life. Like ants, its desires are not frustrated by its being killed painlessly, nor is the lack of frustration altered by the fact that it possesses a potential that ants do not.

We have seen, then, that contractarianism can generate distinctions between kinds of beings relevant to conclusions about how they ought to be treated. I have not worked through completely where contractarianism would take us on the moral status of infants as this would require an investigation of a range of factual issues of no direct bearing on the present enquiry. Nonetheless, enough has been done to show that contractarianism can lead to particular moral judgements without presupposing the truth of either the simple or the complex theory of personal identity. All that is needed is that the parties behind the veil consider the case of a rational self-conscious agent B1 S20 whose body B1 at T20 either is, or is believed by B1 S20 to be, spatiotemporally continuous with a particular infant body at T1 such that he believes any harm to B1 at T1 frustrates or hampers the implementation of his plans at T20. He does not need to believe, nor does it need to be the case, that he is an individual in any sense other than the same bodily individual L1 B1 S1 to L1 B1 SN.

These conclusions also apply to impartialist contractarianism as well as to Rawls' version, as the symmetry condition performs the same role for impartialism as the veil does for Rawls' theory.

13.5   Continuity of Suffering

Haksar argues that any theory which requires the pursuit of utilitarian goals to be constrained by nonutilitarian rights must presuppose the simple view and reject the complex view. As contract theories are intended to generate such nonutilitarian moral constraints they must presuppose the simple theory.   In fact, Haksar suggests, the complex theory is incompatible with any humane morality because its denial of the persistent individual seems to commit it to the view that on-going suffering and murder are not the evils that most of us think they are. After all, if the complex theory is right, then the self which suffers at T1 is not the one that is still suffering at T20 and the self that is alive at T1 is not the self that dies at T20 (p.111).

Does impartialist contract theory, then, agree with Haksar that it is much worse for the same individual to go suffering on and on than it is for the same amount of suffering to be divided among different individuals? Whichever it is, is it the case that impartialist contract theory can only arrive at its answer by presupposing either the simple or the complex view of personal identity?

Earlier I said that the self B1 SN believes itself to be the same suffering individual as B1 S1 when it believes that B1 S1's suffering is the same as its suffering. Any particular self (say, Ben) B1 S1 may believe that he is the same suffering individual as the self B1 S20 or he may not. He may also believe that he is the same suffering individual as B2 S20, but I will limit my discussion for the moment to cases where the selves that regard themselves as belonging to the same individual are all located in the same body.

The self B1 S1 may be wrong in believing that he is the same suffering individual as B1 S20. He will be wrong if the simple theory of personal identity is false and the complex theory true. Nonetheless, regardless of the truth or falsity of either theory, B1 S1 regards himself as the same suffering individual as the selves B1 S2 to B1 S20. This belief has certain consequences for how he regards the suffering of B1 S20. Granted that B1 S1 is a rational self-conscious agent, he will want to minimise his suffering, unless, in some way, greater suffering achieves his plans better than lesser suffering.

This exception, however, raises questions about what is to count as a rational agent rather than whether our judgements about the wrongness of suffering depend on one theory of personal identity rather than another. I will assume, then, that B1 S1 wants to minimise his suffering. As he regards himself as the same individual as the selves B1 S2 to B1 S20 he will also want to minimise the suffering of B1 S2 to B1 S20.

He doesn't need to believe that his later selves will remember his thoughts, experiences, emotions or intentions or even that these later selves will have relevantly similar thoughts, intentions, etcetera. While a self B1 S1 (Ben) may believe he is part of some suffering individual L1 this doesn't mean that he is right. Contract theory would have to beg the metaphysical question against the complex theory if it needed to assume that B1 S1's belief was true before contractarian moral conclusions could be derived from it.

The parties behind the veil, however, do not know whether they are a self that believes it is part of an suffering individual or not. This means they will have to consider a different contract for each of the following cases:- (1) a contract governing how the selves of a particular suffering individual L1 should treat other suffering individuals L2, L3 to LN; (2) a contract governing how suffering individuals should treat the selves of nonsuffering individuals, and vice versa; (3) a contract governing how the selves of a particular suffering individual LN should treat each other; (4) a contract governing how the selves located in the body of one nonsuffering individual should treat each other; (5) a contract governing how selves located in different nonsuffering individuals should treat each other.

In Case (3) each self will be out to minimise the suffering of each other self because it regards this suffering as its own and it wishes to minimise its own suffering. The various selves of a suffering individual can be treated as one self with respect to minimising suffering. This is how the parties behind the veil would contract for the selves of the one suffering individual to treat each other, that is, they would contract that a self that believed itself to be identical with respect to suffering as a number of other selves would minimise suffering across all of those selves considered as a unit.

In case (1), I can talk of how individual L1 should treat L2 to LN rather than use the terminology of selves and the BN SN notation. (Individual L1 SN is understood to be located in body B1.) The parties behind the veil do not know which of LI to LN they are, therefore they will want to enter into whichever contract offers the best chance that they will minimise suffering no matter who they are. This means that they will contract to ensure that, as far as possible, suffering is distributed equally between L1 to LN. This means that they will contract for L1 to LN to be bound by laws that have this effect. Offenders will be penalised to discourage the offence, because the offence is a case where the offender has benefited him or herself at the cost of a greater than equal suffering to someone else.

The parties behind the veil, then, can enter into a contract about how individuals of the kind L1 to LN should treat each other. This contract supports the particular moral judgement that it is worse for the one individual to go suffering on and on than for the same amount of suffering to be distributed among a number of individuals, provided the selves of each individual concerned have a concept of themselves as members of the same suffering individual, and provided inequalities in suffering are due to the deliberate acts of other suffering individuals or are remediable by the deliberate acts of suffering individuals.

This particular moral judgement has been reached, however, without presupposing the existence of individuals (in a deep sense) or without presupposing their non-existence. It has been arrived at instead by investigating what contracts the parties behind the veil would negotiate to cover the case of selves that regarded their own suffering as that of the same suffering individual. It was not even assumed that there actually are such selves.

As it happens, there are such selves, namely the selves of nearly every adult human capable of participating in moral discussions. Consequently, the particular moral judgements that follow from the hypothetical contract are binding on all such humans, provided we adopt contract theory as our moral basis. Even though there are such selves, it doesn't follow that the metaphysical theory that there really are suffering individuals is true. It may be that there is no metaphysical basis to this belief. The complex theory could be true instead, with the consequence that any self that believed its suffering to be that of a suffering individual would just be mistaken. Whether such selves are mistaken or not, until they have been convinced that they are mistaken, they will continue to behave as if they were selves of one suffering individual, therefore the parties behind the veil can negotiate contracts about how the individuals which such selves believe themselves to constitute should treat each other.

Nonetheless, it may seem a weakness of contract theory that the force of the contract depends on whether or not a particular self remains convinced that it is a member of a suffering individual, especially if this belief cannot be rationally justified or can be shown to be false. After all, if it can be shown to be false, then rational selves will abandon this belief, thereby exempting themselves from the contract governing the behaviour of selves who conceive of themselves as suffering individuals. This means that they are no longer required by this contract to regard it as worse that one individual goes suffering on and on than that the same amount of suffering be divided amongst a number of 'bodies'.

The availability of the complex theory of personal identity, then, enables any particular individual B1 (say, a man) to claim exemption from the contract and its penalties on the grounds that he does not regard the suffering of future selves of his body as his suffering. The parties behind the veil, however, will not be convinced that he is entitled to exemption merely because he claims to be a nonsuffering individual. They know that suffering individuals will not want other suffering individuals to pretend to be nonsuffering in order to be exempt from the contract and its penalties. It will have to be the case that the claimant really does not regard himself as a suffering individual. There will need to be evidence of this. If he is exempt merely because he claims to be nonsuffering without support of sufficient evidence then this will lead to pretenders bringing about a reduction in their fair share of the equal distribution of suffering at the cost of someone else's increase.

The parties behind the veil will not consent to this, consequently they will require that the claim to be nonsuffering be consistent with the way that the claimant has behaved or will behave. The claimant, for example, the human B1, will have to have acted in the past as if he was indifferent to his likely suffering in the present. There can be no indications that his past selves continuously planned to minimise suffering for his later selves. Just as importantly, he cannot appeal in the present to the consequences for him in the future of his being treated as a suffering individual because, if he is truly nonsuffering, it shouldn't worry him that there is some future self of his body that is penalised for the actions of this present self.

It is possible, however, that a suffering individual (say a woman) at T1 will become nonsuffering in the future. Should this occur, the parties behind the veil will not want her penalised as if she had remained a suffering individual. This is because the point of the penalty is twofold. Firstly, it is to deter the offender and others from breaking the law. Secondly, it is to prevent the offender getting away with a benefit she has gained at someone else's expense. She cannot be permitted to have created an imbalance in the distribution of suffering such that she preserves the benefit she has hurt others to get.

There is no point, then, in penalising someone who will not be deterred and who, in a sense, does not gain a benefit at someone else's expense because she is not the same individual as the offender. The offender did not plan that the benefit be her benefit. Admittedly, the benefit was enjoyed by someone, and that someone had no right to it, but neither is that someone guilty of improperly obtaining this benefit. The parties behind the veil will not want beings of this kind to be a threat to the lives, safety, property, etcetera, of suffering individuals, but they also will not want such a being treated as if she were responsible for her acts in the way suffering individuals are. They will want her to be able to live her life in a manner that maximises the satisfactions of each of her selves, while minimising her risk to other people.

This will mean that she will become a cost to society. Just in case they turn out to be a nonsuffering individual they will require suffering individuals to contribute something to her maintenance and, possibly, cure. They would seek to return a nonsuffering individual to her former suffering condition if the former suffering individual's expressed wishes or actual behaviour indicated that this is what she would have wanted. Nonsuffering individuals are indifferent to the suffering of their future selves so they will not oppose such a contract. As nonsuffering individuals are indifferent to the suffering of their future selves, they will be indifferent about which contracts exist to regulate the behaviour of their future selves, or the treatment given to their future selves.

There will be no point, therefore, in the parties behind the veil negotiating special contracts to govern the behaviour of nonsuffering individuals because nonsuffering individuals are no more capable of honouring contracts than animals or very young children. Unlike animals and young children, nonsuffering individuals fully understand what a contract is, and how it governs future behaviour. They will not oppose contracts governing how suffering individuals treat nonsuffering individuals because they do not regard the suffering such contracts may bring their future selves as, in any sense, their suffering.

We have seen, then, that the parties behind the veil will be able to negotiate contracts which govern the behaviour of both suffering and nonsuffering individuals, even given that they must assess the acceptability of these contracts from the viewpoints of both kinds of individual. In negotiating these contracts, they did not need to assume the truth or falsity of either theory, although they were only able to negotiate these contracts because they took into account the viewpoint of beings that believed themselves to be suffering individuals. The applicability of the contract, then, depends on the actual existence of beings that believe themselves to be suffering individuals.

As I indicated earlier, most humans regard themselves in this way. The contract negotiated by the parties behind the veil, then, applies to most humans, that is, to all who regard themselves as suffering individuals. We have also seen that those human beings who do not regard themselves as suffering individuals will not oppose this contract, regardless of the truth or falsity of the simple or complex theories of personal identity.

Let us suppose, however, that the simple theory is false. This merely shows that there is no metaphysical entity enduring from T1 to TN in which the experiences of S1 and S2 both subsist, or which subtends these experiences. Must B1 S1, who has regarded itself as part of a suffering individual, now cease to do so? It must certainly cease to believe that there is such an individual, but it can, without an error of reason, continue to value the experiences of B1 S1 to B1 SN in a way that it does not value the experiences of B2 S1 to B2 SN.

There are, however, factors that reduce the arbitrariness of B1 S1's valuing more the avoidance of B1 S2's suffering than B2 S1's, even if the complex theory is true. After all, B1 S2's suffering occurs against a background of contents of consciousness continuous with B1 S1's but not with B2 S1's. The self B1 S1's visual, tactile, etcetera, experiences, its pains, tickles and other sensations, are all experienced from a perspective located in B1 as are B1 S2's, whereas B2 S1's are in B2. If the complex theory is true, then the presence of all these factors provide the basis for adopting the conventions that B1 S1 and B1 S2 are the same suffering individual but the important point is that they, or something similar, have to be present to give the convention a foothold.

The more of them that disappear the less the selves of B1 are likely to regard themselves as the 'same' individual along any of the axes of individuality, for example, if B1 S2 remembers none of B1 S1's experiences then B1 S2 will not regard itself as the same remembering individual as B1 S1. If B1 S2 no longer has desires of the same kind as B1 S1 then it will not regard itself as the same intending individual as B1 S1, and so on. The fewer types of individual that B1 S2 believes it and B1 S1 are both parts of, then the less likely B1 S2 is to regard itself as the same as B1 S1.

Williams, however, argues that a particular self B1 S1 could believe that future selves B1 S2 to B1 SN could share no memories, intentions, emotions, etcetera, and yet B1 S1 still believe itself to be the same suffering individual as B1 S2 to B1 SN. Even if Williams is not right about all humans, he only needs to be right about some for it to be the case that contract theory applies, whatever the metaphysical truth.

What, then, of the person (say, a man) in an actual philosophical argument who either holds the complex theory of personal identity or who is agnostic about the truth of either theory. Can this person claim exemption from the contract? He is, after all, one of the real people involved in an argument about how we should act, and he is unconvinced of the truth of the simple theory. Have the rest of us abrogated our impartialist contractarian responsibility if we proceed to negotiate contracts that will govern his behaviour as well as ours because we negotiate as if we were suffering individuals, even though we have not provided metaphysical proof that there are any such things?

The answer to this question is much the same as the answer given to how suffering individuals should treat nonsuffering ones. The difference here is that the person in the real situation is not pretending to be a nonsuffering individual, nor is he claiming to be a nonsuffering individual. Instead, he has philosophical doubts about the existence of suffering individuals. His philosophical doubts, however, can be either serious ones or speculative ones. If they are serious, this means he is not prepared to regard himself as an suffering individual until they are resolved. He then becomes a nonsuffering individual and the parties behind the veil have already negotiated a contract about how his suffering fellows in the real world should treat him. If his doubts are speculative, in that he still regards himself as an suffering individual but wonders how he can prove that he really is one, then he is bound by the contract governing the behaviour of all beings that regard themselves as suffering individuals.

13.6   Continuity of Memory

It may be that the moral judgements made by impartialist contractarians presuppose a particular metaphysical theory about whatever it is that has B1 S1's memories being the same as whatever has B1 S2's memories, that is, that B1 S1 and B1 S2 are parts of the same remembering individual. I will briefly consider whether or not this is so.

Contract theory would treat memory much as it treated suffering. The parties behind the veil need to consider two types of beings, namely, those that believe themselves to be remembering individuals and those that believe themselves not to be. A self B1 S1 believes itself to be part of the same remembering individual L1 B1 S1 as the self B1 S2 when it believes that the contents of consciousness that B1 S2 will remember will actually be those of B1 S1, that is, when B1 S1 believes that there is a 'direct' relationship, to use Parfit's term, between its contents of consciousness and B1 S2's memories.

Let us consider a case where B1 S2 believes that the thoughts it remembers are those of B1 S1. Suppose, for example, that B1 S2 believes it remembers an argument which has the steps A1, A2, A3. It could be the case that there really has been one remembering individual remembering all the steps A1 to A3 or it could be the case that there is no such individual but merely a series of selves such that S1 had A1, S2 had A2, S3 had A3. In this latter case, B1 S4 thinks it remembers A1 but it is mistaken. This means that S4 was just born ex nihilo with a knowledge of A1 to A3. There seems no logical impossibility in this. Nonetheless, when the parties behind the veil come to consider what contracts to conclude from the viewpoint, firstly, of beings with genuine memories of the thoughts of past selves and, secondly, of beings with pseudo-memories of thoughts of past selves, they would have to treat both kinds of beings as the same for all practical purposes.

What matters is not that S4 really does remember S1's production of A1 as opposed to S4's having a pseudo-memory of this, but rather that S4 knows of S1's production of A1 by some means or other. If S4 doesn't know of S1's production of A1, then the task of the parties behind the veil does get difficult, especially if there are lots of these gaps in lots of these beings that the parties behind the veil had hoped to bind by a contract.

This, however, is not a metaphysical issue but an empirical one. If there are such beings, then they are bound by a particular contract. If there are no such beings, then what beings there are will be either bound by a different contract, or by no contract at all. Contract theory can tell us what our obligations are if the facts are a certain way. The remaining problem is to determine whether the facts are this way or not. There can be no serious doubt that it is a fact that there are beings who believe themselves to be remembering individuals, whether this belief is due to their having genuine or pseudo memories of the contents of consciousness of previous selves.

There can be no serious, as opposed to speculative, doubt about this because we have just been engaging in precisely the situation where each of us was an S1 considering A1, then S2 considering A2 in the light of A1, and so on. There is an ad hominem here against anyone who claims serious doubts. Anyone who is truly a nonremembering individual could not be a person behind the veil. Such people would lack the abilities necessary to conduct an argument on any matter, therefore they would not be capable of arguing about which contract should govern their own behaviour. In fact, as they were not capable of deductive reasoning, they would not be able even to conduct their life in accord with a contract.

13.7   Continuity of Intention

It may be that the moral judgements made by impartialist contractarianism presuppose a particular metaphysical theory about whatever it is that has B1 S1's intentions being the same as whatever it is that has B1 S2's, that is, that B1 S1 and B1 S2 are parts of the same intending individual. If the complex theory is true then, Haksar (p.114) claims, moral theories are committed to treating selves of the same body in the same way as they treat selves of different bodies. In effect, there is little moral difference between punishing a son for the crimes his father committed and punishing later selves of the father for the acts of his earlier self. The son may be innocent of the crimes the father committed but so is the later self of the father with respect to the crimes of the earlier self.

Haksar (p.118) admits, however, that there can be a contractarian justification for punishing a later bodily self for the actions of an earlier bodily self, namely, that, just as the son must pay out of the capital he inherits whatever debts his father incurred, so must the later self with respect to the earlier one.

While Haksar (p.118) agrees that this strategy provides the contractarian with a justified basis to punish later selves of the same bodily individual for the actions of earlier ones for some cases, it is, he thinks, by no means adequate. What if the earlier self commits a murder and the later self is given life imprisonment? Such a case is equivalent to one where the son is required to pay all his father's debts, even when they exceed the capital he inherited. If the latter is morally wrong, so is the former.

We have already seen one way in which the parties behind the veil could legitimately draw up a contract that required a later self of the same bodily individual to be punished for the crimes of an earlier self, that is, when the contract governs how suffering individuals should treat each other. If L1 murders L2 in order to avoid some suffering, then self L1 B1 S2 is legitimately punished for L1 B1 S1's attempts to avoid some suffering for L1 at L2's expense.

This contract, however, only covers the case of beings each of whom regards itself as a suffering individual located in one body. The parties behind the veil would have to negotiate quite a different contract for beings each of whom regarded itself as a suffering individual located in two bodies, either simultaneously or consecutively. While there may be such cases, we do not need to investigate how the parties behind the veil would deal with them unless such cases can be shown to make a difference to the cases that do interest us. The case of punishing the son for his father's crimes is not a case of the same suffering individual located in two bodies. It is, rather, the case of two sets of selves B1 S1 to B1 SN and B2 S1 to B2 SN, where each of B1 S1 to B1 SN regards itself as the same suffering individual as the others, and each of B2 S1 to B2 SN regards itself as the same suffering individual as the others, but none of B1 S1 to B1 SN regards itself as the same suffering individual as B2 S1 to B2 SN.

The parties behind the veil dealing with beings of this kind will treat the crimes of B1 S1 as the crimes of a quite distinct individual to the crimes performed by any of the selves B2 S1 to B2 SN. Instead they will treat them as the crimes of the same individual as the crimes of the selves B1 S2 to B1 SN, at least when B1 S1's motivation for these crimes is the avoidance of suffering to any of B1 S2 to B1 SN.

Avoidance of suffering is not the only motivation behind B1 S1's actions that can serve to identify B1 S1 as the same individual as B1 S2 to B1 SN. Any intention whatsoever will do, as long as B1 S1 believes that whatever intends its actions is the same as whatever will intend the actions

of some other self B1 SN. If B1 S1 believes this then I will say that it
believes itself to be part of the same 'intending' individual as B1 SN.

The parties behind the veil will draw up contracts to govern the
behaviour of intending individuals. The intentions of no individual will be
given superior treatment to those of anyone else when it came to the
distribution of costs and benefits consequent upon these intentions.
Anyone (Ann, say) performing an act intended to gain a benefit beyond her
entitlement or to avoid a cost she is required to bear by a fair distribution
of costs will be appropriately penalised. The parties behind the veil will
want the contract to ensure that individuals are not able to advantage
themselves at the expense of other individuals. This means they will want
to be able to distinguish between criminal individuals who really do not
believe that their various selves are selves of the same intending
individual, and those who merely pretend this.[1]

The parties behind the veil will have to consider a number of
possible relationships that can exist between the intentions of a self B1 S1
and the intentions of some later self B1 SN. Each of these different
possibilities may require a different kind of contract. These relationships
include the following:- (1) B1 S1 believes itself to be a member of the
same intending individual as B1 SN and it matters to B1 S1 that B1 SN's
intentions are not hampered but, rather, are facilitated in their achievement
by the actions of B1 S1; (2) B1 S1 believes itself to be a member of the
same intending individual as B1 SN but it doesn't matter to B1 S1 what
effects its actions have on the achievement B1 SN's intentions; (3) B1 S1
doesn't believe itself to be a member of the same intending individual as
B1 SN but behaves as if it did; (4) B1 S1 doesn't believe itself to be a
member of the same intending individual as B1 SN and doesn't care what
effects its actions have on the achievement of B1 SN's intentions.

The kind of contract the parties behind the veil would negotiate for
Case (1) will be the same as the contract they negotiate for Case (3). In
either case, B1 S1 will perform actions at T1 intended to facilitate the
achievement of B1 SN's intentions at TN, whatever those intentions may
be. In R.M. Hare's terminology (1981, pp. 101-2) B1 S1 (say, a man) will
display signs of evaluating the relative merits of his 'now-for-now'
preferences and B1 SN's 'then-for-then' preferences. This will manifest
itself in his modifying actions based on his own now-for-now preferences
in order to balance their demands against B1 SN's then-for-then
preferences.

As long as B1 S1 reveals this kind of thinking in his choice of the actions open to him, he will be covered by the contract that the parties behind the veil draw up for intending individuals, whether B1 S1 believes himself to be the same intending individual as B1 SN or not. The point is that he thinks and acts as if he and B1 SN were members of the same intending individual. If B1 SN claims that he should not be punished for the actions of B1 S1 because B1 S1 did not believe himself to be the same intending individual as B1 SN, then B1 SN must also be able to show that B1 S1's actions were not intended to facilitate the achievement of B1 SN's intentions in just the way B1 SN would have done had he been present in B1 at T1. The contract, then, is not affected by B1 S1's belief that he is not the same intending individual as B1 SN if B1 S1 behaves exactly as B1 SN would have if he had been present in B1 at T1. Likewise for each of B1 S2 up to B1 SN himself.

This, however, doesn't show that the contract is independent of the truth or falsity of either the simple or complex theory of personal identity because exactly the same analysis could be offered for B1 S1 and the selves of some other body B2. The problem Haksar has posed is why we shouldn't punish the son for his father's crimes. What if the father behaved towards his son as we have described B1 S1 behaving towards B1 SN? If there is no metaphysical basis for saying that the father is a quite distinct individual from the son then why can't we adopt a convention and treat the father and the son as the one individual, as Parfit's complex theory seems to allow us to do?

What we need to do here is distinguish the conventional from the contingent. It is a purely contingent matter that we do not regard different bodily individuals as the same intending individual. It is a contingent matter because, were the facts to be different, we would treat two bodily individuals as the one intending individual. This, however, need not be merely a matter of convention. It is, rather, that different facts mean we have to pursue the same kinds of interests and concerns in different ways. If the facts were such that the father behaved towards his son as if he and his son were the same intending individual, then it would not be a mere matter of convention that we treated them as the same intending individual. It would be a requirement of our desire to ensure a fair distribution of costs and benefits between individuals as applied to the particular facts of the case.

As it turns out, it would be most unlikely that the facts of the case would ever be such as to warrant our treating the two bodily individuals as the one intending individual, given the kind of universe we find ourselves in. Given a different universe, such treatment might be warranted. The behaviour of father and son would have to be much more co-ordinated and inter-dependent than it is in our universe. It would have to be rather like the situation that John Wyndham describes in his novel, *The Midwich Cuckoos*, where there are a group of children, all of whom act as if they were merely different bodily limbs to the one mind. Whatever happens to one is known to the others. They never disagree with each other. Their interests never conflict, and so on. Something similar would have to be the case with the father and son after the father committed the crime for the son to be treated as the same intending individual as the father.

In our kind of world this rarely if ever occurs. Not only does the father at TN perceive the world from a location in B1, but the father's self at TN, that is B1 SN has no 'direct' relation with the perceptions or intentions of the son's self at TN, that is, B2 SN. The self B1 SN cannot act through the body B2. It cannot control B2's arms or legs, etcetera, as it can B1's. It cannot make B2 a vehicle of its will, nor does it believe it can, nor does it believe that B2 SN can make B1 a vehicle of B2 SN's will.

It is also the case that B1 SN (say, Ann) remembers the intentions of B1 S1 to B1 SN. It is as if she had been an observer to the contents of consciousness of each of these selves whereas she had never been an observer to the contents of consciousness of B2's selves. Her memories not only involve her observation of these contents of consciousness but they also are accompanied by the belief that she was not merely an observer. While B1 S1 in fact had a particular set of intentions at T1, the self B1 SN believes that these intentions would have been different if she, B1 SN, had so desired. The self B1 SN can only believe this if she regards herself as the same intending individual as B1 S1. She does not, however, believe it of B2 S1 or even of B2 SN.

These, then, are all contingent facts that, when they obtain, will lead the parties behind the veil to negotiate a particular kind of contract in which a son will not be liable to be punished for his father's crimes. This is so whether or not there is really a metaphysical substratum linking the son's various selves and a quite different substratum linking the father's various selves. It is not, however, merely a matter of convention. Given that these are the facts of the situation, the parties behind the veil could not regard themselves as free to adopt some radically different criterion of personal identity.

The irrelevance of the metaphysical theories to the calculations of the parties behind the veil can be seen by considering a universe in which the facts warranted the father and son being treated as the same intending individual. The parties behind the veil will still want to ensure that innocent parties are not punished for the crimes of the father-son, even if the only beings available for consideration are all multiple-bodied.

For example, the parties behind the veil have to take into account that they could be the innocent mother-daughter. They will, therefore, still want to establish procedures by which to determine guilt and innocence, enforce penalties, and so on. They will not regard as acceptable a contract which advantages the father-son at the expense of other members of the community by refusing to punish the son for the crimes of the father on the grounds that they are distinct intending individuals when the facts have each of them behaving as the one intending individual. In this sense, they are not free to adopt whatever convention they like about what is to count as an intending individual.

Nonetheless, what is to count as an intending individual may still be conventional in Parfit's sense in that there may be no metaphysical substratum linking the various selves of the father-son. Even if the parties behind the veil believed there to be no such substratum, they would still insist that the empirical facts of the case required father and son to be treated as the one intending individual. Their metaphysical theory would make no difference to the contract. Similarly, even if they believed that personal identity depended on a unifying metaphysical substratum, the facts of the case would lead them to postulate that there was such a substratum linking father and son. The metaphysical theory would be tailored to accommodate the empirical facts.

Contract theory, then, need not presuppose any particular metaphysical theory of personal identity in order to generate substantive moral judgements about whom it is proper to punish for the commission of a crime. There can be nonutilitarian right-based constraints on who is to be punished. It can be the case that B1 S1 and B1 SN are linked in such a way that B1 S1 licenses us to punish B1 SN at TN for the murder B1 S1 committed at T1, whereas there is no similar link between B1 S1 and the selves of his son or his wife. Contract theory can refuse to sacrifice the individual for utilitarian ends without thereby begging any metaphysical questions.

Even if the individual is a construct out of separate experiences, contract theory does not have to focus on the separate experiences but can meaningfully negotiate contracts as if there were individuals who had these experiences. What is more to the point, in the cases I have examined, the parties behind the veil would show a blatant disregard for the facts if their contract governed separate selves rather than intending individuals.

We have looked so far at two of the four possibilities I listed earlier, that is, we have looked at:- (1) B1 S1 believes itself to be a member of the same intending individual as B1 SN and it matters to B1 S1 that B1 S1's intentions are not hampered but, rather, are facilitated in their achievement by the actions of B1 S1 and (3) B1 S1 doesn't believe itself to be a member of the same intending individual as B1 SN but behaves as if it did.

The other two cases were:- (2) B1 S1 believes itself to be a member of the same intending individual as B1 SN but it doesn't matter to B1 S1 what effects its actions have on the achievement of B1 SN's intentions, and (4) B1 S1 doesn't believe itself to be a member of the same intending individual as B1 SN and doesn't care what effects its actions have on the achievement of B1 SN's intentions.

Case (2) is likely to occur where B1 S1 believes that B1 SN will remember its contents of consciousness and those of the selves from B1 S1 to B1 SN. It will also believe that B1 SN could have changed what B1 S1 thought and did. The self B1 S1, then, is to be treated in much the same way as the case where B1 S1 doesn't believe itself to be the same suffering individual as B1 SN. Bodily individuals like B1 S1 (say, a man) will not want to oppose a contract that treats BI S1 to B1 SN as the same intending individual because he is indifferent about whether or not B1 SN is punished for his acts. If he does oppose such a contract, then this is prima facie evidence that he does not really fall under Case (2).

The parties behind the veil, however, would be disinclined to punish B1 SN for the crimes of B1 S1 because, from the viewpoint of B1 SN, they would not want to be punished for the crimes of a self that acted with such a blatant disregard for their interests. Also, intending individuals who might become nonintending individuals would be concerned to ensure that their later selves of their non-intending phase were not punished for the crime of an earlier phase. The parties behind the veil, then, would contract to do much as we do, that is, isolate nonintending individuals so that they cannot harm intending individuals, providing them as far as possible with a nonpunishing environment.

Case (4) would be treated much as Case (2). In this case B1 SN's sense of injustice at being held responsible for B1 S1's crimes would he even greater than in Case (2). These cases, then, are consistent with the points made against Haksar in my discussion of Cases (1) and (3).

We have seen, then, that contractarian theories can provide substantive ethical conclusions without making particular controversial metaphysical assumptions about personal identity. This does not, in itself, show that contractarian theories can remain uncommitted on all contentious metaphysical matters but it does outline a strategy they can adopt to try to defuse such charges.

In the next chapter I will look at another, possibly suspect, position which I have assumed throughout this book, namely, that it is rational for a person to be a partialist, either as an egoist or a sectarian. I have argued that these are immoral positions but I have been at pains to insist that what is not at fault is their rationality. There is no link between value on the one hand and empirical fact on the other such that it is self-contradictory for the partialist to accept some empirical fact and still be a partialist. We are faced with a genuine choice between impartialism and partialism. There are, however, writers who want to argue that egoism is irrational, in either its particularist or universalist form or both. I will now turn to the task of showing why they are mistaken.

Note

1   There is a considerable literature on the notion of multiple selves or personalities. Much of it now seems to suggest that the phenomenon is actually an artefact of the therapeutic situation rather than a genuine entity. In particular, see R. Ofshe and E. Watters, *Making Monsters*, Chapter 10.

14 Egoism and Rationality

14.1 Introduction

So far, I have cast conflicts of desires in terms of the wants of Ann and Ben, say, in the real world, then used the parties in a position of equal power to arrive at the principles which tell us what Ann and Ben ought to do. In this chapter I wish to describe what I believe to be the logic of the word 'ought'. I have used it as a hypothetical imperative, that is, the 'ought' conclusions that the parties in the position of equal power reach are what the people in the real world 'ought' to do *if* they endorse impartialism. I will argue that all uses of 'ought' are hypothetical. Supposed categorical 'oughts' are really disguised want claims. I will show that even egoists use universalizable 'oughts' without contradiction in spite of arguments from various philosophers to the contrary. It is my contention that egoism is an unacceptable moral theory, not because it is irrational, but because it would not receive unforced agreement.

14.2 The Universalist Egoist

Egoists have been charged with irrationality because it has been claimed that the logic of the word 'ought' is such that an egoist (say, Ben) who says that he ought to act egoistically is guilty of a contradiction. One way in which this charge has been sustained is by the claim that categorical 'ought' statements either uttered by, or endorsed by, the egoist are not universalizable. My strategy will be to see whether these supposed logical difficulties disappear if egoism is recast in terms of hypothetical oughts. To begin with I'd like to look at an argument used by both Frankena and Kalin against a certain kind of egoist, namely, the kind I called the 'particularist' egoist back in Chapter 1.

      The particularist egoist, according to Frankena (pp.17-20) believes:-
(a) if Ann is judging about herself, then she is to use this criterion 'Ann

ought to do Y if and only if Y is in her overall self-interest'; (b) if Ann is a spectator judging about anyone else (say, Ben), then she is to use this criterion 'Ben ought to do Y if and only if Y is in Ann's overall self-interest'.

Kalin (1968, p.68) sets out to show that anyone (say, Ann),who believes (a) and (b) also must believe that she ought both do and not do a particular action, therefore the principles fail to be a guide to action. His demonstration of this is as follows:- (i) suppose Ann is the evaluator, then what ought she to do? She ought to do what's in her interests (by (a)) What ought Ben to do? He ought to do what's in Ann's interests (by (b)) What ought some third person (say, Colin) do? He ought to do what's in Ann's interests (by (b)), and so on, therefore, everyone ought to do what's in Ann's interests (by (a) and (b)); (ii) suppose, however, that Ben is the evaluator, then what ought Ann to do? She ought to do what's in Ben's interests (by (b)) What ought Ben to do? He ought to do what's in his own interests (by (a)) What ought Colin to do? He ought to do what's in Ben's interests (by (b)), and so on. Therefore, everyone ought to do what's in B's interests (by (a) and (b)). The conclusion to be derived from the above, in Kalin's view is that everyone ought to do what's in Ann's interests, and everyone ought to do what's in Ben's interest, and so on; (iii) Ann's interest is at least sometimes incompatible with Ben's. When this occurs, it will be the case that Ann ought to do what is both in her interest and against it (namely, what is in Ben's interest at her expense). Under these circumstances, particularist egoism gives self-defeating advice. It therefore fails as a moral theory.

This argument clearly depends on the use of categorical 'oughts'. What I wish to do now is to investigate how the Kalin-Frankena argument against the particularist egoist works if we turn the categoricals into hypotheticals. In other words, can an egoist consistently refuse to countenance the existence of categorical imperatives? If he can, does he thereby rescue the rationality of his egoism?

14.3   Deducing Action

The egoist could maintain that he will interpret all categorical 'oughts' as the conclusions of arguments in which the categorical 'ought' is the consequence of a hypothetical imperative whose antecedent is also the minor premise. For example:-

Argument 1

(a) If Ben's self-interest is to be maximised, then he ought to do what he believes is in his self interest.
(b) Ben's self-interest is to be maximised,
therefore:-
(c) Ben ought to do what he believes is in his self-interest.

This has the standard form of modus ponens, namely,
If p then q.
p,
therefore:-
q.

When 'p' and 'q' are propositions, the fact that 'p' appears as the minor premise indicates that its truth is no longer to be considered as hypothetical but as actual. Argument 1 could be given the following 'propositional' interpretation.

Argument 2

(a) If 'Ben's self-interest is to be maximised' is true, then 'Ben ought to do what he believes is in his self-interest' is true.
(b) 'Ben's self-interest is to be maximised' is true,
therefore:-
(c) 'Ben ought to do what he believes is in his self-interest' is true.

Here 'p' appears to be a prediction that it will be the case that Ben's self-interest is maximised and 'q' is a statement to the effect that he is likely to have done what he believed was in his self-interest. Both 'p' and 'q', however, can be interpreted as having a prescriptive component. When this occurs, I will use upper case letters such as 'P'and 'Q' to represent sentences with a prescriptive component It is, however, logically improper to substitute 'is prescribed' for 'is true' in Argument 2. This would give us Argument 3, the major premise of which will in many cases be false, thereby making the argument unsound.

Argument 3

(a) If 'Ben's self-interest is to be maximised' is prescribed, then 'Ben ought to do what he believes is in his self-interest' is prescribed.
(b) 'Ben's self-interest is to be maximised' is prescribed,
therefore:-
(c) 'Ben ought to do what he believes is in his self-interest' is prescribed.

For it to be the case that 'Ben's self-interest is to be maximised' is prescribed, there must be someone who prescribes it, that is, who wants Ben's self-interest maximised. Just because someone wants Ben's self-interest maximised, it doesn't follow that he wants Ben to do what Ben believes is in Ben's self-interest. Consequently, the major premise may well be false, thus making Argument 3 unsound. There is a parallel here with propositional arguments. Consider Argument 4, assuming it to be true that all haemophiliacs are male.

Argument 4

(a) If 'Ben has haemophilia' is true, then 'Ben is a male' is true.
(b) 'Ben has haemophilia' is true,
therefore:-
(c) 'Ben is a male' is true.

If we replace each 'is true' in Argument 4 with 'is believed', then we have the same kind of problem I discussed with 'is prescribed' in Argument 3, that is, some one has to do the believing and just because he believes that A is a haemophiliac it doesn't follow that he believes that A is a male. So, while the major premise of Argument 4 is true when each proposition in it is treated as 'true', it may no longer be true when each proposition is treated as 'believed'. See Argument 5.

Argument 5

(a) If 'Ben has haemophilia' is believed, then 'Ben is a male' is believed.
(b) 'Ben has haemophilia' is believed,
therefore:-
(c) 'Ben is a male' is believed.

Nonetheless, in both the propositional case and the imperative case, the premise of Arguments 1 and 4 'entail' their conclusions, in Hare's sense of 'entail'. As Hare defines 'entailment' a sentence P entails a sentence Q if and only if the fact that a person assents to P but dissents from Q is sufficient reason for saying he has misunderstood one or the other of the two sentences (1952, p.25).

In Argument 1, the two premises can be treated as a single sentence consisting of two clauses. Together with the minor premise they entail the conclusion in the sense of 'entail' defined above. The relationship between the premises and the conclusion is such that, were Ann, say, to refuse to assent to the conclusion after assenting to the premises, then this is normally sufficient for us to say that she has misunderstood one or the others of the sentences. The only exception here is if there is some state of affairs more strongly desired than, and incompatible with, that indicated in the antecedent of the first premise. This exception can be dealt with by treating the minor premise as infelicitous when a state of affairs is more strongly desired, and incompatible with, that indicated by the minor premise. When this occurs, Ben will be regarded as not having assented to the minor premise, which means that he has not assented to the conjunction of the major and minor premises as a whole. He does not really want the state of affairs indicated by the minor premise because he prefers some other state of affairs when the two conflict. With this modification, anyone who really assents to the major and minor premises yet refused to assent to the conclusion, behaves in a way that is incomprehensible except on the hypothesis that he doesn't understand one or the other of these sentences. As Hare points, we find out what people think their remarks mean when they use words on different occasions in apparently different senses by asking them what they see their remarks as entailing (1952, p.25).

Using this test, if people don't see the premises of Argument 1 as entailing its conclusion, then they and I have different understandings of the terms in these sentences, just as we would do if they assented to the proposition 'If A has haemophilia then A is a male and A has haemophilia' yet denied that A was a male. The propositional and imperative cases seem quite parallel here. For the purposes of this discussion, I will treat them as parallel, regarding counter-examples to the imperative case as unsuccessful if they also apply to the propositional case. If the relationship between imperative premises and conclusion is no tighter than that between propositional premises and conclusion then it is tight enough.

14.4   Defending the Particularist Egoist

The particularist egoist, it will be remembered, believes:- (a) if Ben is judging about himself, then he is to use the criterion 'Ben ought to do Y if and only if Y is in Ben's overall self-interest'; (b) if Ben is a spectator judging about anyone else (say, Ann), then Ben is to use the criterion 'Ann ought to do Y if and only if Y is in Ben' overall self-interest.'

It is, however, odd to operate on a criterion which requires Ann to do what is, in fact, in Ben's overall self-interest. The best we mere mortals can manage is for Ben to do what he believes is in his own self-interest, and I will modify all future cases to take this into account. I will take Ben as believing that Ann ought to do Y if and only if Ben believes Y is in Ben's overall self-interest because this is the formulation that would strike any actual egoist as most likely to be true.   Admittedly it could be formulated as, 'Ann ought to do Y if, and only if she believes that Y is in Ben's overall self-interest' but Ben would be rather worried that Ann's concept of his self-interest could be a long way away from his own.

The particularist egoist, as we have seen, believes the following: 'If Ben's self-interest is to be maximised, then everyone ought to do what he believes is in his self-interest and if Ann's self-interest is to be maximised, then everyone ought to do what she believes is in her self-interest' and so on for Colin or whoever.

This, however, is merely a technical belief, that is, a belief about the means by which different ends will be achieved. As a technical belief it is probably true. Ben's self-interest is much more likely to be achieved if everyone does what Ben believes is in his self-interest than if only he does. Nonetheless, it is logically possible that his self-interest is better achieved by other means, as we mentioned earlier. The particularist egoist, then, is someone who has the technical belief, which he thinks is as true of others as of himself, that each person's self-interest will be maximised if everyone pursued it. In addition, any particular such egoist, Ben, wants his own self-interest maximised, being either indifferent or hostile to the self-interest of other people.

Given our previous analysis, this means that he is not so much entitled to, but required to, acknowledge that everyone ought to do what they believe is in his self-interest, or else he is irrational, but it is only a hypothetical 'ought' here. See Argument 6.

Argument 6

(a) If Ben's self-interest is to be maximised, then everyone ought to do what Ben believes is in his self-interest.
(b) Ben's self-interest is to be maximised,
therefore:-
(c) Everyone ought to do what Ben believes is in his self-interest.

Ben, however, does not want Ann's self-interest to be maximised, therefore he is not committed by the hypothetical to the conclusion that everyone ought to do what is in her (or Colin's or whoever's) self-interest. Counter to Kalin and Frankena, then, he is not committed to self-defeating courses of action by his egoistic principles.

14.5 Vicious Universalisation

The anti-egoist will probably accept that, if Ben's self-interest is to be maximised, then everyone ought to do what he believes will maximise his self-interest, but the anti-egoist will also want to know why Ben's self-interest ought to be maximised. In other words, where a categorical imperative is detached from a hypothetical imperative by means of prescribing the antecedent of the hypothetical, the anti-egoist is always entitled to ask why the action prescribed in the antecedent 'ought' to be done, hoping to produce a situation where the 'ought' used in the answer can't be universalised but produces instead the kind of self-contradiction Kalin and Frankena thought that they had found a method for producing such a situation. I will call this method 'vicious universalisation'[1] in that the anti-egoist pursues a regress of universalisations until he or she gets a 'vicious' consequence. Let us see if it works on the particularist egoist Ben.

     'Why', says the anti-egoist, 'ought Ben's self-interest be maximised?' Our particularist egoist only believes in hypothetical imperatives, so he sees this question as a request for a goal, end or purpose for which the maximisation of his self-interest is a means. He might produce the hypothetical, 'If Ben is to be happy, then his self-interest ought to be maximised'. This is a contingent causal claim. Perhaps he will be happier if his self-interest isn't maximised. Perhaps it is part of human nature only to be happy in self-sacrifice. Nonetheless, Ben happens to believe he will be happy if his self-interest is maximised and his answer is at least logically respectable. He would arrive at it via Argument 7.

Argument 7

(a) If Ben is to be happy, then his self-interest ought to be maximised.
(b) Ben is to be happy,
therefore:-
(c) Ben's self-interest ought to be maximised.

Ben is not committed to wanting other people to be happy, especially where this prevents his happiness, nor is he committed to wanting other people's self-interest maximised, especially where this prevents the maximisation of his own self-interest. Nonetheless, the anti-egoist could still ask, 'Why ought Ben to be happy?' At this point Ben will probably not want to claim that he ought to be happy. After all, he believes that 'ought' statements properly derive from hypotheticals, which means he would need to find some goal or end which his being happy serves. This he will be reluctant to do because he is likely to regard his own happiness as the most basic goal, the final justification for behaviour. If the anti-egoist can commit Ben to believing that Ben 'ought' to be happy, then the anti-egoist may be able to show that this universalises to 'Everyone ought to be happy'. Ben does not believe that everyone ought to be happy, nor does he want everyone to be happy, so he will not want to take any step that commits him in this way. Ben, therefore, will refuse to say that he ought to be happy. He doesn't believe he ought to be or, for that matter, that anyone else ought to be either. He just wants to be.

Logically, though, this puts him on a par with the anti-egoist. Suppose the egoist goes on the attack, asking the anti-egoist (say, Ann) why she believes something ought to be the case, for example, that people ought to keep their promises. She will have to show either that people keeping their promises is a means to some end, for which further justification could be asked, or else she has to say that there is no such further end but that keeping promises is an end in itself. It ought to be done just because it ought to be. As an argument to the unconvinced this is singularly unpersuasive. What the anti-egoist has done is use the 'ought' claim as a substitute for a want claim. All she is entitled to do is assert that she wants everyone to be happy but she substitutes a categorical 'ought' statement instead to give the appearance that she is appealing to some objective realm of moral facts.

Unlike Zimmerman (1969), I am not proposing that we can reject 'ought' statements and replace them with 'want' statements. Instead my position is the same as that expressed by MacIntyre (pp.11-22). MacIntyre claims that emotivism should be understood as a theory of the use of moral language rather than a theory of its meaning. MacIntyre agrees with the critics of emotivism that judgements such as 'This is right' or 'This is good' do not have the same meaning as 'I approve of this; do so as well' or 'Hurrah for this!' or any of the other proposals suggested by the emotivists. Nonetheless, it might still be the case that, in using such sentences with whatever their meaning actually is, a person (say, Ann) is, in fact, doing nothing other than expressing her feelings or attitudes and attempting to influence the feelings and attitudes of others. Just from listening to what she said in voicing a moral judgment, we could not safely infer what she was doing. In fact, she may not be fully aware of it herself. Her very self-consciousness about the meaning of her words might lead her to think that she was invoking independent impersonal criteria, when all she was actually doing was manipulating others in how she expressed her feelings (p.13).

The egoist might well regard the anti-egoist as doing precisely this when the anti-egoist says that the reason why you ought to keep your promises is just that you ought. If MacIntyre is right, then the egoist is no worse off than the anti-egoist. The egoist has traced through a chain of 'oughts' until he has arrived at a position where he no longer says that something ought to be the case. He merely says that he wants it to be. The anti-egoist ends her chain with the claim that something ought to be done because it ought. The anti-egoist will be hard-pressed to explain what the difference is.

This does not mean that there are no reasons for rejecting egoism as a moral theory but merely that these reasons are not to be found in either the self-defeating nature of egoistic principles or in the egoist's supposed inability to describe his theory without contradiction. Egoism is not to be rejected because it is irrational or incoherent but because it would not be accepted by unforced agreement. The egoist, of course, is free to ask why ought we reject what is not accepted by unforced agreement. If this is answered by reference to some other goal, the same question can be asked again, and so on. While we cannot escape this regress entirely, I have shown in Chapter 1 that ultimately all goals effectively reduce to two - the goal of resolving conflicts of desire by force or the goal of resolving them by argument and reason. I will develop this point further in the final chapter.

14.6   The Universalist Egoist

Although Kalin believes, wrongly as we have seen, that the particularist egoist holds a self-contradictory principle, he does believe 'universalist egoism' is defensible. According to Kalin, the universalist egoist believes the following two principles, the first being identical with the first principle of particularist egoism:- (a) if Ben is judging about himself, then he is to use this criterion 'Ben ought to do Y if and only if Y is in his overall self-interest'; (b) if Ben is a spectator judging about someone else (say, Ann), then he is to use this criterion 'Ann ought to do Y if and only if Y is in Ann's overall self-interest.' In future statements of these principles I will modify them, as indicated earlier, by talking of someone, such as Ben, doing Y if and only if he believes that Y is in his overall self-interest.

Medlin claims that even universalist egoism is self-contradictory. His argument, briefly, is as follows:- if Ben believes that he ought to do Y if and only if he believes that Y is in his overall self-interest, and his belief that he ought to do so means that he approves of his doing so, or wants himself to do so, then the principles (a) and (c) cited earlier will lead to contradictory advice because his believing that Ann ought to do what is in her interest also commits him to wanting Ann to do what is in her interests even when this conflicts with his interests.

Kalin replies to this criticism by denying that Ben's belief that Ann ought to do Y implies that Ben wants Ann to do Y. Kalin argues for this claim by showing that there are perfectly respectable precedents for this kind of position. He uses the example of games. If Ben is a chess-player, then, in Kalin's view, he can believe that his opponent Ann ought to move her bishop yet not want her to do so. Kalin's argument has been criticised by Carlson who argues that what Ben really believes is this is how Ann ought to move if she is to win the game but, because he does not want her to win the game, then he does not really believe that she ought to move the bishop.

Carlson, I believe, is correct. Ben holds the causal hypothetical, 'If Ann is to win, then she ought to move her bishop'. If he proceeds to the categorical 'Ann ought to move her bishop' he can only do so via the minor premise, 'Ann is to win', which, as we have seen, is not to be interpreted as a prediction but as an imperative indicating the speaker's desire to have that state of affairs realised. [2]

Even though Carlson's point is correct, it doesn't follow that Medlin's criticism of the universalist egoist works. The universalist egoist can be regarded as believing the following:- if Ben's self-interest is to be maximised, then Ben ought to do what he believes is in his self-interest and if Ann's self-interest is to be maximised then Ann ought to do what she believes is in her self-interest and so on for Colin or whoever.

As Ben prescribes the imperative 'Ben's self-interest is to be maximised' but does not prescribe that Ann's, or Colin's or whoever's self-interest is to be maximised, he is only committed to the conclusion, 'Ben ought to do what he believes is in his self-interest'. He accepts all the other 'ought' statements hypothetically. The anti-egoist could try to perform the same vicious universalisation on him as on the particularist egoist, with the same effect, namely, that ultimately the universalist egoist would assert that, if he is to be happy, then his self-interest ought to be maximised, but denying that he ought to be happy. Perhaps he, and even the particularist egoist, might agree that everyone ought to pursue their own happiness, but only because he regards this as definitive of 'rationality'. Here the imperative isn't causal but, in Harsanyi's sense 'formal'. Again, the egoist need not believe that everyone ought to be rational.

The universalist egoist, therefore, is not vulnerable to Medlin's criticism. Just because Ben believes that he ought to do Y if and only if he believes Y is in his self-interest, and this means that he wants himself to do what is in his own interests, he is not committed to wanting other people doing what they believe to be in their interests, especially when this frustrates his own self-interest. He is merely considering hypothetically how others ought to behave if they prescribe to themselves the same kinds of imperatives about their interests that he prescribes to himself about his own.

The universalist egoist, then, only appears to differ from the particularist egoist in his opinion about the best means to his own self-interest, and neither is guilty of any logical fallacy. The particularist egoist, who entertains the hope that everyone wants to do what is best for him, believes that their doing so would maximise his self-interest. The universalist egoist, who doesn't entertain the hope that everyone wants to do what's best for him, believes that his self-interest is most likely to be maximised if at least he pursues it. It is odd, therefore, that Kalin ever thought that one could be logically defensible when the other was not, as logically they are counterparts of each other. In fact, the particularist egoist is probably closer to the truth than the universalist egoist, at least as concerns what would be the desirable situation for an egoist to find himself in. He would, however, have to have the power of a Caligula, so the universalist egoist is probably more realistic.

14.7 Motivating by Practical Arguments

I'd now like to clear up some points raised in the discussion of 'vicious universalisation'. When the anti-egoist asks either kind of egoist 'Why ought your self-interest be maximised?' it is undoubtedly the case that she will not regard as satisfactory the answer which the egoist gives her, namely, 'Because it maximises my happiness'.

On the analysis given so far, her dissatisfaction should not be surprising. She is looking for an answer that will enable her, too, to prescribe the categorical imperative. What she needs is both a hypothetical major premise and a prescriptive minor premise from which she can deduce the conclusion 'Ben's (the egoist's) self-interest ought to be maximised'. The trouble is that the prescription that Ben uses as a minor premise, that is, 'Ben's happiness is to be maximised' is not one that the anti-egoist, unlike Ben himself, has any obvious reason to prescribe. Nor, of course, does it provide other egoists with a reason why they should want Ben's happiness to be maximised. This draws our attention to an important feature of the way in which I have handled sentences containing the word 'ought'. I will now spend some time elucidating this feature and its implications.

Consider the belief of the particularist egoist Ben to the effect that everyone (Ann, Colin, whoever) ought to do what is in his interest. He believes the following hypothetical:-

Argument 8

(a) If Ben's self-interest is to be maximised, then Ann ought to do what Ben believes is in Ben's self-interest.
(b) Ben's self-interest is to be maximised.
Therefore:-

(c) Ann ought to do what Ben believes is in Ben's self-interest.

Ann will not find this argument convincing unless she prescribes the minor premise, that is, unless she wants Ben's self-interest to be maximised. Even though she may well accept the truth of the major premise and the validity of the argument form, it is unlikely that she will accept the conclusion. This fact, however, does not render Ben's argument invalid. It merely renders it unsound in Ann's eyes because she regards the minor premise as false. Were she to become a slave to Ben's charisma, she might well find the argument perfectly sound, prescribing both the minor premise and the conclusion. As a slave the only reason she might not regard the argument as sound would be if she doubted the truth of the major premise, thinking perhaps that Ben's self-interest would he better served if she did what she thought was in his self-interest. (See the discussion of superfans in Chapter 1.)

Be this as it may, the point to be noted is that the soundness of the argument depends on the psychological state of the person responding to the minor premise. The truth of the minor premise is always person-relative, making the argument sound if the person who ought to do the action indicated in the consequent also prescribes the end indicated in the antecedent, provided that the means proposed truly is the best one for attaining that goal. (Subject to qualifications made in the last chapter about being 'fully rational'.)

As we have seen, however, the person who ought to do the action indicated in the consequent need not be the person whose self-interest will thereby be maximised. A person (Ben, say) may, for example, wish to maximise the interests of some sectional group. He might argue as follows:-

Argument 9

(a) If Group G's interest is to be maximised, then everyone (or some particular person) ought to do X.
(b) G's interests are to be maximised.
Therefore:-
(c) Everyone (or some particular person) ought to do X.

We will only agree that his argument is sound, however, if we also prescribe the maximisation of G's interests, that is, if we share his patriotism, or religious or political convictions or whatever. We can meaningfully argue with him about the truth of the major premise and, if we can produce factual evidence to show that G's interests are more likely to be maximised if everyone does Y rather than X, he will change his argument. He is, therefore, rational in the appropriate sense. Rather than maximise the interests of some group, however, he may wish to maximise the achievement of some ideal. A suitable substitution of 'maximising the achievement of ideal I' for 'maximising the interests of Group G' could be made in Argument 9 to produce Argument 10, with similar comments as made on Argument 9.

We can even extend the model to cover what are claimed to be 'moral' arguments, for example,

Argument 11

(a) If people are to act as would be determined by rational contractors in a position of equal power (or behind a veil of ignorance or who are benevolent ideal observers) then everyone (or some particular person) ought to do X.
(b) People are to act as would be determined, etcetera.
Therefore:-
(c) Everyone (or that particular person) ought to do X.

If utilitarianism and rational contractor theories are to be counted as typical moral systems, then even morality has no categorical imperatives. As Mrs. Foot (1972) maintains, if morality is a system of imperatives, it must be a system of hypothetical imperatives. Nonetheless, the analysis I have given of the use of 'ought' explains why philosophers have thought of morality as a system of categorical imperatives. Moral systems like utilitarianism or Rawls' contractarianism are systems that provide their believers with ideals. In utilitarianism the ideal is the state of affairs in which happiness has been maximised. This provides a standard against which to measure any act a person (say, Ben) performs. There is the act he actually did and the act he ought to have done if the state of affairs in which happiness had been maximised was to obtain. Likewise, with Rawls' model, the acts we actually do can be compared with the acts we would have done if we had acted in accord with the contractors' principle.

Once one is within such a system, there is no need to preface every 'ought' statement with the antecedent of the conditional. It can just be assumed. As a result, 'ought' statements look categorical even though they are really hypothetical. It is only when Ben, say, from one system argues with Ann from another that it is essential that both parties realise the hypothetical nature of their 'ought' statements. Within any moral system, once its believers have adopted categorical 'oughts', all the moral judgements within the system take on the appearance of descriptive judgements. There may, for example, be certain categories of killing that transgress the ideal. These may be similar to that category of killings we call 'murder'. They all fall under the concept of 'murder', however, because of their relationship to the ideal, not because of any common empirical features they happen to possess. It may be that they all transgress the ideal because they are similar in their empirical properties but it is not this that makes them 'murder'. Anyone who tried to find what made an act a 'murder' by looking for empirical properties common to all murders would not have grasped the concept of murder.

It may be, for example, that someone thinks up a new kind of killing which transgresses the ideal in the way the others did. It still falls under the concept 'murder' even though its empirical properties differ from those of other murders. Anyone who refused to call it a murder because of its lack of the usual empirical properties associated with murder would have mistaken what Kovesi (p.4) calls the 'material' element of the concept of murder for its 'formal' element. Within the one moral system, then, there would develop an inter-related set of moral notions that appear to describe the world. When making moral judgements, we do not appear to ourselves to be applying an ideal. We appear to be more concerned with whether an act falls under a notion such as 'murder' or 'manslaughter'.

These notions, however, derive from some standard that we think actions ought to meet. As a consequence, we cannot both classify an act as a case of 'murder' or whatever and remain free to value it or detest it as we wish. Given our ideal, we must detest it if it is properly classified as 'murder'. When we say that murder is 'wrong' or 'bad' the words 'wrong' and 'bad' are used as reminders, to use Kovesi's term, (p.26) rather than as providers of additional information, or as a discriminator (p.109). People who do not share our ideal can legitimately wonder whether to value or detest an act we classify as 'murder' but they cannot use the word 'murder' in the same sense as we use it without also committing themselves to detesting acts of 'murder'. They will have to find a new vocabulary to express their attitudes or else give our vocabulary a new meaning.

Foot (1978, p.137), for example, claims that ordinary English words like 'father' or 'daughter' determine criteria of goodness in the sense that, if a foreign language said of a person that she was a good X when she denounced her parents to the police, then X could not be translated by our word 'daughter'. A difference in meaning, however, is not the only explanation available for this phenomenon. An alternative one is that the noun associated with the word 'good' sometimes is used just to pick out an individual without the speaker having any intention that the adjective attached to the noun is meant to modify the noun. This difference can be marked by how we stress the adjective or noun. What we mean when we say of a particular person that she is a *good* daughter may not be the same as when we say that she is a good *daughter*. Whereas the second kind of case fits Foot's model, the first does not. What we are saying in the second case is that she is good *as a daughter*. The word 'daughter' is used, not only as an identifier which indicates who it is we are talking about, but also as the term modified by the word 'good'. In the first case, the word 'daughter' is used solely as an identifier and the word 'good' is not intended to apply to her under the description 'daughter'. Rather, it means some thing more like 'See that woman over there, you know, Mary's daughter, I can't remember her name, well, she's a good person.'

Geach, like Foot, also thinks the grammar of words can lock us into particular moral judgments. In his case, he appeals to a distinction between 'attributive' and 'predicative' adjectives. 'Red' is a predicative adjective whereas 'big' is not because a sentence such as 'What I can see is a red car' can be split into 'What I see is a car' and 'What I see is red' but 'What I see is a big car' does not split up into 'What I see is a car' and 'What I see is big.' According to Geach, 'good' is always attributive. If true, this supports Foot's claim about phrases like 'good daughter' in that 'good' always modifies a person or thing under a description. As phrases like 'good man' or 'good person' seem perfectly meaningful, this suggests that the content of goodness in such cases is to be found in the term 'man' or 'person'. It suggests that these terms pick out their references on the basis of functional criteria, contrary to what non-Aristotelian philosophers might think. If so, then goodness as a man or as a person is determined by the function of 'men' or 'persons'.

However, as my discussion of Foot makes clear, 'good' can have a purely predicative use. We can use the adjective 'good' both attributively and predicatively in a phrase such a 'good man'. It is used predicatively, (that is, it is stressed as '*good* man') when we just use the term 'man' merely as an indicator and say of him that he is morally good. It is used attributively when we stress it 'good *man*' - which does require us to give 'man' a functional sense, as in the sense of human 'stud' or in the sense of human with the kinds of qualities that make men rather than women useful in a particular situation, such a physical strength. In order to escape Foot's examples, there is no need for the prescriptivist to invent a new language that does not have these value judgements built into it, as Montefiore suggests. (For a more detailed discussion of the case against Foot and Geach, see Woolcock 1972.)

At the most, then, the examples adduced by Foot and Geach show that criteria of goodness can be extracted from certain nouns when the noun is not merely used as an indicator but is also used to convey a function for the person or thing indicated. This functional use is not to be confused with what these words mean. It is only because the roles of daughters are reasonably similar from society to society that there might seem to be translation problems when the role of daughters in a particular society gives us criteria of good daughters for that society that do not involve caring for or being obedient to, their parents, etcetera. Whether 'daughter' really is translatable into another language, however, depends on whether or not that language has a word that picks out a person because she is the offspring of the person whose 'daughter' she is claimed to be, that is, that 'identifies' her or 'indicates' her on that basis. It may appear, then, within a particular society, that our moral notions 'describe' the world and that our moral imperatives are categorical ones but this is because the antecedents of the hypotheticals are assumed by all, or most, of us.

The problem, however, is to identify what the common goal is that directs the application of these apparently descriptive notions. Kovesi calls it 'the moral point of view'. He distinguishes it from other points of view in that the notions we form from this point of view are not only formed by ourselves but they are about ourselves and they are about ourselves in so far as we are rule-following rational beings. As Kovesi notes, however, there are also other notions that are about ourselves in so far as we are rule-following rational beings, like 'clever', 'consistent', 'learned', which are not necessarily moral notions (p.147).

Theories like utilitarianism and Rawls' rational contractor theory can be seen as attempts to try and specify what it is that makes moral notions different from these other notions. Utilitarianism postulates that moral notions derive from our concern with maximising happiness. Rawls postulates that they derive from our concern with our status as free and equal beings. The moral notions we would develop to describe the world from a utilitarian point of view would not necessarily be the same as those we would develop from a contractarian point of view, yet they will share what Kovesi (p.148) believes to be a crucial requirement of any moral notion, namely, that they about those features of our lives that can be the features of anyone's life and that they are formed from the view point of anyone.

Whenever we have concepts which have these two features they could derive from either the utilitarian or the rational contractor point of view, or there may even be other points of view that satisfy these conditions. Kovesi (p.26) himself appears to consider the moral point of view to be *sui generis*. Anyone who asks what is wrong with murder or stealing thereby shows that they haven't understood the rules that govern these concepts and which enable us to agree on which other concepts are moral and which are not. This, however, merely shows that there is a concept called 'wrongness' that is internal to what Kovesi calls the 'point of view of right and wrong', that is, the moral point of view. It doesn't show that this concept of 'wrongness' is one that rationally requires us not to do acts that are 'wrong'. In fact, this kind of claim about the unquestionability of the wrongness of murder is precisely what we would expect with the apparently descriptive terms that have been generated from within a single moral system. Anyone who says, 'What's wrong with murder?' either doesn't understand the meaning of the word 'murder' or else is outside the moral system in which acts that the system calls 'murder' are automatically wrong.

There is, then, a danger that those within a particular moral system will refuse to debate the justification for their moral judgements on the grounds that anyone who challenges these judgements thereby demonstrates that they have misunderstood them. This is a moral version of Tertullian's paradox, with the egoist playing the same role with respect to the moral point of view as the atheist does with respect to the religious point of view. As a consequence, they run the risk of regarding themselves as possessing a faculty which enables them to follow rules that those who lack this faculty cannot follow, whereupon they begin to look very like non-naturalists.

Unfortunately, however, the egoist, like the atheist, cannot accept it as a reason against his position that he just doesn't understand the view he thinks he is opposing unless he can see that believers possess a rule-following ability that he lacks that is more than just a case of verbal rule-following. In fact, there is no reason to believe the egoist or, for that matter, the atheist, cannot follow the rules of the system they oppose. They can use words in the same way as believers. They can even say how believers will act under certain circumstances if the believers are sincere. What the egoist needs to be shown is that there is something akin to the practical consequence of being colour-blind that follows from his not agreeing with the judgements of those who are committed to the moral point of view. Unless this can be shown, then there is a conflict of desires between egoists and holders of the moral point of view that can only be resolved by force.

There is a similar problem within the moral point of view. There appear to be irreconcilable differences between nonegoists over issues such as abortion, euthanasia, the scope of individual liberty and so on. Different moral theories produce different answers to these questions. Which set of nonegoists has got the rules that link concepts to particular judgements right? It is a strategy open to either side of any contentious issue to claim that the other just fails to understand the rules that govern the moral point of view. What is needed is some more objective decision procedure by which to arbitrate between these various theories or between egoism and the 'moral point of view'.

Rawls (1951) proposed a set of conditions he believed such a decision procedure needed to meet. His own candidate for a decision procedure meeting these requirements he calls 'reflective equilibrium'. This decision procedure requires that we already have consensus on some matters. Rawls says that mere proof is not justification because it simply displays the logical relations between propositions. To amount to a justification, a proof must rest on agreement about the appropriateness of its starting point and the compelling nature and comprehensiveness of its conclusions (1972, p.581). In the next chapter I will examine whether or not reflective equilibrium is an appropriate procedure by which to justify either our particular moral judgements or the theories by which we hope to render these judgements consistent.

Hare is unconvinced that Rawls' justification of principles should begin from a consensus. He asks why consensus should not be the end, rather than the beginning of the process - an end brought about by argument? He accepts that such a justification must assume a consensus on matters of logic and on matters of fact, including facts about the (possibly conflicting) interests of the parties but it should not assume, as Rawls seems to, a consensus on substantial moral questions. In his view, all that moral argument needs to reach normative conclusions are facts, singular prescriptions and logic (1975, pp.84-85). In the next chapter I will also look at whether Hare's decision procedure is any better able to produce consensus than Rawls'.

Notes

1   I use Kalin's definition of 'universalisation' here, namely, what is reasonable for one person to do in a particular set of circumstances is reasonable, if sufficiently similar, for any similar person to do in similar circumstances (1970, p.66). Hudson (1970, p.184) interprets Hare's notion of universalisability in much the same way. He gives an example of how 'ought' judgements must be universalizable, namely, that to say that we ought to encourage immigrants to return to their countries of origin is to say that anyone else, placed as we are, ought also to encourage them to return home. The viciousness of the universalisation only takes effect if the 'ought' is used categorically.

2   Kalin (1975), in his reply to Carlson, tries to avoid this criticism by distinguishing a teleological and a deontological sense of 'ought'. If my arguments are correct this is unnecessary. The word 'ought' can be treated as unambiguous in meaning, although the different kinds of hypotheticals in which it can occur may make it appear as if there is a different sense of 'ought' at work in each case.

15 Reflective Equilibrium and Moral Logic

15.1   Introduction

A state of 'reflective equilibrium' is one where there is a harmonious fit between our considered judgements about what ought to be done and the principles from which these judgements are derived. Our judgements are arrived at intuitively, then given due thought. Rawls (1972, p.20) says that such a fit is an 'equilibrium' because our principles and judgements are in an harmonious balance. It is 'reflective' because we know to what principles our judgements conform and the premises of their derivation.'

A distinction needs to be drawn between what I will call 'personal' and 'communal' reflective equilibrium. Personal reflective equilibrium obtains when the harmonious fit is between the judgments and principles of just one individual. Communal reflective equilibrium obtains when the fit is between the judgements and principles of more than one individual. Both the advocates of reflective equilibrium discussed in this book, namely Rawls and Haksar, are concerned with communal reflective equilibrium. They each engage in argument with other people in order to arrive at a consensus on which judgements and principles are right. With personal reflective equilibrium, an individual (say, Ben) is not concerned to harmonise his judgements and principles with those of other people so he has no need of arguments by which to persuade them to adopt his personal balance. He merely needs to satisfy himself that the relationship he has achieved between judgements and principles is the best from his own point of view. Arriving at a personal equilibrium, then, would appear to be a much easier proposition than arriving at communal reflective equilibrium. In this chapter I want to investigate under what conditions communal reflective equilibrium is possible and what the status is of those judgements and principles that actually achieve a communal reflective equilibrium. Does the fact that there is consensus within a particular community show anything about the rightness, or if appropriate, the truth, of these judgements and principles?

15.2   The Scientific Model

There are a number of models of how consensus can be achieved between individuals on some disputed matter, including mathematics, the various sciences such as physics, and sciences such as linguistics. Hare (1975, p.86) dismisses the mathematics and linguistics models as inappropriate models by which to arrive at moral consensus. In his view, the analogy with these sciences fails because neither yields substantive conclusions, whereas moral philosophy is supposed to do so. Hare's comments here should not be regarded as settling the matter, however. As I have argued in Chapter 1, the analogy with mathematics is stronger than Hare thinks. What impartialism does is develop a set of axioms, then derive substantive moral conclusions from them, but the impartialist set of axioms is not the only possible set. In this respect, morality is rather like the axioms of geometry, of which there are least three competing sets, namely, the Euclidean, the Riemannian and the Lobachevskian. The issue for physicists is which of these sets of axioms best models the physical universe. The issue for moral theorists is whether there are grounds for preferring the impartialist axioms to partialism, given that impartialism and partialism are mutually exclusive and the only two possibilities. I have already explored what such grounds could be in Chapter 1 and will take the issue up once again in the final chapter.

Linguistic theory is an unsatisfactory model because it, in effect, merely seeks to systemise our intuitions about what uses of words in our language are meaningful and grammatically standard. Whatever consensus we achieve in the grammar of our language is not thought to be a consequence of the fact that our linguistic intuitions are a form of sensation that we can use as a guide to the reality that has caused them to take the form they do, as we might think was the case with our sensory experiences. This leaves the model of sciences such as physics. I now wish to explore what parallels there are, if any, between reflective equilibrium and physics as methods of obtaining a consensus by rational means, where the goal to which the methods are a means is the goal of having true beliefs. Rawls himself does not propose the physics model but, if our aim is to arrive at communal reflective equilibrium, it might be thought to be the most promising candidate.

There seems, at least at first sight, to be considerable parallels. Intuitive judgements might play a similar role in moral theories as perceptions do in physics. In physics, there is a fixed point of comparison between theories, namely, what is observed.[1] Admittedly, each theory may have its own terms to describe what is observed, these terms being comprehensible only in the context of the theory as a whole, but this rarely, if ever, is the cause of a disagreement between theories about the ordinary language features of what was observed. No matter how a theory describes red flashes on a screen, for example, as electron traces or whatever, if the holders of the theory refused to acknowledge that the flashes on the screen looked red because their theory required that the flashes looked yellow, then this would be regarded by scientists in general, regardless of their theoretical persuasion, as a case of intellectual dishonesty. The holders of this theory may wish to argue that the flashes would look yellow if initial conditions were properly controlled, but what would definitely make their theory scientifically disreputable would be their insistence that the colour the flashes appear to be to the observer depends on the theory he or she holds.[2] Ultimately, scientific theory has to fit with how people perceive things in controlled conditions. If an advocate of a theory wishes to claim that things are not as they appear, then he or she does not do this by denying that this is how they actually do appear but by explaining why they appear like this.

Similar considerations apply to reflective equilibrium theories. A moral theory does not deny that people make certain intuitive judgements. Instead, it suggests that, when these intuitions cannot be fitted into the best set of principles, then these intuitions can't really be intuitions of moral reality. While they truly are the intuitions that some people have they are not intuitions of the moral truth, consequently they are to be abandoned as descriptions of what morally ought to be the case, just as the description of the colour an object looks to have under abnormal conditions is to be abandoned as a description of the colour it really has.

There is, however, a radical difference between how scientific theories relate to perceptions and how moral theories relate to intuitive judgements. With a true scientific theory we could correctly predict how things would appear to people when all variables are controlled, including the internal states of the observers and the conditions under which the observations take place. The more accurately a scientific theory enables us to predict how things will appear to people under controlled conditions, the more the theory behaves as we would expect of a true theory, therefore the more rational it becomes for us to treat the essential components of the theory as true, particularly if no other theory is as successful over the same, or a similar, range of kinds of phenomena. A completely true scientific theory would enable us to correctly predict that, under certain circumstances, there would be a total consensus among truth-tellers about how things appeared. The presence of the predicted consensus under specified conditions is the test of the truth of the theory (although how the truth of a theory is tested is not to be confused with what it *means* for a theory to be true). If the theory says that things have properties different from those they appear to have, then the occurrence of the predicted consensus under specified conditions is confirmation that things really have properties other than those they appear to have. If a theory enables us to predict more accurately than any other theory the consensus that will be reached on how things appear to be under specified conditions, then there will be a consensus among rational people concerned to believe a true scientific theory that this particular theory is closer to the truth than any of its rivals. The consensus among rational people as to which theory is closer to the truth depends on which theory enables us to predict most accurately the consensus that will obtain on how things appear to be under specified conditions in the greatest range of kinds of cases.

As we saw earlier, reflective equilibrium permits the distinction between how things really are morally, and how they appear to be. Reflective equilibrium, however, is not like science in providing us with a method for discriminating between theories with different claims as to which properties are the ones things really have and which are the ones they merely appear to have. It is not part of a reflective equilibrium approach to moral theories to use a theory to predict that there will be a consensus on how things morally appear to be under given conditions, then determine from the success or failure of this prediction whether it is rational to accept the theory's claims as to what properties things morally really have and what properties they merely appear to have. Reflective equilibrium, then, cannot use the presence of a consensus on how things morally appear to be to produce a consensus on how things morally are.

The significance of the difference between scientific methodology and reflective equilibrium becomes apparent when we see how each handles the case where our predictions fail, either because a consensus doesn't occur that should if the theory is true, or a consensus does occur that shouldn't. When a scientific theory fails in test conditions where there is no instrument or observer error, etcetera, then the theory has to be modified so that the properties it claims things actually have are made consistent with the properties that things appear to have. If a scientific theory fails to explain those cases of how things appear to be that were inconsistent with the predictions based on it, this is a weakness in the theory. We may still prefer this theory to its competitors because they are even less successful but, nonetheless, we acknowledge that this theory has a mistake in it somewhere.

When a moral theory, however, says that things morally really are a particular way yet there is no consensus that they morally appear to be as the theory requires, then reflective equilibrium does not demand that the theory be modified so that its claims about how things morally are be made consistent with how things morally appear. It does not even demand that the variables be more rigorously controlled so that we find out under what conditions we do get consensus on how things morally appear. It does not direct us to obtain enough information on the various relationships between initial conditions and consensus on how things morally appeared to be so that we can use this data base to hypothesise about how things morally really are. If we did do this, however, I suspect that all we would get would be theories about the psychological causes that lead to consensus on how things morally appear to be. The use of a truly scientific methodology would lead us to theories of what empirical reality is behind people's beliefs about morality rather than theories about what moral reality is behind these beliefs. This is of little help in our current enterprise. We are after theories about what makes people's moral beliefs true or false, not theories about what makes them have these beliefs.

Reflective equilibrium, then, does not provide us with the same kind of fixed criterion of theory preference as scientific methodology does. The consequences of this are fatal to its pretensions as a method for obtaining consensus on particular cases of moral judgement. With scientific methodology, advocates of a theory that cannot be used to predict correctly how things will appear under specified conditions have the onus of explaining away this predictive failure. They can appeal to instrument error, observer error, unknown variables, etcetera, but they must make some appeal. If they can offer nothing, their theory has been shown to be seriously flawed. Reflective equilibrium places no such onus on advocates of a moral theory whose claims about how things morally are is at odds with how things morally appear to some people. The advocates of the theory can, if they wish, take into account only how things morally appear to those who agree with them. It is as if those who believed in ESP only took into account the experiments whose results agreed with what they had observed, rather than taking experiments with contrary results as possible evidence that controls hadn't been rigorous enough, or observer error had been a factor, or some such.

Suppose Ann holds particular moral judgements J1 to J10 whereas Ben holds J4 to J14. Both Ann and Ben will want principles that generate J4 to J10 but it may be that some of these principles generate some or all of J1 to J3 while others generate some or all of J11 to J14. If Ann adopts the principle or maxim M1 that generates J1 to J10 whereas Ben adopts M2 that generates J4 to J14 there is no onus on Ben to show that Ann only had intuitive judgements J1 to J10 because some variable relevant to moral perception hadn't been controlled such that, had it been, she would have had intuitive preference J4 to J14, thereby showing that M2 was closer to moral reality than M1. In fact, the only way that reflective equilibrium can contribute to consensus between two or more parties on moral matters where they initially disagree is if the parties themselves are more committed to arriving at consensus with each other than they are to keeping their intuitive judgements intact. If they value certain intuitive judgements more than they value consensus they will need to have these in common. This means they are only prepared to reach consensus on those intuitive judgements that matter less to them than consensus itself does. The more intuitive judgements there are that are valued more than consensus the more theories there will be whose advocates cannot reach consensus with each other. Some of these intuitive judgements may be very far-reaching, such as Rawls' intuitive preference for liberty over utility. Anyone who prefers utility to liberty will be unable to reach consensus with Rawls, nor does Rawls have the kind of method available to science that would enable him to show that his intuitive judgements correspond with moral truth whereas the utilitarian's doesn't.

In physics, Theory A may enable us to predict that flashes on a screen will appear red and theory D that they will appear yellow. It may turn out that either some people see red and others see yellow or that the same people sometimes see red and sometimes see yellow. The theories lead us to predict different results in the properties things appear to have to people because they postulate different properties that things actually have. If the advocates of A wish to accommodate the fact that some flashes appear yellow, which contradicts predictions based on A, they need to show that there is some variable present when the flashes appear yellow that, if controlled, results in the flashes appearing red, and that the real properties attributed to things by Theory A would lead one to predict that things would appear yellow to people if this variable wasn't controlled. If Theory B failed to do this, then rational people concerned with truth will prefer A to B, provided A doesn't have any other failings that B lacks. This ability to eliminate counter examples to the theory by identifying an uncontrolled variable which produces the predicted result when controlled in a way to be expected if things really are as the theory says they are is an ability not present with moral theories on a reflective equilibrium model. This means that reflective equilibrium doesn't provide moral theories with a methodology which achieves consensus by showing that one theory accommodates better than other theories a set of facts that must be accommodated by any true theory.

Reflective equilibrium allows a moral theory to ignore the fact that things do not appear morally to people as the theory says they should. Instead of attempting to find a theory that fits a set of facts that must be accommodated, a group of individuals seeking consensus can pick and choose which facts their principles will accommodate. This, however, creates the possibility of endlessly diverging groups, each of which has made a different choice at each branch in the decision-tree. While there is consensus within each group, there is nothing that pulls all the groups back towards a common theory, as the facts about how things appear to people do with a scientific theory. There is nothing that leads all groups to a consensus about what the properties of moral reality are through the avenue of a consensus on how they appear to be. In fact, there is nothing that leads to such a consensus by any other means. Even if the strongest intuition of every member of every group is the desirability of consensus, reflective equilibrium gives no clues as to which intuitive judgements are to be preferred as the basis of theorising when these intuitions clash. The problems this generates can be seen by looking at how Haksar tries to arrive at consensus on the status of the human foetus as a rights-bearer.

15.3   Haksar and the Foetus as a Rights-Bearer

Haksar believes that any human has a right to equal respect and consideration. Whenever he considers a particular case where there is a dispute about how some human should be treated, his intuitive judgement will be that this human should get the same treatment as any other. These intuitive judgements can be derived from the principle that all humans have a right to equal respect and consideration. I will call this the principle of 'human equality'. Haksar now has two problems if he is to obtain consensus. He must get people to accept his intuitive judgements in this area, and he must get them to derive these judgements from the principle of human equality. There are, however, people who do not intuitively judge in accord with the principle of human equality, for example, those who do not believe that human foetuses have the same rights as other humans.

Unlike the scientific case, this difference about how things morally appear to be does not provide Haksar with an unavoidable datum that his theory must explain predictively. There is no attempt to uncover a variable that, were it controlled, would empower the theory to predict a consensus on how things morally appear whenever the variable is controlled in this way. What we have instead is a branch in the decision-tree where the possessors of each kind of intuition can go their own way unrestrained by any requirement to accommodate the differences in intuition.

The search for consensus need not be abandoned here, however. Suppose Haksar puts his principle of human equality to 2000 people, and 1000 accept it because they have his kind of intuitive judgements in particular cases. Haksar has to try to obtain consensus from the remaining 1000. He cannot just postulate the principle of human equality as an axiom. Those who disagree with it will be unpersuaded by this kind of question-begging. He therefore needs to derive the principle of human equality from some higher principle, but not any old higher principle will do. Whatever it is, it must prove attractive to the 1000 unbelievers. He will need a principle, then, that states that all members of some class X have a right to equal respect and consideration such that the class X includes all humans but need not be identical with the class of all humans, where 'human' merely means members of 'homo sapiens'.

Haksar, then, will need to find some property E possessed by all members of X that is not logically limited to humans. As I said earlier, not any old property of this kind will do, however. Whatever it is, it must be of a kind likely to eliminate or, at least, drastically reduce the categories of opposition to the principle of human equality. In other words, most of those who were unhappy with the principle that all members of 'homo sapiens' have a right to equal respect, etcetera, will need to be happy with the principle that members of the class X, all of whom possess property E, have a right to equal respect, etcetera. This amounts to getting people to agree that the reason for giving beings a right to equal respect is their possession of property Q. In the first instance, Haksar will try to find a property whose presence is empirically demonstrable because this increases the chances of consensus about which beings possess it and which don't.

Reflective equilibrium, then, does find itself tested by the facts after a fashion. If there is absolutely no empirical property Q that can be embodied in a principle from which the principle of human equality can be derived, then Haksar will be forced by the facts to abandon the principle of human equality. Nonetheless, the way the facts test his moral theory is quite different to the way that facts test scientific theories. Having decided which intuitive judgements his moral theory is to accommodate, Haksar must now find some property Q possessed by all humans that enables him to postulate a principle that all possessors of Q have a right to equal respect and consideration that will be accepted by the 1000 remaining unbelievers.

If we used this method in science, we would decide which perceptions our scientific theory was to accommodate, for example, we will accommodate the cases of people who see red flashes on the screen rather than the case of people who see yellow flashes. Our choosing to accommodate those who see red flashes is a consequence of our theoretical commitment to the view that the flashes really are red, just as Haksar's commitment to intuitive judgements giving foetuses a right to equal respect and consideration is a consequence of his theoretical commitment to the view that it morally really is the case that foetuses have such a right. Having chosen to treat the flashes as really being red, we will then look for some property Q, as Haksar does, that is common to all cases of people seeing red flashes. When we find Q, we will try to show that Q's being common to all cases of people seeing red flashes is exactly what you would expect if the flashes really were red.

This still involves getting a consensus, for it involves getting the people who believe the flashes really are yellow, to see that they experience the flashes as red under conditions which would be predicted by a theory that treated the flashes as really being red but not by a theory that treated the flashes as really being yellow. It is this last step that is missing from Haksar's methodology. The 1000 unbelievers will not experience an intuitive judgement that foetuses have a right to equal respect and consideration under conditions which would be predicted by a moral theory that treated foetuses as having this right but would not be predicted by a moral theory that didn't treat them as having this right. The role, then, of the property E, will be quite different in reflective equilibrium methodology to what it is in scientific methodology.

When Haksar finds his property Q, he will not be able to show that its being common to all cases of people experiencing the intuitive judgement that foetuses have a right to equal respect and consideration is what you would expect if it morally really was the case that foetuses had this right. He would not be able to show this because it lacks the appropriate kind of prediction. It is not predicting an experience someone would undergo who was ignorant of the theory. In fact, it usually doesn't even predict the experiences of those who are familiar with the theory because it has no interest in accommodating all the original moral intuitions people have. It is interested, rather, in getting people to convert to new intuitions in those cases which don't fit the theory. This is as if the proponents of red flashes appealed to those who saw yellow flashes to try their hardest to see the flashes as red because this is a lot easier than changing the theory to accommodate the case of those who see yellow.

If the proponents of red flashes did try this, it would show that their theory wasn't really a theory about empirical reality. Likewise, when reflective equilibrium theorists do this, it shows that their theories aren't really about moral reality. If there is a reality, and we can perceive it, then we should be able to use a consensus about how it appears to us as a means for arriving at a consensus about how it really is. Reflective equilibrium pretends to be a method for arriving at such a consensus but provides no unavoidable datum which a true theory must accommodate. As a consequence an indefinite, possibly even an infinite, number of equally consistent moral theories can be generated with no criterion for choosing between them.

Reflective equilibrium, then, is too weak to achieve consensus about what principles should resolve conflicts of desires. It is unable to restrict the options available to disparate groups. Instead, it proliferates options. If there were a moral reality, it would not be able to lead us to it. Given the more likely alternative that there is no moral reality, it does not provide us with a method that, if successful, eliminates all but one uniform system of principles for deciding which desire should be satisfied in any conflict of desires. If reflective equilibrium is to help us arrive at consensus, we need to correspond in our intuitions at each of many branches of the decision-tree. Hare (1975, p.85) thinks that he can avoid this dependence on intuition by a reliance on facts, singular prescriptions and logic. I shall now consider the extent to which Hare's methodology is any less 'intuitionist' than Rawls'.

15.4   Hare's Methodology

Hare (1975, p.85) refers us to his book *Freedom and Reason*, especially Chapters, 6, 7, 10 and 11, for an exposition of his views on the logic of moral argument. In these chapters, he claims that a 'moral' judgement is one in which a person universally prescribes some action. To say, for example, 'I ought to put A into prison' is, according to Hare, to be understood in ordinary English as entailing the universal prescription, 'Let anyone who has done what A has done be put into prison', where the fact that I utter this prescription means that I want it to be the case that the state of affairs so prescribed comes about.

So far this thesis is a purely linguistic thesis. As such, its truth or falsity is a matter for the lexicographer to determine. Does the ordinary speaker of English (say, Ben) think that 'I ought to put A into jail' entails 'Let anyone who has done what A has done be put into jail' (with suitable riders about the conditions being 'relevantly similar')? If he doesn't, then 'ought' can't have universal prescription as part of its ordinary language meaning and Hare's analysis of the 'ordinary language' meaning of 'ought' would fail. Hare (1963, p.96) himself recognises this.

However, even if Hare's analysis of the meaning of 'ought' failed to capture ordinary usage, it could still be the case that there are good reasons why people should engage in universal prescription, and this is the crucial thing that Hare needs to establish if his position is not to be just as intuitionist as Rawls.

There are three alternatives to universal prescription, namely, prescribing without universalising, universalising without prescribing and, finally, neither universalising nor prescribing. Hare provides reasons for rejecting the first two alternatives.

15.5   Prescribing Without Universalising

If a person uses the word 'ought' to prescribe but not to universalise then, in Hare's view, he or she is not using the word 'ought' in its moral sense. For the sake of the argument, I will accept that the word 'ought' is used morally if, and only if, it is used to make a universalisable prescription. Consider the case where a person Ben says, 'Ben ought (nonuniversalisably prescriptively) put his debtor Ann into prison but his creditors ought (nonuniversalisably prescriptively) not put him in prison'. It may appear that he is in substantial moral disagreement with people who say 'Ben ought (morally) put his debtor Ann into prison and his creditors ought (morally) put him in prison'. In Hare's view, however, there is only a verbal disagreement between them, even though their utterances involve quite different prescriptions. According to Hare (1963, p.99), when we understand what Ben really means, our apparently substantive moral disagreement with him, that is, our universal prescriptive disagreement, turns out to be merely verbal because Ben does not intend his opinion to be about the morality of the action at all. Such a manoeuvre means that Ben can go on prescribing to himself to put Ann into prison, but the downside of this strategy is that he has to abandon the claim that he is justifying the action morally, as the word 'morally' is normally understood.

The nonuniversalising prescriber, then will presumably endorse the prescription, 'Let me jail Ann if she owes me money but can't pay but let Colin, say, not jail me if I owe him money and can't pay', whereas the universal prescriber will presumably endorse either 'Let anyone who owes another person money and can't pay be jailed' or 'Let anyone who owes another person money and can't pay not be jailed'. Depending on which universal prescription is endorsed, the universal prescriber will either endorse. 'Let me jail Ann if she owes me money and can't pay but also let Colin jail me if I owe him money and can't pay' or 'Let me not jail Ann if she owes me money and can't pay but let Colin not jail me if I owe him money and can't pay'. Now, if Hare's position is not ultimately to rest on pure intuition, he needs to supply us with a good reason why we should endorse either of the courses of action recommended by the universal prescriber rather than that recommended by the non-universalising prescriber.

15.6   Universalising Without Prescribing

According to Hare, the moral judgement 'Colin ought to put me into prison' entails the singular prescription, 'Let me be put into prison'. It presumably does so because 'Colin ought to put me into prison' entails 'Let anyone who is in position X (Colin's position) perform some action (for example, put in jail) anyone who is in position Z (my position)'. With the factual minor premise 'I am in position L and Colin is in position X' it is possible to deduce the singular prescription 'Let me put into jail (by Colin)'. This conclusion does not follow, however, if I use 'ought' universalisably but not prescriptively. This is because 'C ought to put me into prison' does not entail 'Let anyone who is in position X (C's position) Y (jail) anyone in position Z (my position)'. Consequently, even if I'm in position Z in relation to Colin, it doesn't follow that I am committed logically to endorsing the injunction 'Let me be jailed'.

Hare dismisses this difference between the universalising prescriber and the nonprescribing universaliser as, again, purely verbal. In one sense as with the nonuniversalising prescriber this is true. In neither case is the disagreement a 'moral' one, in Hare's sense. If the disagreement were kept within the 'moral' framework that Hare imposes, the nonprescribing universaliser's conclusion that he was not committed to 'Let me put in jail' would no longer hold. By definition, in merely uttering 'Colin ought to jail me' he has prescribed 'Let me be jailed by Colin'.

Hare, however, has merely shown what would follow for the universal prescriber. He has not shown us why we should be universal prescribers. What" wrong with being a nonprescribing universaliser? It is time to turn to his answer to this question, and to what's wrong with being a nonuniversalising prescriber.

15.7   Why be a Universal Prescriber?

Hare (1967, p.201) asks where can a man such as Ben flee to if he wants to flee from Hare's universalisable, prescriptive concepts? He can take refuge in either singular prescriptions expressing selfish desires or in universal but non-prescriptive judgements. Neither refuge helps him because neither results in his being in dispute with us about what *ought* to be done, even if we remain in dispute with him about the facts or about what to do.

This hardly solves our problem, that is, why be a universalising prescriber. True, it points out to those who are not universalising prescribers that they are not using a particular kind of 'ought', that is, a universalisable and prescriptive 'ought' but it hardly provides them with a reason to use such an 'ought'. Hare (1963, p.202) suggests that we are better off than someone like Ben who isn't a universalising prescriber because our language is more general than his. We can say whatever he wants to say but, unlike him, we also can also express universal prescriptions, that is, we can moral and other evaluative judgements.

In one obvious way, this argument fails. Let us imagine three languages. Language 1 contains a universalisable prescriptive 'ought', language 2 contains a non-universalisable prescriptive 'ought' and language 3 contains a non-prescriptive universalisable 'ought'. Each language contains only its kind of 'ought'. If this is so, it is not at all clear how language 1 can say all that can be said in language 2 and 3. After all, in language 1 a person can't say 'You ought to do X' in a nonprescriptive universalisable way nor can he say 'I ought to do X' in a nonuniversalisable prescriptive way. If we have language L4, which has all three kinds of 'ought', then the universal prescriber is no better off than his attackers. Each has three kinds of 'oughts' to appeal to if they wish.

Furthermore, even if Hare's point was true, all that has been established is that the universal prescriber can make universal prescriptions in his language, as well as nonuniversalisable prescriptions and nonprescriptive universalisations. Whatever the others can do he can do better, but why should the nonuniversalising prescriber or the nonprescribing universaliser want to make universal prescriptions? Fair enough, if Hare is correct, he will need to choose a language that has the apparatus to make universal prescriptions if he wants to make them but surely he isn't going to want to make them just because there's a language around that allows him to. There's a set of concepts around called 'theology' that allows me to make statements about God, if I want to, but why should I want to? The mere fact that the language makes it possible for me to is hardly a reason. Hare, therefore, appears to have supplied no reason why anyone should be a universal prescriber. His preference for universal prescribers, therefore, appears to have no more basis than Rawls' particular set of intuitions.

This is not a happy conclusion to reach at the end of our examination of the justifications underlying two of the major influential moral views in ethics today. As we saw in Chapter 1, however, and as I outlined earlier in this chapter, impartialism provides another option, one closer to the mathematical model. In the next chapter, which is also the final one, I will take up the role of public reason-giving as a criterion for choosing between rival moral theories, taking the work of R.S. Peters as a guide.

Notes

1   For an overview of the current debate in philosophy of science about the relationship between theory and observation, see Couvalis (1997).

2   This point, and the others made in this chapter, holds against writers like Werner (1983) and Flanagan (1982) who try to use the naturalist and holistic epistemology developed by Quine (1960, 1978) to defend the claim that there is as much justification to believe in a moral reality as there is to believe in a scientific one.

16 Public Reason-Giving

16.1 Introduction

We have seen that neither reflective equilibrium nor universal prescription provides us with a decision-procedure that rational people have good reasons to adopt as the means of achieving consensus. Reflective equilibrium of its very nature lets rational people with conflicting desires dissent from each other in their choice of the principles to govern the conflict, provided that each person (say, Ann) can harmonise her principles with her other principles and her intuitions about particular cases. Rawls gives no reason to believe that there could not be an indefinite number of such 'reflective equilibria', each equally coherent. Universal prescription fails to give any good reasons why a person should be a universal prescriber rather than a nonprescribing universaliser or a nonuniversalising prescriber. Even if it did not give such reasons, it still allows universal prescribers to adopt any of an indefinite number of ideals or, as Hare calls them, 'fanaticisms'.[1]

It seems, then, that if we are to arrive at a consensus we must find a decision-procedure that is neither pure formal, as Hare claims his to be nor that already presupposes consensus on substantive moral matters, as Rawls says that his does. A purely formal procedure, as Foot (1959) and other have argued, admits principles that seem to have nothing to do with morals, or, as I said above, lets in conflicting moral principles. A method like Rawls' that presupposes a consensus on substantive moral matters just begs the question against those who hold positions not encompassed by this consensus. In Rawls' case, even with an initial consensus, Rawls' reflective equilibrium procedure will soon have people departing from consensus down endlessly branching, but consistent, interconnections of principles and intuitions about particular cases.

R.S. Peters provides us with an example of a different model. I do not think that Peters' own application of this model is successful but I believe it is an example of the kind of strategy we need to adopt to show why impartialism should be preferred to any of the alternative moral systems.

16.2   Peters' Methodology

Peters[2] (p.115) suggests that it would be a powerful justification for a principle that it is necessary to assume it for a form of discourse to have a point or be given meaning or application. If this were so, then anyone who was serious in their use of the form of discourse would automatically be committed to accepting the principle. Peters goes on to argue that the principles of equality, freedom and the considerations of interests are presupposed in this way by anyone who sincerely asks the question, 'What ought I to do?' or 'Why do this rather than that?' He (p.116) thinks that these principles are presupposed in the sense that we can only avoid being committed to them by refusing to talk or think about what ought to be done, which would amount to a refusal to participate in a mode of thinking to which everyone in our society had been introduced to some extent. We would be excluding ourselves from the practice of guiding our conduct by appealing to reasons.

I will concentrate on his arguments for how engaging in discourse about what to do presupposes two principles, namely, the principle of consideration of the interest of others and the principle of freedom. I will show that this kind of discourse does not presuppose a commitment to these principles, in the sense that the person must either endorse these principles or abandon discourse about how to act. Nonetheless, the reasons why Peters' arguments fail do provide us with an understanding of the nature of moral argument and the extent to which its conclusions can escape a reliance on intuition.

16.3   The Consideration of Interests

Peters (p.171) begins his discussion of the consideration of the interests of other people by asking what is wrong, if anything, with only appealing to egoistic reasons. His answer is worth analysing in detail. It begins with the claim that we can only ask the question 'Why do this rather than that?' seriously if we presuppose consideration of the interests of other people. Prima facie, this claim is false. If I ask myself, 'What is there in it for me if I do A rather than B?' I am asking a specific example of the question, 'Why do this rather than that?' yet I am quite clearly excluding consideration of the interests of others. How does Peters propose to enforce such consideration on me? How do I presuppose such consideration?

Peters claims that I do so because the question I have asked is part of public discourse. As such, it assumes a situation in which people want to find the answers to matters of public policy where the help of other people is essential. In one sense, this claim is true. Such a form of words would not have entered a language unless there were issues of shared interest that warranted such a form of speech. In another sense it is false, if it is meant to show that the question is only legitimately asked when we need the help of others. All Peters can establish here is that a particular linguistic practice will not get off the ground unless it is in the common interest of the group of language speakers to have such a practice. This, however, makes language no different from any other institution, for example, money. Unless it were in the common interest of a group to have a standard means of exchange the group would not have instituted the custom of 'money', but it does not therefore follow that a person who uses money must want the interests of others to be achieved. The public nature of the institution of money does not make the egoistic use of money irrational.

Peters seeks to reinforce his argument with the claim that none of us would bother to engage in a public discussion about how we ought to act if we thought that our interest in a worthwhile life for ourselves would just be ignored. Our participation presupposes that we expect to be given due consideration. This makes clear that Peters is talking about the presupposition of the *public* debating of why do this rather than that. It can be accepted that public debating of why do this rather than that must historically precede private debating, that is, debating with oneself or thinking through for oneself the options open to one. It isn't clear, however, why this commits one to the consideration of the interests of others. The explanation, I believe, lies in the fact that Peters has conceived the public debate in a particular way, namely, as a debate among people who are more or less equal in power. Also, I believe, he is using the word 'consider' in an ambiguous manner.

It is true that if Ann, say, is going to feel that a debate with Ben or Colin or whoever about whether to do this or that is going to be worthwhile to her, then it must be the case that the debaters attentively discuss the interests of all the debating members. None of them need care tuppence for each other, but in order to get help from the others on their own problems they have to be prepared to exchange advice. This will be true, anyway, if Ann, etcetera, are all egoists. If the group contains Ann and her non-autonomous slaves Ben, Colin, etcetera, then in this debate the slaves will not necessarily want advice on their own affairs, although they may well wish to exchange views on how best to help Ann.

If they are in a position of equal power, then Peters is right when he says that consideration of the interests of others is a presupposition of asking the question, 'Why do this rather than that?' seriously but this doesn't show, as he intends it to, that an egoist (say, Ben) cannot properly ask himself 'What ought I to do considering only myself?' At least, it doesn't show that the egoist cannot ask himself. 'What ought I to do considering only myself or, if others, only as a means to my ends?' He may have to give lip service to the interests of others but this hardly limits his egoism in any significant manner.

What has not been established is that the egoist is logically committed to giving his own interests no more status than anyone else's. Peters goes on to note that there may well be occasions on which it is shown that the interests of some are more important than those of others. Nonetheless, he insists, this needs to be shown. But to whom is it to be shown? If the question is asked privately then does Ben have to show to himself that his interests are more important than those of others? Why does he have to? If he is an egoist, he will already believe they are. The only sense in which he will need to show himself this, perhaps, is to convince himself that he is logically consistent, as we have already seen that he can be. Peters seems to suggest this interpretation when he states that, just as a private language presupposes a public one, so private ploys are dependent on public practices. But we saw in Chapter 14 how the egoist escapes self-contradiction if the 'oughts' in the public language are hypothetical.

16.4   The Principle of Freedom

Peters (p.180) argues that it is a presupposition of doing what one ought to do or what one has reasons for doing that one expects others not to interfere in one's doing it. Consider the egoist. Is it the case that such a person, if he sincerely asks this question, must (as Peters claims he must) clearly expect no interference in his doing whatever there are reasons for doing? The problem here is - to whom is he going to make this demand? It makes little sense for him to demand absence of interference from himself, so he must be demanding it of other people. If this is so, then we need to distinguish between categories of other people, namely, egoists, sectarians or impartialists.

Suppose an egoist (Ben) demands of other egoists that they do not interfere with his pursuit of his own interests. They will be unimpressed because as far as they are concerned their interests, not his, are the only reasons for action. It seems that he would be foolish to make such a demand of other egoists unless he can back it up with force. He would be better advised to get his way by secrecy and deceit therefore it is not obviously true that he must demand absence of interference.

Suppose, on the other hand, that he makes this demand of impartialists. They would only accept his demand for freedom from interference in pursuing his interests if his interests are compatible with impartialism. However, he wants no interference at all, even in his partialist actions. Yet if he demands freedom to do what he has no impartialist right to do, then impartialists will not accept his demand. Therefore it is again the case that such a demand would be foolish. There is no reason, certainly no obvious reason, why he must demand absence of interference, even if he wants it.

The final possibility is that he make this demand of sectarians. Two types of sectarians are relevant here. Those who share his own cause and those who don't. Those who don't will treat him as the impartialists do. As the others regard his ideal as their most important goal there is no need for him to demand that they do not interfere. They would not want to. So once again, Peters' claim has no force.

Perhaps Peters means that, if a person is seriously asking what he ought, in his own overall self-interest, to do, then he must obviously want absence of interference in doing whatever there are reasons for doing. Again, this is not true, for Ben may ask what he ought to do if he is to maximise his overall self-interest but discover that this is not what he ought to do if he is to meet the requirements of impartialism. It is not obvious that he want absence of interference in doing what he ought (in his overall self-interest) to do because he may want to be an impartialist more than an egoist. He would, then, be grateful to anyone who stopped him doing what he ought (in his overall self-interest) to do if this was incompatible with what he ought (as an impartialist) to do. He may welcome efforts to bolster his resistance to temptation in situations where his present desire overcomes what he knows in the long-run is what he really wants.

From this discussion it would appear that, if Ben is asking seriously what he ought to do (in his overall self-interest), then it will only be true that he will want to be free to do what he ought to do (in his overall self-interest) if what he most wants to do is what he ought to do (in his overall self-interest). This would appear to be true enough, but does not show he must also want freedom for others.

Similar considerations would apply if the person seriously asked himself what he ought to do as an impartialist. If the word 'seriously' is understood to mean that he asks the question because he most wants to do what he ought to do as an impartialist, then it will be the case that he does not want to be stopped from doing it. Here, however, there is more point to the use of the word 'demand' because within impartialism, a person has the right to do what he ought to do and the right to be allowed to do it by others.

The problem for Peters here, however, is that he has tried to show that freedom to do what there are reasons for doing is justifiable to all people. This, however, is not so, as our argument has shown. The impartialist will only accept that a person is justified in doing what there are impartialist reasons to do, whereas each egoist will accept that he in particular only has reasons for doing what is in his interests to do. Consequently, the egoist will not accept that other people should be free to do anything that must interfere with his freedom. Of course, he will not be able to give them any reason why their freedom should be limited, but they will not be able to give him any reason he finds convincing why they should not have their freedom limited (other than force). The egoist will see the issue entirely in terms of how much freedom he can force or trick others into surrendering so that he will be better off. As a justification, then, this argument of Peters is a failure.

Let us return to the case where Ben is a person who most wants to do what he ought to do in his overall self-interest. Peters (p.181) says of such a person that it would be silly of him to ignore the advice of others about what there are reasons for doing, simply on prudential grounds. It would be even sillier to make it impossible for them to advise him. We have already seen that there are at least three different kinds of rational beings who might have views about what there are reasons for doing, that is, the egoist, the sectarian and the impartialist. Would the egoist be foolish to impose constraints on members of each of these classes so that they cannot give him advice. Should he listen to them all? If Peters' argument is to go through, he must.

Does the egoist have any reason to listen to the advice of other egoists and therefore reason to allow them freedom? What kind of advice could he ask of them? As an egoist, he only wants to know what is in his own best interests. As egoists, they will only give him such advice if they believe it to be in their best interests. Each bit of advice they give him is likely to be planned to give them some advantage. He could not trust them to give him honest answers therefore there is no reason why be should want their advice and therefore no reason why he should want them to be free to give it.

Does the egoist have any reason to listen to the advice of impartialists? Provided he acts on behalf of his own interests in an impartialist way, they will give him honest and often helpful advice. The problem with impartialists, however, from his point of view, is that they will also give him impartialist advice, which he doesn't want. Not only that, they will give each other advice on how to stop him doing what he has no right to do, therefore they are a mixed blessing, particularly as they are likely to act on that advice. The only advice the egoist really wants is not advice on what personal goals are desirable but how to achieve the goals he already has or how to organise them to maximise their chances of being achieved or else what are the consequences of various planned courses of action so that he can choose the one that he prefers. As a result, he may wish to live in a society neither of other egoists, nor of impartialists, but of sectarians whose cause is to service his every wish. Unfortunately for him, there are few such people, but this is no reason why he should not seek great political power, repress and render unfree the vast majority of the population while keeping relatively free a body of fawning technical advisers who are too intimidated by his power to do anything other than provide him with instrumental information about the means to his goal. In other words, the true egoist might want to be a Nero, or a Hitler, an absolute despot. He may even want to be a Svengali who controls their desires but leaves their minds free to calculate what will maximise his self-interest. All Peters' arguments about the need for freedom would fail to have any effect on him, not because he is irrational, but because Peters' arguments do not give him a reason to have reasons of a particular sort.

A deeper understanding of the different constraints imposed on us by public, as opposed to non-public, reason-giving can be gained from an examination of the arguments put forward by Michael Smith in his 1994 book, *The Moral Problem*, which I will examine in the next section.

16.5　Michael Smith's *The Moral Problem*

Plato, in *The Republic*, tells the story of the shepherd Gyges who obtains a ring that makes him invisible. He uses the advantage this gives him over other people to seduce the queen of his country and, with her help, murder the king and seize the throne. This is a *locus classicus* of the idea that it is perfectly rational to be an egoist, in the sense of someone who places no value on the interests or welfare of others. In fact, the story can even be taken to illustrate the idea that it is perfectly rational to actively want to harm the interests of others for one's own advantage, that is, that there is nothing irrational in behaving maliciously or malevolently.

Smith proposes an account of morality which contests this view of rationality. He considers a case parallel to the Gyges case, namely, that of the successful criminal. According to Smith (pp.94-98), the successful criminal (say, Ben) may think that he is acting rationally in pursuing wealth for himself regardless of the cost to others in that he may think that he has a normative reason for behaving this way, where a 'normative reason' is a justificatory reason and is to be understood in opposition to an explanatory or motivating reason. However, Smith (p.195) claims, the successful criminal is mistaken. He would only have a normative reason to behave this way, that is, it would only be *right* for him to behave this way or it is only the case that he *ought* to behave this way, if this behaviour is what fully rational creatures would want to do were they in the same situation. In Smith's opinion, fully rational creatures would not want to behave in this way.

My argument throughout this book, however, has assumed that fully rational creatures might well want to behave this way. This is precisely what an egoist or a coercionist would want to do if accumulation of wealth was what mattered to them most. Moreover, while the accumulation of wealth as such would not be what mattered to a sectarian (say, Ann), she, too, would count the interests of others as nought compared to the achievement of her particular sectarian cause. Even so, I do not want to deny Smith's claim that the action that Ann has a normative reason to do, that is, that is the right one for her to do, or that she ought to do, is the one that a fully rational creature would want to do in her situation. This account does overcome many of the problems associated with trying to analyse rationality in terms of manifest desires. Nonetheless, in my view, Smith has failed to appreciate the different conditions placed on our reasoning by whether it is conducted externally, that is, as part of our justifying ourselves to others, or whether it is conducted internally, that is, as part of justifying a particular course of action to ourselves. (This distinction could also be labelled 'public' as opposed to 'private' justification, provided the 'private' was understood to mean 'inside one's own head', rather than to just one other person.) There is nothing in the concept of a 'fully rational creature', it seems to me, that requires such a creature to treat all justification as external.

Smith (p.156) wishes to argue that those who believe that Gyges, say, has a normative reason to murder the king are committed to a 'relative', as opposed to a 'non-relative' conception of reasons. A relative account of reasons makes the reasons of an agent (say, Ann) relative to her actual desires, the agent being regarded as fully rational (in the relative sense) provided she has no false beliefs, has all the relevant true beliefs, and she deliberates correctly. It is a consequence of such a view, Smith thinks, that it is also what I will call a 'non-convergence' account of rationality, that is, that it is not part of rationality as a concept that all fully rational agents will converge on the same desires about what is to be done in a particular situation (p.165). On such an account of rationality, then, it follows that, when we try to decide whether or not a claim such as 'It is desirable that some action A be performed in a particular set of circumstances C' is true, we first of all need to find out from whose point of view the claim is thought to be true (p.167). If this account of rationality is correct, then there is no such thing as 'desirability' or 'rational justification' *simpliciter*.

Smith thinks the relative, non-convergent account of rationality fails to reflect how we actually talk about reasons for action and rational justification. In his view, none of our other normative concepts such as 'truth', 'meaning', 'support', and 'entailment' plausibly generate claims whose truth conditions are relativised. They all have normative force *simpliciter*. With these concepts, he points out, we are not able to dissolve apparent disagreements by discovering that both sides are speaking truly when one says that the proposition p supports or entails some conclusion q whereas the other denies it (p.168). This makes all our other normative concepts very different from the concept of 'desirability' as the relativist understands it. To Smith's mind, this raises the suspicion that those cases where desirability appears to be relativised have been misconstrued. One such case is where Ann, say, likes wine whereas Ben likes beer. This seems to suggest that Ann has a reason to go to the local wine bar after work because it sells better wine than the local pub whereas Ben has a reason to go to the pub because the wine bar doesn't sell beer, the difference in their reasons being a function of the difference in their psychologies (p.170).

This seems to be a case where Ben can say 'The quality of the wine at the wine bar is a reason for you to go there rather than to the pub, Ann, but it's not a reason for me', that is, it seems to be a case where Ben's reason, in the normative or justificatory sense, is relative to his desires. Given his preference for beer over wine, he is justified in going to the pub because any fully rational person with such a preference would also want to go to the pub rather than the wine bar if these were the only factors taken into consideration. While it may seem to be a case of the relativity of what is desirable, Smith argues that it is not because a relevant feature in the case of both Ann and Ben is their particular preference. All people with no false beliefs and all the relevant true beliefs who had Ann's preference for wine would converge on the judgement that it is desirable that she go to the wine bar in the circumstances. Equally, such fully rational people would agree that it desirable that Ben go to the pub. Ben cannot say that the quality of wine is a reason for Ann to go to the wine bar rather than the pub, given her preferences but, were he to have the same preference, and all the other circumstances remained the same, that it would not be a reason for him.

But this example undermines Smith's whole project. In exactly the same way as it is desirable for Ann to go to the wine bar, it may be desirable for a person (say, Colin) to harm another person (say, Deidre) for his own benefit. It may not be desirable, in this sense, for another person (say, Eileen) to harm Deidre in relevantly similar circumstances to those that Colin is in but this is because her predilections are not the same as his. In the language of the evolutionary ethicists, it may that the two of them have radically different 'deep preferences' when it comes to resolving conflicts of desire between people. What Colin may want is to maximise his pleasure, regardless of its effect on others. This allows him two kinds of non-relative justification of the kind allowed Ben and Ann in the example above. He can either justify his harming Deidre on the grounds that anyone who held no false beliefs, and had all the true relevant beliefs, and whose preference was to maximise Colin's pleasure, would act as he did in these circumstances. This is the particularist version of egoist rationality, which is only likely to be adopted as a justification by his superfans. Alternatively, he could justify his harming Deidre on the grounds that all fully rational people whose preference was to maximise their own pleasure, and whose pleasures were similar to Colin's, would, in relevantly similar circumstances, harm Deidre or someone relevantly like Deidre. This is the universalist egoist version of egoist rationality. A parallel example could be constructed for particularist and universalist sectarians.

Of course, Colin may not want to offer such a justification in public unless he was in a position of very superior power but even this can be given the kind of analysis that Smith requires, that is, any fully rational person who happened to be an egoist or a sectarian not in a position of very superior power should not make the real reason for their behaviour public. What justifications, then, are offered in public will nearly always appear to be categorical rather than hypothetical, even though they are actually hypothetical in nature. They are hypothetical in nature because they are justifications in terms of goals, but only goals that it is rational to let other people know that you have. This feature of the selection of justifications that are offered publicly, however, is not itself offered as part of the justification so such justifications give all the appearance of categoricality. (See Chapters 1 and 14 for elaboration of this point.)

Fully rational people, then, will converge on judgements about how people with certain kinds of basic preference 'ought' to act, or are 'right' to act, but the convergence will be on what means they ought to choose or which option is the right one for them, given their preferences. There will not, however, be a convergence on preferences. Not all fully rational people who find a wallet in the street will converge on the rightness of returning it to its owner, for example.

Smith (p.193) notes that the word 'ought' has motivational force such that anyone who judges an act right is either motivated to do it or else is irrational. This point can be granted him, but this creates no problems for the rationality of the egoist (Ben, say) who behaves in ways that we regard as immoral. It creates no problems for Ben because he does not regard the fact that an act is the one that morality demands as a rightness-making feature of it. He is certainly motivated to do whichever act maximises his self-interest and he can accept that the right act for him to do would be the one that people with no false beliefs and all the relevant true beliefs and who deliberated correctly would want to do in the particular circumstances in which he finds himself. We can acknowledge that it would be irrational of him to do any other act but this means saying that it would be irrational of him to do an act that did not maximise his self-interest in the circumstances.

Smith (pp.195-196) suggests that the successful criminal (say, Ben) suffers from intellectual arrogance because he doesn't feel the force of arguments that come from others at all. As we have seen, however, even an egoist such as the successful criminal must take account of the force of arguments about the best means to his ends if he is to be rational, regardless of where they come from - although it will usually only be rational of him to get them from his superfans. It is not a failure to feel the force of *argument* that is his problem. Rather, it is that he doesn't feel the force of the preferences of others. He doesn't respect them as valuers whose worth should be given equal consideration with his own.

Smith, then, has failed to link rationality and morality. We cannot determine which option is the moral option in a particular situation by identifying which option would be wanted by fully rational agents. What is lacking from his account is the fact that people have different attitudes to how they should behave if they have superior power. As we have seen, noncoercionists in a position of equal power are likely to converge on a single option, but not everyone is a noncoercionist, nor does there seem to be any demand of reason that requires one to be. There is nothing self-contradictory in using a position of superior power to force your preferences on others. In fact, we should be very cautious of arguments that try to link morality and irrationality because those who convince themselves there is such a link seem to make themselves vulnerable to the view that a person (say, Ann) who performs what they regard as an immoral act is not fully rational. This suggests that, in their view, Ann cannot know what her true interests are, that the wants or preferences she has are the wants of her manifest self rather than those of her real (that is, 'fully rational') self. It is out of such moves that arrogationism is spawned.

There is nothing, then, in the nature of reason-having that requires the reasons one has for one's actions to be the reasons one would be prepared to give publicly. That one's reasons are of the kind that one will not give publicly may reflect on the morality of such reasons but not on their status as justifications of the rationality of what one does. Just because rationality itself may sometimes require one, given one's preferences, not to make one's reasons public, does not, in itself, make those reasons irrational. Nor, for that matter, does the fact that the kinds of reasons one has for one's actions make it unlikely that one will converge towards the same set of wants as other people. The only convergence that rationality itself seems to require is that people would converge towards wanting to perform the same acts if they had the same preferences and were fully rational in that they had no false beliefs, had all the relevant true beliefs and made no errors of logic. What is crucial in morality, then, as has been argued from Chapter 1, is that one have preferences of a particular kind - namely, the overriding preference to resolve conflicts of desires by unforced argument. In a speculative discussion, as in a context where our interest is clearly a philosophical or theoretical one, it is not irrational of us to ask whether or not we have good reasons for being moral but in a serious discussion, that is, in a discussion where people take us to mean that we do not regard ourselves as having such reasons, then it will be irrational of us to reveal our amorality unless we are in a very secure position of superior power. As it happens, very few of us appear to be amoral in this way. We do seem to have as our overriding preference a desire to act in ways that can be justified publicly. Before I conclude this chapter, and the book as a whole, I will briefly examine the issue of how impartialism relates to modern evolutionary explanations of moral behaviour.

16.6   Impartialism and Evolutionary Theory

Michael Ruse has suggested that natural selection has favoured those humans with a genetic tendency to altruism. He has even gone so far as to postulate that there has been a survival advantage for those of us with a disposition to regard morality as objectively true. (For criticisms of his arguments to this effect see Woolcock 1998b.)   This seems to me, however, to be too strong a thesis. All we need at the biological level if people are to act as though morality were objectively true is that there be a genetic disposition to believe privately what we offer as the public reasons for our behaviour. This amounts to our being susceptible to socialisation. When this is joined with the general components of rationality such as the ability to deduce and to predict consequences, it is likely that any expansion of the groups to whom we have to justify our actions will result in our making our reasons for action more inclusive. The demand to respect only the lives of our own tribe members becomes difficult to maintain when we have to negotiate with other tribes who can inflict serious injury on us unless we cooperate with them.   The more that technology puts us into contact with groups we had not previously had to take into account the more general we will find our public reason-giving becoming. In fact, we will find ourselves having to reason with strangers in terms of fairness, universalisability and the other standard norms of morality. While each of us will tend to accept the customs and beliefs we have been socialised into, we will still possess our own perception of the world, our own logical abilities and our capacity to recognise inconsistencies between what our socialisation has told us and how we individually perceive things to be. This leaves open the possibility of both moral and cognitive reform.

All of this is compatible with the claim that natural selection has instilled into us an innate disposition to altruism, although of a very general kind, otherwise how to we explain the sort of facts that James Q. Wilson draws to our attention, for example, the fact that, while theft may be more common than we may wish, it is far less common than we might expect, given that only one in four thefts are reported to the police and, of these, only three in a hundred lead to the culprit being jailed. Likewise, parental neglect of children is much less widespread than the difficulties of parenting might suggest. David Hume in 1772 made much the same point when he said that it would be absurd to deny 'that there is some benevolence, however small, infused into our bosom; some spark of friendship for human kind; some particle of the dove, kneaded into our frame, along with the elements of the wolf and the serpent.'

Granting this, however, does not amount to granting that there is a genetic disposition to favour kin over non-kin or those can reciprocate over those who cannot, as many sociobiologists wish to argue. Nor need we grant Ruse's claim, mentioned earlier, that there is an inherited inclination to treat moral claims as matters of fact. The same phenomena can be explained on weaker, less contentious assumptions. Interestingly, the kind of disposition to socialisation that I described above, combined with a general disposition to benevolence, would seem to have exactly the same kind of reproductive advantages as the evolutionary ethicists have proposed for the innate tendencies they favour. The two dispositions I have postulated might well be sufficient to explain why people honour the moral codes of their societies, without our needing to hypothesise the existence any specific moral instincts.

16.7   Conclusion

The aims that I set myself in this book have now, I believe, been met. The conditions under which unforced agreement on the resolution of conflicts of desires is possible have been identified. They are that people must argue as if they are nonmonist noncoercionists in a position of equal power who offer each other offer principles that do not presuppose that they are the ones in a position of superior power in the real world. Only if they argue like this are they impartial about whose desires are to be satisfied.

I have also spelt out some of the principles on which, I believe, the parties in a position of equal power would reach agreement. These, however, should not be seen as an essential part of the theory as such. I would not wish to find people conflating the conclusions I have drawn from my theory with the theory itself, as they seem to have done with Kant. In Kant's case, his critics have focused on the conclusions he drew from his theory as if the fact that he believed his theory had these consequences was holy writ, rather than a possibly faulty deduction from a theory that, when applied correctly, produced much more plausible outcomes. As I warned earlier, even if our values are such that we want to live in accordance with what the parties would agree in a position of equal power, we are not infallible impartialists. Our arguments can only result in provisional positions, although some of them may be so universally supported that it is difficult to see that an error in our reasoning will subsequently be revealed, for example, in the position that torturing people for fun is wrong. Nonetheless, I think that a good case can be made in favour of the view that the parties in a position of equal power would agree to each of the proposals mentioned below.

I argued that there were important differences in the kinds of freedom that a person might pursue, demonstrating that those, such as utilitarians, who see freedom primarily in terms of the capacity to satisfy interests, have ignored the vital freedom involved in being as much the maker of one's life as other people are of theirs - a freedom that, it seems to me, is integral to the idea of being a rational agent engaged in a conflict of desires with other rational agents. In the context of this discussion, I noted that, while paternalism is a constant danger to the survival of the kinds of liberal-democratic institutions valued by impartialists, arrogationism also presents a serious contemporary threat.

Another conclusion reached was that a contractarian-type theory of right does not need to make contentious assumptions about the metaphysics of personal identity, nor does it need to presuppose a particular epistemology or operate on unacknowledged perfectionist premises about the value of autonomy or potentiality or being human. Nonetheless, the contract situation itself does impose considerable restraints on the kinds of positions people will adopt on these issues.

It was also shown that a number of substantive normative principles are derivable from the impartialist axioms, such as the relativities principle, the error principle, the independence principle, the autonomy principle and the degustibus principle, as well as a number of particular moral judgements about the wrongness of murder and theft. We have also shown that impartialism provides some parameters in which to determine issues such as the rights of indigenous peoples and the rights of nonpersons such as foetuses and animals. It also gives substantive advice on the basic structure of the ideal political and educational systems, as well as enabling us to make judgements across the ages, and across different cultures, as to what kinds of acts or institutions would have been morally acceptable given that the ideal ones were not viable in the circumstances of a particular time or place.

It was also demonstrated that the extent to which moral judgements are grounded in subjective preferences is very limited indeed. In fact, the only preferences available to us with respect to resolving conflicts of desires are either to do so by force or by argument. If our preference is the impartialist one, then the constraints imposed by the presuppositions of unforced agreement give our moral reasoning much the same kind of objectivity as mathematics has, making consensus on particular moral judgements a real possibility. It was also pointed out that morality cannot be reduced to rationality, that there is a significant difference between it not being rational to tell the truth publicly about one's reasons for one's actions and it not being rational to have such undeclarable reasons in the first place. A course of action that is not justifiable to others may still be justifiable in that it is the action that others, too, would choose if they had the same preferences as oneself and were fully rational.

I have, however, only been able to apply the impartialist axioms to a small range of moral problems. Even there, given the programmatic nature of this book, I have often only been able to sketch the kind of answer that I think an impartialist would give. I look forward to developing a fuller picture of impartialist morality in the future and hope that others have found the programme convincing enough to motivate them to do likewise.

Notes

1   Hare now argues (1976; 1981) that universal prescription leads only to utilitarianism. His arguments are criticised by McCloskey (1979) and McDermott (1983).
2   His argument here is a development of the argument in Benn and Peters (p.31).

Bibliography

Baier, K. (1965), *The Moral Point of View*, Random House, New York.

Barrow R. (1976), *Commonsense and the Curriculum*, Allen and Unwin, London.

Barrow, R. (1980), *Happiness*, Martin Robertson, London.

Barry, B. (1963), *Political Argument*, RKP, London.

Barry, B. (1967), 'On Social Justice', *Oxford Review*, 5.

Barry, B. (1973), *The Liberal Theory of Justice*, Clarendon Press, Oxford.

Barry, B. (1989), *Theories of Justice,* University of California Press, Berkeley.

Barry, B. (1995), *Justice as Impartiality,* Clarendon Press, Oxford.

Bayles, M. (1972) 'A Concept of Coercion' in Pennock, J.R. and Chapman, J.W. (eds) *Coercion,*, Chicago, Aldine, Nomos XIV.

Beatty, J. (1983), 'The Rationality of the Original Position: A Defense', *Ethics,* 93, April.

Beauchamp, T. (1980), 'Distributive Justice and the Difference Principle' in Blocker, H.G. and Smith, E.H. (eds) *John Rawls' Theory of Social Justice*, Ohio University Press, Athens, U.S.A.

Beauchamp, T. (1991), Philosophical Ethics, McGraw-Hill, N.Y., (Second Edition).

Benn, S.T. and Peters R.S. (1959), *Social Principles and the Democratic State*, Allen and Unwin, London.

Benn, S.T. (1975/76), 'Freedom, Autonomy and the Concept of a Person', *Proceedings of the Aristotelian Society,* 1975/76.

Bentham, J. (1948), *Introduction to the Principles of Morals and Legislation,* Hafner Publishing Co, N.Y. (First published 1789)

Berlin, I. (1969), 'Two Concepts of Liberty' in his collection, *Four Essays on Liberty*, Oxford University Press, Oxford.

Berlin, I. (1978), *Russian Thinkers*, Viking, New York.

Berndt R., Berndt C., and Stanton J.E. (1993), *The World that Was: The Yaraldi of the Murray River and the Lakes, South Australia*, Melbourne University Press, Melbourne.

Blocker, H.G. and Smith, E.H. (eds), (1980), *John Rawls' Theory of Social Justice*, Ohio University Press, Athens, U.S.A.

Bourke, U.J. (1978), 'Ethical Role of the Impartial Observer', *Journal of Religious Ethics*, Vol. 6, Fall.

Bowie, N. (1980), 'Equal Basic Liberty for All' in Blocker, H.G. and Smith, E.H. (eds) *John Rawls' Theory of Social Justice*, Ohio University Press, Athens, U.S.A.

Braithwaite, R.B. (1955), *Theory of Games as a Tool for the Moral Philosopher*, Cambridge University Press, Cambridge.

Brandt, R.B. (1979), *A Theory of the Right and the Good*, Clarendon Press.

Buchanan, A. (1982), *Marx and Justice : The Radical Critique of Liberalism*, Methuen, London.

Carlson, G.R. (1973), 'Ethical Egoism Reconsidered', *American Philosophical Quarterly*, Vol. 10, No. 1, January.

Charvet, J. (1996), 'The Place of the Nationality Principle in the Contractarian Perspective on International Society', in Wright, M. (ed), (1996), *Morality and International Relations*, Avebury, Aldershot.

Constant, B. (1819), 'Ancient and Modern Liberty' in *Political Writings*, Cambridge University Press, N.Y. (1988).

Cooper, D. (1982), 'Equality and Envy', *Journal of Philosophy of Education*, Vol.16, No. 1.

Corrado, G. (1980), 'Rawls, Games and Economic Theory' in Blocker, H.G. and Smith, E.H. (eds) *John Rawls' Theory of Social Justice*, Ohio University Press, Athens, U.S.A.

Couvalis, S.G. (1997), *The Philosophy of Science: Science and Objectivity*, Sage, N.Y.

Croker, L.G. (1963), *Jean-Jacques Rousseau: the Prophetic Voice*, Methuen, London.

Daniels N. (ed), (1975), *Reading Rawls*, Basil Blackwell, Oxford.

Daniels, N. (1975), 'Equal Liberty and Unequal Worth of Liberty' in Daniels, N. (ed), *Reading Rawls*, Basil Blackwell, Oxford.

Daniels, N. (1979a), 'Wide Reflective Equilibrium and Theory Acceptance in Ethics', *Journal of Philosophy*, pp.276-83.

Daniels, N. (1979b), 'Moral Theory and the Plasticity of Persons', *Monist*, No 62, July.

Davies, B. (1991), 'The Concept of Agency: a Feminist Postructural Analysis' in Yeatman, A. (1991), *Postmodern Critical Theorising*, Department of Anthropology, University of Adelaide.

Dworkin, G. (1975), 'Non-Neutral Principles' in Daniels N. (ed), (1975), *Reading Rawls*, Basil Blackwell, Oxford.

Dworkin, R. (1975), The Original Position, in Daniels N. (ed), (1975), *Reading Rawls*, Basil Blackwell, Oxford.

Dworkin, R. (1977), *Taking Rights Seriously*, Duckworth, London.

Dworkin, R. (1981a), 'What is Equality?' *Philosophy and Public Affairs*, 10/3-4, pp.296-9.

Dworkin, R. (1981b), 'Two Concepts of Liberty', in Morgenbesser, S. and Lieberson, J. (1991), *Isaiah Berlin*, Hogarth Press, London.

Edgley, R. (1969), *Reason in Theory and Practice*, Hutchinson, London.

Farrell, D.M. (1980), 'Dealing with Justice in a Reasonably Just Society,' in Blocker, H.G. and Smith, E.H. (eds) *John Rawls' Theory of Social Justice*, Ohio University Press, Athens, U.S.A.

Feinberg, J. (1974), *Rights of Animals and Future Generations: Philosophy and Environmental Crisis*, W. Blackstone, London.

Feinberg, J. (1975), 'Rawls and Intuition', in Daniels N. (ed), (1975), *Reading Rawls*, Basil Blackwell, Oxford.

Feinberg, J. (1977), 'Ethical Theory and Utilitarianism', in Lewis, H.D. (ed), (1976), *Contemporary British Philosophy 4*, Allen and Unwin, London.

Fergie, D. (1995), 'Whose Sacred Sites? Privilege in the Hindmarsh Island Debate', *Current Affairs Bulletin*, August/September.

Feyerabend, P. (1975), *Against Method*, Verso, London.

Fishkin, J.S. (1979), *Tyranny and Legitimacy*, John Hopkins University Press.

Fisk, M. (1975), 'History and Reason in Rawls' Moral Theory', in Daniels N. (ed), (1975), *Reading Rawls*, Basil Blackwell, Oxford.

Flanagan, O. (1982), 'Quinean Ethics', *Ethics*, Vol. 97, No. 1., October.

Foot, P. (1959), 'Moral Beliefs', *Proceedings of the Aristotelian Society*, Vol. 59.

Foot, P. (1961), 'Goodness and Choice', *The Aristotelian Society Supplementary Volume*.

Foot, P. (ed), (1967), *Theories of Ethics*, Oxford University Press, Oxford.

Foot, P. (1972), 'Morality as a System of Hypothetical Imperatives', *Philosophical Review*, Vol. 81, July.

Foot, P. (1978a), *Virtues and Vices*, Oxford, Blackwell.

Foot, P. (1978b), 'Moral Arguments', *Mind*, Volume 67, 1958.

Francis, L.P. 'Responses to Rawls from the Left', in Blocker, H.G. and Smith, E.H. (eds) *John Rawls' Theory of Social Justice*, Ohio University Press, Athens, U.S.A.

Frankena, W. (1973), *Ethics*, Prentice Hall, Englewood Cliffs, (Second Edition).

Freire, P. (1972), *The Pedagogy of the Oppressed,* Penguin, Harmondsworth.

Galston, W.A. (1980), *Justice and the Human Good*, University of Chicago Press.

Gardenfors, P. (1978) 'Fairness Without Interpersonal Comparisons', *Theoria*, 2.

Garnsey, P. (1996), *Ideas of Slavery from Aristotle to Augustine*, Cambridge University Press, Cambridge.

Gauthier, D. (1963), *Practical Reasoning*, Clarendon Press, Oxford.

Gauthier, D. (ed), (1970), *Morality and Rational Self-Interest*, Prentice Hall, Englewood Cliffs, NJ.

Geach, P. (1967), 'Good and Evil', in Foot, P. (ed), (1967), *Theories of Ethics*, Oxford University Press, Oxford.

Gert, B. (1966), *The Moral Rules*, Harper and Row, N.Y.

Gert, B. (1972), 'Coercion and Freedom,' in Pennock, J.R. and Chapman, J.W. (eds) *Coercion,,*, Chicago, Aldine, Nomos XIV.

Glover, J. (1977), *Causing Death and Saving Lives*, Penguin, Harmondsworth.

Gray, J. (1995), *Isaiah Berlin*, Harper Collins, London.

Gray, T. (1991), *Freedom*, Macmillan, London.

Grice, G.R. (1967), *The Grounds of Moral Judgement*, Cambridge University Press, Cambridge.

Habermas, J. (1973), *Theory and Practice*, Polity Press, Cambridge, U.K.

Haksar, V. (1979), *Equality, Liberty and Perfectionism*, Clarendon Press, Oxford.

Hampton J. (1980), 'Contracts and Choices : Does Rawls Have A Social Contract Theory', *Journal of Philosophy*, Vol. LXXVII, No. 6.

Hare, R.M. (1952), *Language of Morals*, Oxford University Press, Oxford.

Hare, R.M. (1967), *Freedom and Reason*, Clarendon Press, Oxford.

Hare, R.M. (1975), 'Rawls' Theory of Justice', in Daniels N. (ed), (1975), *Reading Rawls*, Basil Blackwell, Oxford.

Hare, R.M. (1976), 'Ethical Theory and Utilitarianism' in Lewis, H.D. (ed), (1976), *Contemporary British Philosophy 4*, Allen and Unwin, London.

Hare, R.M. (1981), *Moral Thinking*, Clarendon Press,Oxford.

Harsanyi, J.C. (1976), 'Ethics in Terms of Hypothetical Imperatives', in his collection, *Essays on Ethics, Social Behaviour and Scientific Explanation*, Utrecht, Reidel.

Hart, H.L.A. (1975), 'Rawls on Liberty and its Priority', in Daniels N. (ed), (1975), *Reading Rawls*, Basil Blackwell, Oxford.

Hegel, G.W.F. (1967), *The Phenomenology of Spirit*, Harper and Row, N.Y.

Held, V. 'Coercion and Coercive Offers', in Pennock, J.R. and Chapman, J.W. (eds) *Coercion,*, Chicago, Aldine, Nomos XIV.

Henberg, M.C. (1978), 'Impartiality', *Canadian Journal of Philosophy*, Vol. 8, December.

Hirst, P.H. (1974), 'Liberal Education and the Nature of Knowledge,' in his collection, *Knowledge and the Curriculum*, Routledge and Kegan Paul, London.

Howard, N. (1971), *Paradoxes of Rationality*, MIT Press.

Hubin, D.C. (1979), 'The Scope of Justice', *Philosophy and Public Affairs*, Fall, Vol. 9, No.1.

Hudson, W.D. (ed) (1969), *The Is-Ought Question,*, MacMillan, London.

Hudson, W.D. (1983), *Modern Moral Philosophy*, MacMillan, London.

Hume, D. (1772), Enquiries Concerning Human Understanding and Concerning the Principles of Morals, edited by L.A. Selby-Bigge, revised by P.H. Nidditch, Clarendon Press, Oxford, 1975.

Hume, D. (1978), *A Treatise of Human Nature*, (London, 1740); (ed) Selby-Bigge, L.A., Clarendon Press, Oxford, bk 111, pt 111,sct 11.

Hunt, I. (1991), 'Freedom and its Conditions', *Australasian Journal of Philosophy*, 69, pp.288-301.

Hunt, I. (1995), 'A Note on Woolcock's Defence of Berlin on Positive and Negative Liberty', *Australasian Journal of Philosophy*, 73, pp.465-471.

Kalin, J. (1968), 'Two Kinds of Moral Reasoning : Ethical Egoism as a Moral Theory', *Canadian Journal of Philosophy*, Vol V., No. 3, November.

Kalin, J. (1970), 'In Defense of Egoism', in Gauthier, D. (ed), (1970), *Morality and Rational Self-Interest*, Prentice Hall, Englewood Cliffs, NJ.

Kant, I. (1948), *Groundwork of the Metaphysics of Morals*, translated and analysed by H.J. Paton as *The Moral Law*, Hutchinson, London.

Kant, I. (1963), *Lectures on Ethics*, translated by Louis Infield, Harper, N.Y.

Katzner, L.I. (1980), 'The Original Position and the Veil of Ignorance', in Blocker, H.G. and Smith, E.H. (eds) *John Rawls' Theory of Social Justice*, Ohio University Press, Athens, U.S.A.

Kekes, J. (1981), 'Morality and Impartiality', *American Philosophical Quarterly*, Vol. 18, October.

Kovesi, J. (1967), *Moral Notions*, Routledge Kegan Paul,London.

Kymlicka, W. (1990), *Contemporary Political Philosophy*, Oxford University Press, Oxford.

Lakatos, I., and Musgrave, A. (1970), *Criticism and the Growth of Knowledge*, Cambridge University Press, Cambridge.

Lewis, C.I. (1946), *An Analysis of Knowledge and Valuation*, Open Court, London.

Lewis, H.D. (ed), (1976), *Contemporary British Philosophy 4*, Allen and Unwin, London.

Liston, D.L. (1990), *Capitalist Schools: Explanation and Ethics in Radical Studies of Schooling*, Routledge, N.Y.

Locke, D. (1981), 'The Principal of Equal Interests', *Philosophical Review*, Vol. 90.

Lucas, J.R. (1976), 'The Principles of Politics', Clarendon Press, Oxford.

Lyons, D. (1975), 'Nature and Soundness of the Contract and Coherence Arguments', in Daniels N. (ed), (1975), *Reading Rawls*, Basil Blackwell, Oxford.

MacIntyre, A. (1981), *After Virtue*, Duckworth, London.

Mackie, J.L. (1977), *Ethics*, Penguin, Harmonsworth.

Martin, D.B. (1990), *Slavery as Salvation*, Yale University Press, New Haven.

Marx, K. (1967), *Writings of the Young Marx on Philosophy and Society*, in Easton, L.D. and Guddat, K.H. (eds.), Anchor Books, N.Y.

McCallum, G.C. (1991), 'Negative and Positive Liberty' in Miller, D. (ed), (1991), *Liberty*, Oxford University Press, Oxford.

McCloskey H.J. (1979), 'Universalised Prescriptivism and Utilitarianism: Hare's Attempted Forced Marriage', *The Journal of Value Inquiry*, Vol. XIII, No. 1, Spring.

McDermott, M. (1983), 'Hare's Argument for Utilitarianism', *Philosophical Quarterly*, Vol 33, No 133.

Medlin, B. (1957), 'Ultimate Principles and Ethical Egoism', *Australasian Journal of Philosophy*, XXXV. Also In Gauthier (1970).

Mill, J.S. (1971), *Utilitarianism*, Dent, London.

Miller, D. (1979), 'Moral Theory and the Plasticity of Persons', Monist, Number 62, July.

Miller, D. (1983), 'Moral Arguments and Social Contexts', *The Journal of Philosophy*, Vol. LXXX No, 10, October.

Miller, D. (ed), (1991), *Liberty*, Oxford University Press, Oxford.

Montefiore, A. (1961), 'Goodness and Choice', *The Aristotelian Society Supplementary Volume*, pp.61-80. This a reply to 'Goodness and Choice' by Philippa Foot in the same volume.

Morgenbesser, S. and Lieberson, J. (1991), *Isaiah Berlin*, Hogarth Press, London.

Murphy, J.G. (1982), *Evolution, Morality and the Meaning of Life*, Rowman and Littlefield, Totowa, N.J.

Nagel, T. (1970), *The Possibility of Altruism*, Clarendon Press, Oxford.

Nozick, R. (1974), *Anarchy, State and Utopia* , Blackwell, Oxford.

Ofshe, R. and Watters, E., (1995), *Making Monsters*, Andre Deutsch, London.

Papineau, D. (1979), *Theory and Meaning*, Clarendon Press, Oxford.

Parfit, D. (1984), *Reasons and Persons*, Oxford University Press, Oxford.

Partington, G. (1995), 'Determining Sacred Sites: the Case of the Hindmarsh Island Bridge', *Current Affairs Bulletin*, February/March.

Pennock, J.R. and Chapman, J.W. (eds), (1972) *Coercion,*, Chicago, Aldine, Nomos XIV.

Peters, R.S. (1966), *Education and Ethics*, Allen and Unwin, London.

Pettit, P. (1997), *Republicanism*, Clarendon Press, Oxford.

Plato (1955), *The Republic*, Penguin, Harmondsworth.

Pring, R. (1976), *Knowledge and Schooling*, Macmillan, London.

Quine, W.V.O. (1981), *Theories and Things*, Belknap Press, N.Y.

Rawls, J. (1951), 'Outline of a Decision-Procedure for Ethics', *The Philosophical Review*, 60.

Rawls, J. (1967), 'Two Concepts of Rules' in Foot, P. (ed), (1967), *Theories of Ethics*, Oxford University Press, Oxford.

Rawls, J. (1972), *A Theory of Justice*, Oxford University Press, Oxford.

Rawls, J. (1975), 'Fairness to Goodness', *The Philosophical Review*, 84.

Rawls, J. (1977), 'The Basic Structure as Subject', *American Philosophical Quarterly*,14.

Rawls, J. (1982), 'Social Unity and Primary Goods' in Sen, A. and Williams, B. (1982), *Utilitarianism and Beyond*, Cambridge University Press, Cambridge.

Rawls, J. (1993a), *Political Liberalism*, Columbia University Press, N.Y.

Rawls, J. (1993b), 'The Laws of Peoples', in Shute and Hurley.

Richards, D.A.J. (1971), *A Theory of Reason for Action*, Clarendon Press, Oxford.

Robinson, H.M. (1982), 'Is Hare a Naturalist?' *Philosophical Review*, XCI, No. 1, January.

Rousseau, J.J. (1991), *Emile*, Penguin, Harmondworth.

Ruse, M. (1986), *Taking Darwin Seriously*, Basil Blackwell, Oxford.

Sandel, M.J. (1982), *Liberalism and the Limits of Justice*, Cambridge University Press, Cambridge.

Sanders, T. The Paulo Freire Method, Literacy Training and Conscientisation, Australian Council of Churches on Christian Education.

Saunders, C. (1994), *Report to the Minister for Aboriginal and Torres Straits Islander Affairs on the Significant Aboriginal Area in the Vicinity of Goolwa and Hindmarsh (Kumarangk) Island*, Centre for Comparative Constitutional Studies, University of Melbourne, Melbourne.

Scanlon, T.M. (1975), 'Rawls' Theory of Justice', in Daniels N. (ed), (1975), *Reading Rawls*, Basil Blackwell, Oxford.

Scanlon, T.M. (1982), 'Contractualism and Utilitarianism' in Sen, A. and Williams, B. (1982), *Utilitarianism and Beyond*, Cambridge University Press, Cambridge.

Sen, A. and Williams, B. (1982), *Utilitarianism and Beyond*, Cambridge University Press, Cambridge.

Shute , S., and Hurley, S. *On Human Rights*, Basic Books, N.Y.

Singer, P. (1979), *Practical Ethics*, Cambridge University Press, Cambridge.

Skinner, Q. (1997), *Liberty Before Liberalism*, Cambridge University Press, Cambridge.

Smith, M. (1994), *The Moral Problem*, Blackwell, Oxford.

Sterba, J.P. (1980), *The Demands of Justice*, University of Notre Dame Press.

Taylor, C. (1991), 'What's Wrong with Negative Liberty?' in Miller, D. (ed), (1991), *Liberty*, Oxford University Press, Oxford.

Taylor, C.C.W. (1970), 'Critical Notice of R.M. Hare's Freedom and Reason' in Wallace, G., and Walker, A.D.M. (1970), *The Definition of Morality*, Methuen, London.

Toynbee, A.J. (1974), *A Study of History*, Dell Books, N.Y.

Ullmann-Margalit, E. (1977), *The Emergence of Norms*, Clarendon Press, Oxford.

Wallace, G., and Walker, A.D.M. (1970), *The Definition of Morality*, Methuen, London.

Warnock, G.J. (1971), *The Object of Morality*, Methuen, London.

Watt, A.J. (1974), 'Forms of Knowledge and Norms of Rationality', *Educational Philosophy and Theory*, Vol. 6, No. 1.

Werner, R. (1983), 'Ethical Realism', *Ethics*, Vol. 93, No. 4, July.

Wertheimer, A.P. (1972), 'Political Coercion and Political Obligation', in Pennock, J.R. and Chapman, J.W. (eds), (1972) *Coercion,*, Chicago, Aldine, Nomos XIV.

Whitlock, F.A. (1973), *Criminal Responsibility and Mental Illness*, Butterworth, London.

Williams, B. (1973), 'Ethical Consistency', in his collection, *Problems of the Self*, Cambridge University Press, Cambridge.

Williams, B. (1980), 'The Self and the Future', *Philosophical Review*.

Wilson, J. Q. (1993), *The Moral Sense*, Free Press, Macmillan, London.

Winch, P. (1958), *The Idea of a Social Science*, Routledge and Kegan Paul, London.

Wolff, R.P. (1977), *Understanding Rawls*, Princeton University Press, Princeton.

Woolcock, P. (1972), *Attributive and Predicative Good*, unpublished thesis, University of Western Australia.

Woolcock, P. (1993), 'Ruse's Darwinian Meta-Ethics: A Critique', *Biology and Philosophy*, 8, pp.423-39.

Woolcock, P. (1995), 'Hunt and Berlin on Positive and Negative Freedom', *Australasian Journal of Philosophy*, 73, No 3, pp.458-64.

Woolcock, P. (1998a), 'Objectivity and Illusion in Evolutionary Ethics: Comments on Waller', *Biology and Philosophy*.

Woolcock, P. (1998b), 'The Case against Evolutionary Ethics', in Ruse, M. and Maienstein, J., (eds) *Biology and the Foundations of Ethics*, Cambridge University Press, Cambridge.

Wright, M. (ed), (1996), *Morality and International Relations*, Avebury, Aldershot.

Yeatman, A. (1991), *Postmodern Critical Theorising*, Department of Anthropology, University of Adelaide.

Zimmerman, M. (1969), ' "Is-Ought": An Unnecessary Dualism', in Hudson, W.D. (ed) (1969), *The Is-Ought Question,* MacMillan, London.

Index